Modern PBL

Project-Based Learning in the Digital Age

Daniel Jones

Modern PBL

Published by TeacherGoals Publishing, LLC, Beech Grove, IN
www.teachergoals.com
Cover Design by: Daniel Jones and Tricia Fuglestad
Interior Design by: Heather Brown
Edited by: Dr. John Wick, Ed.D.
Copy Edited by: Heather Brown

Library of Congress Control Number: 2024937472
Paperback ISBN: 978-1-959419-20-4
ASIN: B0D3QZ2TQV
First Printing May 2024

Dedication: To my wife Gretchen, whose support, love, and encouragement are unwavering in every aspect of life, and to my children, Gwyneth, Beatrice, and Oliver, who bring light and joy into my life every day. To Shellie Gorman for her invaluable mentorship, consistently challenging and encouraging me to reach new heights. To Sandra Sutherland and Scott Will, thank you for all the support and encouragement you have provided for my various educational classroom adventures over the years. A heartfelt thank you to Errol St. Clair Smith for providing me with opportunities to engage with thought leaders in education and offering new challenges and perspectives that have been essential to my development. This book reflects the collective support, inspiration, and wisdom you and numerous other educators have shared.

Reviews

"Readers will come away with new ideas for teaching that create more meaningful learning experiences. They will examine many ways to engage students and motivate student learning, build more passion into the teaching and learning experience, and support and implement a PBL learning approach that helps students develop the knowledge and skills necessary for living and learning in a 21st century world."

-Elliott Seif, Ph.D., Author of Teaching for Lifelong Learning: How to Prepare Students for a Changing World

"Modern PBL: Project-Based Learning in the Digital Age will ignite novice and veteran teachers alike...and thereby ignite their students' learning."

-Chris Gareis, Ed.D., Professor of Educational Leadership at William & Mary School of Education, Co-Author of Assessing Deeper Learning and Teacher-Made Assessments: How to Connect Curriculum, Instruction, and Student Learning

"Dan Jones draws from his extensive classroom experience to give readers an in-depth look at what it means to be a PBL teacher, including the experience of students and how to build the right classroom culture. He provides valuable guidance for enhancing PBL with recent developments such as passion-based learning, flipped learning, artificial intelligence, and other new technologies."

-John Larmer, Senior PBL Advisor, Defined Learning, formerly editor in chief at PBLWorks/Buck Institute for Education

"Dan has not only provided step by step details of how to implement project-based learning into our classrooms but he has included countless case studies and anecdotes to help us visualize exactly how and what we need to do to meet with success. After reading Dan's book I feel confident I could introduce my students to project-based learning tomorrow—and most importantly, they'd love it!"

-Jon Harper, Elementary Intervention Specialist at Maple Elementary in Easton, Maryland

Professional Development

In a rapidly evolving educational landscape, Daniel offers powerful PD that empowers educators to seamlessly integrate innovative digital tools into their classrooms through project-based learning. Each session combines strategic insights with practical experiences designed to enhance understanding and fluency with advanced technologies.

Daniel's sessions are engaging, informative, and they enable educators to effectively enhance student engagement and outcomes. By their conclusion, participants are equipped to inspire and guide students in impactful, real-world projects.

Facebook Group

You are invited to join our Facebook group based on the book, which serves as a vibrant community for educators to share their experiences, successes, and challenges with PBL. This group is a valuable resource where teachers can ask questions and receive support from thousands of fellow educators who are equally committed to enhancing PBL in their classrooms. It's an ideal space for ongoing learning and collaboration, further enriching the professional development journey initiated in our series.

Table of Contents

Who is This Book for?

This book is a resource for educators at all stages of their careers, from the skeptical to the weary, from those eager for fresh methods to those still perfecting their craft. It meets you wherever you are in your educational journey and offers targeted insights, actionable strategies, and a supportive framework to navigate your teaching environment.

If you're new to teaching and keen on starting strong, this book is your comprehensive guide. It demystifies the principles of Project-Based Learning and offers a solid foundation in an educational landscape increasingly shifting towards active, student-centric learning. You'll gain the confidence and the know-how to make a lasting impact right from the start.

If you have previously experimented with project-based learning (PBL) and found the initial experience challenging, remember that any innovative approach often requires several iterations and modifications to find the right fit for you and your students. This book is designed to guide you through those challenges by offering practical strategies, real-world examples, and supportive guidance from educators who have successfully navigated these waters. Each chapter addresses common obstacles and presents insights on transforming these challenges into learning and growth opportunities. As you read, think about what hasn't gone well or the challenges you encountered when implementing PBL, and then see if you can find solutions. How are your concerns being addressed?

Skeptical about embracing new educational paradigms? This book will help you confront your reservations head-on. In an era of evolving standards and criticism of traditional methods, it provides foundational principles that shed light on the tangible benefits of PBL. Your doubts will be acknowledged and addressed, paving the way for a fruitful journey into modern pedagogical approaches.

For those of you who have dedicated your energy and passion to teaching but feel consumed by its challenges, this book brings rejuvenation. It introduces a transformative approach that reignites the passion for education, providing strategies and techniques to refresh your teaching practice by effectively integrating Project-Based Learning. It aims to restore the very element you may feel you've lost: time, enabling you to do what truly resonates with educators everywhere—guiding student growth through close collaboration.

If you're an experienced educator who may be wary of "the next big thing," this book offers a fresh perspective worth considering. It invites you to reevaluate your methodologies against the backdrop of significant advancements in both technology and pedagogy. New paradigms are deeply explored, encouraging you to refresh and potentially transform even the most established learning environments. Your expertise cannot be ignored. As you read, highlight those passages that you know to be best practices and underline those things that challenge you to take a step back.

As you know, there is more than one way to approach education, and instead of seeing this as just another initiative, look for pieces and parts that you can start to work into what is already working in your classroom.

Lastly, this book unveils a spectrum of fresh perspectives for veteran teachers looking to shake things up. Drawing on extensive classroom experience and modern research, it presents nuanced strategies beyond PBL basics. Whether you're interested in taking calculated risks, incorporating technology, or developing interdisciplinary projects, you'll find many ideas to revitalize your practice.

Welcoming educators of every experience level, this book initiates a transformative journey, recognizing your challenges and offering a dynamic, student-centric approach rooted in passion and purpose. In the face of unparalleled shifts in education, envision a classroom crafted with insights from your wisdom, transforming students from mere spectators to active participants immersed in a continuous cycle of trial and error. This isn't merely a guide but a partnership pledge in your professional evolution. With pens ready, consider this your invitation: class is in session, and together, we navigate this ever-evolving landscape.

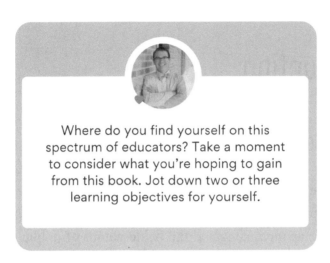

Where do you find yourself on this spectrum of educators? Take a moment to consider what you're hoping to gain from this book. Jot down two or three learning objectives for yourself.

Journal Your Journey

Use the space below to reflect on this question.

Introduction

Since publishing my first book, *Flipped 3.0 Project Based Learning: An Insanely Simple Guide*, the educational landscape has profoundly shifted in the wake of unprecedented global changes. As a current classroom educator, I've grappled with the challenges of engaging students amidst rising apathy, navigated the fickle nature of public opinion, and questioned my place in this evolving world of education. I remember a particular morning, post remote schooling, staring at the school building from my car, questioning if I could muster the strength to continue in this new world of education. While some traditional strategies remain relevant, others demand reconsideration and reinvention in our post-pandemic reality.

Writing this book doesn't imply I possess all the answers or that I stand alone atop a mountain of knowledge. Rather, it suggests that we are intertwined, walking side by side on this enlightening journey. Every time I refer to myself as 'I,' there's an underlying meaning—it's not just about me, but an ensemble of voices and experiences. This "I" is a mosaic of the collective "we." The perspectives shared, the lessons illustrated, and the narratives unfolded are deeply rooted in the contributions of countless individuals who have generously poured into my life. They've offered guidance, shared their wisdom, and pushed me toward horizons I might not have explored. Consequently, my insights are a culmination of this shared wisdom. Along this path, you might find ideas that resonate deeply, kindling a flame of motivation within you. On other occasions, you might encounter revelations that shed light on challenges or dilemmas you've grappled with. It's as if we've been journeying through an intricate labyrinth in the shadows, but together, we are steadily finding our way toward clarity and illumination. The journey is enriched, the insights more profound, and the path clearer when the solitary "I" transforms into the encompassing "we."

Have you had your own "car moment?"

What carried you forward?

Journaling Your Journey

Use the space below to reflect on this question.

_____

_____

_____

_____

_____

_____

_____

_____

_____

_____

_____

_____

_____

As an educator, I staunchly believe that my classroom will not spontaneously improve; I need to be the one to enhance it. Implementing PBL is my proactive solution. It is not just a teaching method; it's a powerful toolkit that empowers me to cultivate a more impactful, engaging, and relevant learning environment for my students. Instead of passively awaiting improvement, PBL enables me to drive change. It is an approach that I need to actively integrate into my plans. PBL fosters active learning, promotes critical thinking, and nurtures creativity and problem-solving skills in my students. With PBL, my classroom becomes a dynamic space for exploration and discovery, where students actively participate in their learning journey. By embracing PBL, I am not merely hoping for an improved educational setting but actively creating it. This perspective guides my role as an educator: acting as a catalyst for change and a facilitator of enriched, student-centric learning experiences.

How can you get the most out of this journey? As we transition into the book's structure and suggested reading experience, it's essential to remember that this book is more than a repository of theoretical information. It's an interactive guide with multimedia elements and hands-on activities designed to engage you from multiple angles and learning preferences. Whether you're a visual, auditory, or text-based learner, there's something here for you. Likewise, the book offers various application, reflection, and discussion opportunities, encouraging you not just to consume but actively engage with the content.

So, as you prepare to delve into project-based learning, know that you are embarking on a multi-dimensional, interactive, and, above all, transformative experience. This is not just another pedagogical text to skim through but a guide to rejuvenate your teaching practice and breathe new life into your classroom. Take your time, engage deeply, and be open to the profound impact this could have on your educational journey.

How to Read This Book

Welcome to a uniquely structured reading experience designed to inform, engage, inspire, and transform. While deep-rooted in theory, this book is firmly attached to practicality, offering a dynamic exploration of project-based learning. As you embark on this journey, here are some suggestions to maximize your experience.

Interactive Content

Throughout this book, you will encounter video segments meant to visually stimulate and engage, inviting you to observe and absorb new ideas actively. Most of these appear at the beginning of the chapters. Be on the lookout for the following symbol as it highlights interactive elements that will add depth to the content.

Each chapter begins with an interview via a QR code featuring a renowned expert in the field. These interviews serve as an introduction, allowing the experts to share their insights and perspectives firsthand. While the interviews themselves do not encompass the entire chapter content, they will highlight and touch upon key topics that will be explored in greater depth throughout the chapter. By opening with these expert voices, you gain valuable context and a deeper understanding of the subject matter before delving into the core concepts and strategies discussed in the subsequent sections.

But do not worry if you are a traditional reader, as each chapter also features thoughtfully articulated text, delivering detailed and comprehensive insights. I encourage you to choose your preferred learning medium or, even better, mix and match them to engage multiple senses. The video will set you up for what you will encounter in the chapter.

Application Opportunities

At the end of each chapter, you will find opportunities to extend and apply your knowledge. These activities are designed to push you beyond passive information consumption and encourage active learning. Through these tasks, you can put theories into practice and experience the power of flipped learning firsthand. When we do something with what we are learning, we internalize it, making it more relevant and meaningful.

Reflective Practice

As you navigate through each chapter, take the time to reflect on your understanding and how the ideas presented can be translated to your specific context. Your reflections will help reinforce new concepts and inspire innovative ways to apply them. Project-based learning is not limited to just one content area. This is your chance to explore how it fits within your classroom, school, or district.

Navigating Your Educational Journey: Engage, Reflect, and Collaborate

As you dive into this journey exploring innovative educational strategies, remember that the path to deep understanding is not just a solitary one. Engage actively with the material, and consider the benefits of discussing your takeaways with others. Engaging in conversation can spark insights, clarify doubts, and deepen your grasp of the concepts. Whether in a formal book club, online forums, or chats with colleagues, embrace the power of shared exploration. Learning thrives as a social endeavor.

Education's evolution isn't a sprint but a marathon. Each chapter, each concept, serves as a stepping stone towards richer comprehension. Prioritize depth over speed, allowing your understanding to evolve organically. As tempting as it might be to rapidly apply every new strategy, a methodical and reflective approach ensures more effective outcomes. Take time with each chapter, reflecting on its implications and pondering its integration into your teaching approach. This thoughtful pace promotes a deeper, tailored understanding, fostering a more robust integration that benefits both you and your students.

To assist in this journey, I've curated a list of actionable steps to enrich your exploration.

1. Find a Reading Partner: Engaging with a fellow educator or curious friend can amplify your understanding through discussions, shared insights, and mutual motivation.

2. Journal Your Journey: Maintain a dedicated journal for your reflections and thoughts. This not only solidifies your grasp but also serves as a valuable resource for future reference.

3. Experiment in Real-Time: Implement strategies as you encounter them. Real-world experimentation, even on a small scale, provides invaluable feedback and deeper comprehension.

4. Participate in Online Discussions: Broaden your horizons by joining online communities discussing this book. Engage with diverse perspectives, gather additional resources, and seek answers to lingering questions.

5. Set Regular Checkpoints: Pause periodically for reflection, ensuring you're genuinely absorbing and applying the book's insights.

Remember, the goal is not just to read but to immerse, engage, and transform. By actively integrating these steps, you amplify the impact of the book and set yourself up for a more enriched and fulfilling teaching experience.

How do you currently pace your professional development? Does this pace align with how you pace your classroom instruction?

Journaling Your Journey

Use the space below to reflect on this question.

_____

_____

_____

_____

_____

_____

_____

_____

_____

_____

_____

_____

_____

_____

Chapter 1
Understanding the Power of PBL

 **Interview with Suzie Boss**
PBL Author & Educational Consultant

"Education is not the filling of a pail, but the lighting of a fire."
-W.B. Yeats

Allow those words to resonate for a moment. Consider how much of our teaching time is dedicated to stuffing every conceivable academic standard into our students' minds before a state examination. How much time do we invest in disseminating all the information? Conversely, how much time do we allocate to simply posing questions, fostering curiosity, and facilitating exploration? This reflection is not a mere exercise but an opportunity to re-center and re-calibrate our understanding of education's true purpose.

Before we delve into the transformative world of project-based learning (PBL), let's acknowledge the initial fire that led us to the classroom. Forget the buzzwords and the jargon for a moment. Remember when you first realized you wanted to teach? That moment wasn't just about a career; it was about a calling. That passion is the cornerstone that can help us embrace innovation, even when faced with challenges or skepticism. This isn't about dredging up some lofty reason you scripted for a job interview; it's about tapping into that real, raw enthusiasm that perhaps even you've forgotten.

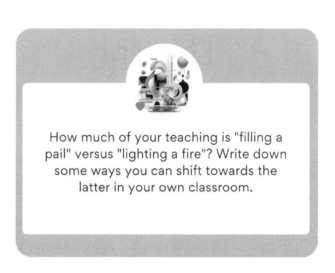

How much of your teaching is "filling a pail" versus "lighting a fire"? Write down some ways you can shift towards the latter in your own classroom.

Journaling Your Journey

Use the space below to reflect on this question.

_____

_____

_____

_____

_____

_____

_____

_____

_____

_____

_____

_____

_____

By revisiting that enthusiasm, we're not just reminding ourselves of a past emotional state; we're equipping ourselves for future innovation. This foundational passion becomes our compass, making it easier to navigate through new methodologies like Project-Based Learning. It helps us approach changes not as hurdles but as opportunities—opportunities that our initial selves would have eagerly embraced. So, let's not just look backward; let's also cast our gaze forward because that initial spark isn't just our origin story, it's our North Star guiding us towards becoming the educators we aspired to be.

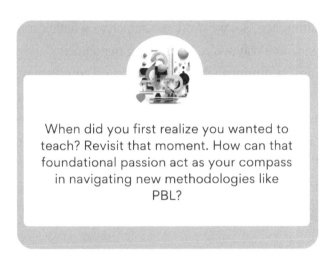

When did you first realize you wanted to teach? Revisit that moment. How can that foundational passion act as your compass in navigating new methodologies like PBL?

Journaling Your Journey

Use the space below to reflect on this question.

_____

_____

_____

_____

_____

_____

_____

_____

_____

_____

The teaching journey is similar to a PBL project: both start with an initial problem or question, followed by an exploration phase and culminate in applying what's been learned. Remember, PBL isn't just a teaching method; it's a mindset. Just as personal passion drives the success of a PBL project, broader educational motivations often drive our commitment to the teaching profession.

A survey carried out by LKMco and Pearson Inc., involving over 1,000 educators, revealed that the primary reason individuals choose teaching as a profession is their desire to positively impact students' lives (McNeil, 2015). However, we often feel ineffective if we perceive that we're not making a substantial difference. So, we must ask ourselves whether imparting knowledge is truly the key way we're influencing our students' lives.

This is not to diminish the significance of conveying subject matter to students – it's undeniably an important part of the equation. We often feel ineffectual if we think we aren't doing that, but the key is not just in imparting facts—it's in shaping experiences that make a real difference in students' lives. This book isn't designed to lock you into one teaching approach but to guide you on how to best serve your students while you continue to evolve as an educator.

Addressing Misconceptions: Beyond Real-World Problems

One of the common misconceptions about project-based learning is that it must exclusively focus on solving real-world issues. This notion can deter some teachers from embracing PBL, as the pressure to constantly find meaningful, real-world connections can be overwhelming. However, PBL is far more flexible and can be incredibly meaningful when it is student-driven, aligned with their passions, and not strictly tethered to global problems.

Furthermore, teachers can encourage students to think beyond the traditional definition of "real-world issues." While projects related to societal problems certainly have their place in project-based learning, it's essential to broaden the scope of what is considered meaningful and relevant. Students can explore personal interests, cultural topics, historical events, artistic expressions, scientific phenomena, and more. The key is to create an environment where students feel empowered to pursue projects that resonate with them on a personal level.

 Identify one topic that could lend itself to a student-driven project. Jot down a few ideas.

Journaling Your Journey

Use the space below to reflect on this question.

_____

_____

_____

_____

_____

_____

_____

_____

By shifting the focus from exclusively real-world issues to student-driven exploration, educators can alleviate the pressure of constantly finding connections for their students. PBL allows for a rich framework where students can delve into topics that genuinely interest them, whether or not these topics have an immediate real-world application. Teachers should consider that a student's passion and interest can be just as compelling a force for learning as any global issue.

More Than Just a Buzz Word

Project-based learning is an intricate concept, rich in nuance and application. This richness, combined with its adaptability across various educational landscapes, makes it challenging to encapsulate in a singular definition. As one sifts through the numerous interpretations by respected institutions, a subtle yet critical observation emerges: many definitions seem to position the student as a passive recipient rather than an active agent. PBL, in these depictions, is something "done to" the student rather than "driven by and through" them. Here are various definitions:

- "A teaching method in which students gain knowledge and skills by working for an extended period of time to investigate and respond to an authentic, engaging, and complex question, problem, or challenge" (The Buck Institute for Education, n.d.).

- "A teaching method in which complex real-world problems are used as the vehicle to promote student learning of concepts and principles as opposed to direct presentation of facts and concepts." (University of Illinois, 2023)

- "A student-centered approach in which students learn about a subject by working in groups to solve an open-ended problem. This problem is what drives the motivation and the learning." (Cornell University, 2022)

A New Definition

When reading those definitions, they are all correct. Each definition includes pieces and parts that the others don't. One aspect of PBL is missing, though, from each. And it is a component that elevates and enhances PBL to be such an intrinsic and dynamic approach: **passion**. My experience with PBL has led me to define PBL as:

> *The act of using a project to develop hands-on engagement where students, fueled by their curiosity and passion, work collaboratively to explore, absorb, and internalize classroom content beyond rote memorization.*

Incorporating passion into our educational definition, echoing W.B. Yeats, ignites a metaphorical flame. I was fortunate enough to have a conversation with Suzie Boss, a prominent author on project-based learning, where she discussed the relationship between passion-based learning (PsBL) and PBL. Boss explained how intertwining student interests within projects can amplify their innate motivation and sense of ownership (Boss, personal communication, June 21, 2023).

In her view, when students are given the opportunity to infuse their unique skills and passions into a project, they experience a heightened level of engagement and purpose. By crafting projects that accommodate individual self-expression and passion, educators can tap into the inherent motivation of students. This, in turn, cultivates profound learning experiences that encourage students to assume responsibility for their educational journey.

In a project-based learning classroom, teachers can encourage students to identify and pursue projects that align with their personal interests and aspirations. This approach acknowledges that students are more likely to be engaged and motivated when they genuinely connect to the project. By embracing student passions as viable avenues for exploration, teachers can tap into their students' intrinsic motivation, curiosity, and creativity.

 Think about your upcoming lessons. Jot down ways to incorporate student interests or passions into at least one project. Share your ideas with a trusted peer.

Journaling Your Journey
Use the space below to reflect on this question.

_____

_____

_____

_____

_____

_____

_____

_____

_____

Project-based learning can be divided into manageable components: formulating essential questions, conducting research, planning, applying knowledge, and presenting findings. What sets PBL apart is that it transitions the teacher from being the central figure to a more supportive role, acting as a coach, mentor, and encourager.

Proven Impact: How PBL Transforms Learning

Making this adjustment can be challenging. Abandoning the traditional stance of lecturing from the front of the classroom and relinquishing control to foster student-led exploration can be quite uncomfortable. This paradigm shift might prompt some teachers to reject the concept altogether, stating, "There's no way I'm letting students just Google everything. This approach is far too unstructured!" This is when we need to set our reservations to the side and take a look at what the research tells us.

Research funded by Lucas Education Research (2021), a division of the George Lucas Educational Foundation, has studied project-based learning for over seven years across various grades and subjects. The findings show that embedding PBL in advanced placement courses significantly increases students' likelihood of earning a passing score on AP tests. Middle school students in California who were taught science through PBL outperformed their peers on a science assessment, while third-grade students in Michigan using PBL for science education performed better than their peers in traditional classes. Second-grade students in Michigan who used PBL for social studies and literacy showed accelerated learning compared to a control group. Furthermore, PBL was found to improve social and emotional learning across different racial and socio-economic groups.

Another study conducted by Mohammed Abdullatif Almulla (2020) identified five aspects of PBL that contribute to student engagement: collaborative learning, disciplinary subject learning, iterative learning, authentic learning, and social and emotional learning. PBL is constructivist in nature, promoting student engagement by actively involving them in authentic tasks and encouraging innovation through resource and knowledge sharing. PBL fosters collaboration and social-emotional learning and is highly effective in higher education settings (Almulla, 2020).

In 2018, Sally Kingston analyzed literature that focused on improving student learning outcomes through PBL. The analysis encompassed

8

studies from 1984 to 2017, covering social studies, science, mathematics, and English/language arts. In social studies, PBL students experienced higher growth, particularly those from low socioeconomic backgrounds. PBL students also performed better on standardized tests and demonstrated greater academic gains and problem-solving skills compared to students in traditional classes. In science, PBL students outperformed their peers on outcome measures aligned with core science ideas and practices. They showed significant improvements in learning goals, application of information, and understanding of relationships between concepts. In physics and chemistry, students demonstrated gains in scientific content knowledge and process skills. In mathematics, students in PBL statistics classes showed significant gains in statistical literacy. They performed comparably or better in rote knowledge and demonstrated a higher application of mathematics in different situations. In English/language arts (ELA), PBL students showed statistically significant higher growth in informational reading (Kingston, 2018).

PBL has demonstrated significant positive impacts across various subjects and grades (Kingston, 2018). It enhances student engagement, improves academic performance, fosters social and emotional learning, and helps students apply knowledge and skills in real-world contexts. If we want to improve student outcomes and engagement, PBL is how we are going to get there. But it's not just the research that underscores the power of PBL; real-life examples from our classrooms bring this to life.

Stories From the Classroom

A few years ago, a creative 8th-grade student, Ava (a pseudonym), with a passion for art, set foot on an educational journey that would drastically reshape her academic landscape. Unknown to her, this transformation would be sparked by the introduction of project-based learning, which provided her with a platform to blend her love for art with her studies.

Ava's world was colored by her artistic inclinations, a refuge from traditional academic challenges that often left her feeling disconnected from her lessons. But by integrating art into her learning process, she discovered a unique pathway to understanding. She began to view academic content through a creative lens, resulting in a noticeable improvement in her comprehension and engagement.

This transformation was beautifully captured during our unit on "Life in the Colonies." Ava produced a pop-up picture book as her project, a creative testament to her in-depth understanding of the subject. More than just an art piece, the book was a tangible reflection of Ava's growth and her ability to express knowledge through creativity.

Ava's academic evolution was not just confined to the application of artistic skills in her projects. Our class moved away from traditional testing, focusing on a project-based approach instead. This learning environment encouraged Ava to delve into her personal interests and hobbies and utilize them to decipher complex academic subjects. Her progress was evident, her understanding deepened, and her confidence soared with each project.

With the introduction of interactive lessons delivered via Google Docs, a shift occurred in Ava's engagement with her studies. Passive content consumption was replaced by active learning, which ignited her intellectual curiosity. Her notes transformed into a blend of intriguing questions, thoughtful reflections, and colorful illustrations, all pointing towards a deeper connection with the subject matter.

Our post-lesson discussions served as a platform for Ava to delve deeper into her understanding. Fueled by her desire to master the content, she raised probing questions and shared insightful observations. These conversations were a testament to Ava's commitment to her learning journey and her passion for understanding, retaining, and applying knowledge.

Despite the academic rigor, Ava's spirit remained undeterred. She maintained an atmosphere of light-heartedness, her laughter and energy radiating throughout the classroom. Her playful demeanor was complemented by her deepening understanding of complex subjects, adding a layer of depth to her academic profile.

Ava's transformative journey is not an isolated case. Over the years, I've witnessed numerous students undergo similar metamorphoses, each with their unique flair and story. These experiences, these narratives of growth and discovery, have been the driving force behind my commitment to education. They serve as constant reminders that when we, as educators, step outside the confines of traditional teaching and embrace innovative approaches, we pave the way for moments of profound realization and lasting impact in our students' lives (Williams, 2020).

In my 19 years of teaching, there are moments that stand out, clear reminders of why I chose this path. One such instance unfolded during a routine day in my classroom. I casually asked my students, "Anyone remember a project from last year's class?" Among the thoughtful faces, Rose (also a pseudonym), always an attentive student, raised her hand. "I recall working on the mosaic for 'The Fall of the Roman Empire,'" she said with a hint of pride. Intrigued, I pressed on, "What details do you remember from that unit?" She paused, thinking, then replied, "Rome fell for a few reasons. There was an attacking group... their name slips my mind."

Jumping in, I said, "You're thinking of the Visigoths." Recognition flashed in her eyes, "Exactly! And there were also economic and political challenges."

As she recounted, I felt a deep sense of satisfaction. "Rose," I said, trying to keep my voice steady, "that was a year ago. You've not just remembered the project but the core of the content. It wasn't just for a grade; it stuck with you."

She looked back, a mix of realization and confidence in her gaze. In that moment, amidst the everyday routine, the true value of project-based learning became even clearer. When students engage, when they take ownership of the content, they don't just learn – they internalize. Rose's reflections were a testament to this. It was a reaffirming nod to the power and impact of PBL.

Plan, Personalize, Pursue

The role of an educator is a dynamic one, shaped by evolving personal motivations, teaching methodologies, and the ever-changing landscape of the educational world. In the quest for maintaining the zeal and passion that drives effective teaching, it's essential to continuously reflect, adapt, and renew one's approach. The pathway to rediscovering and rejuvenating your teaching passion can be seen as a three-phase cycle: plan, personalize, and pursue. This guide aims to lead educators through these stages, prompting introspection and action to maintain and amplify the fervor that makes teaching not just a profession but a calling. Dive in to embark on a transformative journey to reshape your teaching narrative.

Welcome to "Your PBL Pathway," a guide designed especially for you to navigate the multifaceted world of project-based learning. As you journey through the three integral stages—*plan, personalize, and pursue*—you'll be empowered to harness your teaching passions, craft actionable goals, and continuously reflect on your progress. This guide isn't just about understanding PBL's transformative potential; it's about tailoring it to your unique teaching style, strategies, and aspirations. Embark on this journey to refine your teaching approach, foster your professional growth, and elevate the learning experience for your students. Dive in, and let's revolutionize your classroom together with the power of PBL.

Plan

Every educator's journey begins with a simple spark, a driving question that leads you to the noble profession of teaching. It's time to reconnect with that original spark. Begin with a moment of deep self-reflection. Ask yourself, "What was it that drew me to the teaching profession initially? What kept me excited, eager, and curious in those early years?" This introspective exploration will help illuminate the motivations and passions that propelled you to become an educator.

This exploration isn't a passive act; instead, it serves as a platform to engage with your teaching vocation actively. Write down your thoughts, feelings, and experiences that underpin your passion for teaching. Take this time to reminisce on your achievements, challenges, and the joy of witnessing students' growth.

Personalize

As you dive deeper into your past motivations and passion-fueling elements, you may realize that some aspects have changed over time. This isn't necessarily a negative revelation but rather an opportunity to recognize, reassess, and recalibrate your teaching philosophy to reflect the teacher you've evolved into.

Ask yourself, "How have these motivations and elements changed? How has my teaching environment affected these elements? What elements of my initial passion can I still control or reignite?" The answers will serve as a hypothesis. They may not be definitive, but they'll provide you with a preliminary understanding of why you feel the way you do about your profession now.

Based on these reflections and your hypothesis, formulate an action plan. List down actionable steps that you believe can reignite your passion. It could involve reviving old habits that bring joy, adopting new teaching strategies, fostering deeper relationships with your students, or setting new personal development goals. This plan is deeply personalized to you, acting as a roadmap to reignite your passion for teaching.

Pursue

The planning stage is complete; now, it's time to apply. Implement your action plan and make notes of your experiences, observations, and challenges. Remember, the goal here isn't perfection but a journey of rediscovery and growth. Be open to the prospect of evolution, learning, and change as you immerse yourself in this application phase.

During this stage, consider organizing round-table discussions with your fellow teachers who might be undertaking similar journeys. Share your experiences and learn from each other's perspectives. This collaborative approach to professional development could unearth further insights and inspire tweaks to your plan.

After applying your plan, enter the reflection stage. Reflect on the effectiveness of your action steps and the experiences they elicited. Have you noticed a change in your feelings toward teaching? Have certain actions sparked joy or enthusiasm? Document these findings and allow them to steer your ongoing path

CONTINUING THE JOURNEY:
Evaluate and Iterate Your Approach

Finally, take a step back and evaluate. Look at the bigger picture and analyze your journey. Have you reignited your initial passion? If yes, continue to refine and evolve your strategies. If not, don't be disheartened. Reflection and adaptation are core aspects of learning and growth.

Take your experiences, your successes, and the areas needing improvement, and recalibrate your action plan. Remember, this is a pathway, a journey of professional and personal growth. You're not expected to arrive at a final destination immediately. Instead, you should aim for progress, learning, and a deeper connection with your passion for teaching.

This process—plan, personalize, pursue—is a cyclical pathway, not a one-time event. Your teaching environment, students, and personal growth will continuously shift and evolve, requiring you to revisit and revise your plan. In this process, remember to celebrate every small win and reflect on every challenge. By remaining connected with your passion for teaching, you'll create a dynamic, fulfilling, and rewarding teaching career that's uniquely yours.

***

This chapter has traced the transformative impact of embracing passion and curiosity in our classrooms. By tapping into students' innate motivations and interests, educators can facilitate deeply engaging learning experiences that drive comprehension and retention. Now, in our next chapter, we further explore how to create these optimal learning environments, specifically by establishing a supportive classroom culture centered around community, trust, diversity, and growth mindsets. Just as passion serves as the cornerstone for impactful PBL projects, the culture we foster acts as the foundation upon which enriching educational experiences can thrive.

As we transition to the next chapter, reflect on what elements you aim to establish or enhance in your classroom culture. What values and mindsets do you hope your students will internalize? Let these reflections guide you as you broaden your perspective to evaluate and cultivate this critical culture—the fertile soil from which our students' academic and personal growth can blossom.

Chapter 2
Creating Engaging Learning Experiences

 Interview with Dr. Tony Wagner
Writer & Research Fellow

"The principal goal of education is to create individuals who are capable of doing new things, not simply of repeating what other generations have done."
-Jean Piaget

Every classroom is built upon **culture**. Every block that a project-based classroom is built upon can be found in the established classroom culture. I want you to consider if there is a strong sense of belonging among your students?

- Do they feel part of a supportive community where their ideas and contributions are valued?

- Are your students encouraged to embrace challenges and learn from errors? Is there an emphasis on learning and the belief that abilities can be developed through dedication and hard work?

- How is respect for oneself and others cultivated in your classroom? Are students open to diverse perspectives and willing to share their thoughts without fear of judgment?

- Do your students feel trusted and encouraged to take responsibility for their learning? Is there mutual trust between the teacher and students?

- Is the natural curiosity of your students nurtured? Are they encouraged to ask questions, explore, and seek answers?

- Are your expectations and norms for behavior and learning clearly communicated and consistently enforced? Do students understand what is expected of them and why?

- Is diversity in backgrounds, perspectives, and ideas celebrated? Are your students encouraged to appreciate and learn from the diverse experiences of their peers?

As you consider these questions, you sharpen your ability to identify both the strengths and weaknesses in your classroom environment. When I started my journey with project-based learning, I openly admitted that my classroom environment hardly promoted learning. My classroom served merely as a transit point where students entered and exited. Students either understood the content or they didn't—there was no middle ground. Like many teachers, I overlooked the growth concept and focused only on final grades. I wrongly thought that delivering the content fulfilled my role and blamed any lack of comprehension on students' inattention. Curiosity had no place; we followed a rigid curriculum without deviation. Although I set expectations, it was like planting seeds in concrete and expecting them to grow. I failed to see how embracing diversity related to the curriculum. I thought I was teaching objective historical facts, which I believed had no connection to a student's background. In summary, my classroom stifled rather than nurtured creativity and growth; in a word, it was toxic. I failed to recognize that the culture I had created was the source of my frustration, discouragement, anger, and burnout.

Reflection initiates our journey toward improvement. This self-examination serves as the seed for change; it allows us to make the necessary adjustments for growth. Your starting point on this journey doesn't matter, whether you're at a low or high point. What's crucial is beginning with a strong foundation. Understand that your journey is uniquely yours. Don't compare your progress to that of other teachers, whether they are next door, in a different school, on social media, or in academic papers. Your journey belongs to you alone, and any progress, no matter the pace, holds value. Comparing yourself to others can harm your growth, so focus on your path. Here are some first steps that can help you in this journey.

Build Relationships and Get to Know Your Students

As a twelve-year-old boy, there was nothing I looked forward to more than recess. I distinctly remember a day during my 6th-grade year when my teacher said he would play basketball with us on the playground. For the first time, I had a teacher who invested in me relationally. He spent all year investing in us, getting to know us and our families, and ensuring we knew we were valued. This man was not a veteran teacher. He wasn't even an experienced teacher. He was a first-year teacher! His passion permeated everything he did. To this day, I remember the lessons he taught us and the projects he helped bring to life. How did someone with so little teaching experience create such a lasting impact on his students? His secret was knowing the importance of building relationships with his students.

Over the years, I have kept in touch with Mr. Rich Kline. He is still teaching, and his students all have such wonderful things to say about him, but one of the things that rings true for almost all his students is that Mr. Kline cares about them and makes them feel valued. Recently, I had Rich (he asked me to call him that, but I must admit, no matter what age you become, your teachers will always be Mr. or Mrs. So-and-So) come and visit my classroom. It was wonderful to hang out and visit, and we reminisced about his first year of teaching. He looked back with very fond memories, and I could tell he got as much from that year as we, his students, did. As we chatted, he said, "I am proud of you." Those words mean so much to me. Thirty-two years later, he was still investing in and inspiring me.

The invaluable lessons I learned from Mr. Kline about the importance of building relationships in a classroom are echoed in contemporary educational thought. As we pivot from the deeply personal influence of one exceptional teacher, you'll find that the core of what he taught me still reverberates in the educational landscape today. Whether through traditional methods or innovative approaches like project-based learning, the undercurrent remains the same: a meaningful, relational foundation is critical. As you'll soon discover, this foundational truth takes on a new dimension when applied in dynamic, collaborative learning environments. Stay tuned for the conversation ahead that weaves these threads together, offering fresh perspectives on time-honored truths.

From Pedagogy to Practice: Personalized Project

During my conversation with Suzie Boss, we discussed the importance of introducing students to project-based learning. Suzie emphasized the significance of getting to know the students and ensuring they get to know each other. This lays the foundation for a cohesive, collaborative learning environment. She suggested initiating the term with a small project that nudges students to explore learning in new, exciting ways.

Every year in my classroom, I start with a personalized project that allows me to know my students better. They craft a project centered around their interests and passions. Grace's story is one that I hold close to my heart. She was a reserved 7th-grader who blended into the background. When I assigned her this personalized project, I saw a spark ignite in her. She was thrilled at the prospect of creating something truly hers. The result was remarkable: a meticulously crafted potted flower. A newfound confidence enveloped her as she stood in front of the class. The project was more than an object; it reflected her soul. With a beaming smile, she explained, "I made a potted flower because my mom and I love to work in our flower garden." The flowers were not ordinary; their leaves were shaped like books, symbolizing her love for reading, and the petals were in paw prints to express her love of animals.

The class honored her with applause, and as Grace returned to her seat, I realized something magical had happened. Grace had shared a piece of herself with us through her creative expression, and in doing so, she found a supportive environment to open up. This experience embodies what a PBL-focused classroom culture should strive for – creating an environment where students can explore their passions, connect, and embrace vulnerability.

Developing a Growth Mindset Within Your Class

Journeying through the vast landscape of education, I once believed I was the guide, leading my students toward the lofty peak of perfection. Yet, as I navigated this evolving terrain, I realized our true destination wasn't perfection but growth. A compass set to a growth mindset doesn't point to a final endpoint but guides us through an enriching path marked by discovery and introspection.

In a conversation that lit up my understanding, Dr. Tony Wagner shared, "We need to strike the word 'failure' from our vocabulary in educational settings. Let's talk about this as a process of trial and error instead. This isn't about failing but identifying and learning from errors in our methods" (T. Wagner, personal conversation, June 23, 2023).

Bearing these words, I realized I wasn't astray but on a more authentic path. Dr. Wagner's emphasis on trial and error reinforced the idea that a growth mindset celebrates every experience, understanding each 'misstep' as an opportunity for a new revelation.

In the realm of project-based learning, students don't simply follow; they pioneer. They're not walking predefined paths but charting their own courses, discovering terrains filled with challenges and insights. Through Dr. Wagner's lens, it's evident that our journey's richness comes not from its straight stretches but from the unexpected detours that teach us the most.

So, with our compasses set firmly on growth, let's embrace every part of this educational expedition. Dr. Wagner's insights serve as a beacon, highlighting that every step, be it forward or sideways, enriches our collective experience. It's this continuous exploration that makes the entire journey invaluable.

How does Dr. Wagner's suggestion of replacing failure with trial and error shift your perspective in the realm of growth mindsets?

Journaling Your Journey

Use the space below to reflect on this question.

_____

_____

_____

_____

_____

_____

_____

_____

_____

_____

_____

_____

From Pedagogy to Practice: Adventures in Error

If there is one thing that is certain with any projector activity, it is trial and error. In the classroom of Dr. Lois M. Campbell, a K-12 educator at Beaver Island Community School in Beaver Island, Michigan, the principles of a growth mindset come alive in particularly creative ways. Dr. Campbell begins her unit on experimentation with a captivating narrative. To engage her students, she creates a tale using the characters Buzz and

Woody. Buzz and Woody are iconic characters from Disney's *Toy Story* movie, with Buzz being a space ranger action figure and Woody being a cowboy doll. Together, they share adventures and form a deep bond despite their initial rivalries.

The narrative sets up a challenging but relatable scenario: Buzz and Woody are cornered at a stream while escaping from a space alien. Since neither can swim, they must use hanging grapevines to swing across. Students are tasked with figuring out the fastest way for the duo to cross. Should they swing together, thereby adding mass, or swing separately? Also, should they opt for a longer or shorter vine?

This imaginative framework serves as the backdrop for Dr. Campbell's students to engage in hands-on experiments. She provides a range of materials, like washers, sinkers, kite string, scissors, and tape. Using these supplies, the students create test setups to find the quickest method for Buzz and Woody to traverse the stream. Throughout this process, Dr. Campbell actively engages with the students, probing them on their testing methodologies and encouraging them to maintain organized records of their data.

One student, we will call him Derek, exemplifies the growth mindset Dr. Campbell aims to cultivate. Initially, he faced challenges in understanding the experiment's results. Derek believed that the longer string, coupled with greater mass, would surely be faster. His misconception was challenged by both the data and his peers, pushing him to reconsider his assumptions. After multiple rounds of testing, Derek had an epiphany. He discovered that the shorter string allowed for a quicker swing and that additional mass didn't significantly impact the speed.

The look of realization and accomplishment on Derek's face was nothing short of transformational. His journey from misconception to understanding, aided by trial and error, clearly illustrated the benefits of nurturing a growth mindset. By embracing the process of questioning, failing, and iterating, He was able to deepen his comprehension of the scientific principles at hand.

Dr. Campbell's classroom stands as a testament to the transformative power of a growth-focused culture, where trial and error aren't merely accepted but are celebrated. As her students freely navigate their learning paths, embracing mistakes as opportunities, they embody the essence of a truly progressive educational journey. Yet, fostering such a mindset extends beyond these individual practices—it necessitates an environment where every voice is valued, every query honored, and every opinion respected.

Open and Respectful Environment

Creating an open and respectful classroom is like setting the stage for a collaborative performance. Every participant, regardless of their role, has a voice and a space to contribute, much like actors in a theater production. Each day, our interactions range from directed rehearsals to impromptu script readings, ensuring a balance between structure and authenticity.

The power of relaxed and trusting environments cannot be overstated. As we build camaraderie, akin to actors preparing for a play, we begin our dialogues with simple, relatable questions such as, "What did you have for dinner?" These conversations serve as warm-ups, setting the tone for a deeper trust. In such nurturing spaces, teachers are provided the latitude to effectively guide and impact their students' lives as the barriers of formality wane.

Ensuring discipline in this atmosphere mirrors the discipline required in theater rehearsals. With a firm foundation of trust in place, addressing any missteps becomes a constructive exercise in mentorship rather than mere correction. Rita Pierson's impactful TED talk, "Every Kid Needs a Champion," underscores the essence of this approach (TED, 2013). Her advocacy for strong relationships resonates with the ensemble spirit of theater, where each individual's contribution is cherished. This collaborative approach is particularly pivotal in a project-based learning environment, where students, akin to cast members, must be confident, expressive, and open to feedback.

By emphasizing intentional interactions and the power of trust, classrooms become arenas of profound influence and growth. Here, every student not only contributes to the learning process but is also deeply influenced by the mentors guiding their journey.

From Pedagogy to Practice: A Quiet Battle

In a classroom anchored in open dialogue and mutual respect, one truly grasps the deeper, often silent, transformations of education. I remember a student who transitioned into my class during her seventh-grade year. Relocating across the country and then facing the gauntlet of bullying from another school had left marks on her spirit. She walked in with walls built high, a defense against the world that had been less than kind. With each interaction, I tried to bridge that gap, using simple gestures – an inquiry about her weekend, a nod to her passions. Her responses were often guarded, but the aim was clear: let her know she was seen, heard, and mattered.

It was a quiet battle. I had held a hope that our time together would lead to her letting down her guard, but patience was the lesson she'd teach me instead. It was her return the next year that spoke volumes. The initiation of conversations, the trace of a smile — these were subtle indicators of a breakthrough. That evolution resonated deeply with me and made my heart smile. It underscored the profound value of steadfast presence and genuine connection, even when faced with silent resistance.

Consistent, respectful engagement is the key. I continued to chat with her, as with every student, emphasizing that my classroom is a nurturing atmosphere for sharing and emotional growth—not just academic learning. This sustained dialogue gave me a nuanced understanding of her needs and moods. I now recognize when she needs solitude, seeks assistance, and is ready to talk or work on projects. Her emotional walls are gradually coming down, and her smile is a more frequent, heartening sight.

This experience underscores the importance of creating an environment steeped in open communication and mutual respect. Such a setting fosters academic achievement and becomes a sanctuary for emotional and social development. Her growing comfort in seeking help and engaging more openly is a testament to the impact that a nurturing classroom culture can have on young lives.

Building Trust and Responsibility

Creating an effective classroom environment is likened to orchestrating a symphony—each piece, from relationships to growth mindsets, contributes to a harmonious whole. Without these elements, trust and responsibility can waver.

Setting clear expectations is foundational. In a project-based learning environment, it's not just about the teacher setting the pace; students co-create this rhythm. This collaboration ensures a meaningful and engaging learning experience for all involved.

It was during a conversation with Daniel Pink, the renowned author and behavioral science expert, that he underscored the significance of choice, collaboration, and real-world relevance with me. He noticed that teenagers often disengaged in traditional settings, come alive in extracurricular spaces where these elements are present. Bringing these components into the classroom amplifies student engagement and commitment.

Valuing student feedback and perspectives fosters trust, much like a conductor tuning into each musician. Recognizing and valuing their input sets the stage for a cohesive learning experience.

As we move into amplifying student choice, we will see what happens when students take charge of their learning. The dynamics shift significantly. Maralee Scott, a teacher in Aptakisic-Tripp District 102 in Buffalo Grove, IL, has worked with problem-based learning that exemplifies this, revealing the transformative power of student-led choice in education.

From Pedagogy to Practice: Power of Choice

In the 1980s, a young teacher named Maralee Scott had a vision that would reshape classroom dynamics. She saw potential in empowering students, granting them the autonomy to blend their creativity with critical thinking. This innovative approach—allowing students to decide how they'd showcase their understanding—was ahead of its time. By the 2000s, educators would come to recognize this method as problem-based learning (PmBL).

For context, Maralee is no ordinary educator. She has been a National

Board Certified teacher since 2003 and holds a Master of Education degree in Curriculum and Instruction from the University of MN. Further enriching her accolades, Maralee was a recipient of the NASA Endeavor Fellowship at the Goddard Space Center in Rye, NY, earning her STEM Certification through Columbia Teachers College in 2013.

Let's delve into the stories from her classroom that exemplify the transformative power of student choice. One standout moment revolves around Cyrus, a keen 2nd grader. Tasked with exploring Peggy Parish's *Amelia Bedelia* series, instead of being told what to do, his group decided to create a rotating stage for *Play Ball, Amelia Bedelia*, illustrating the multi-meaning words in the story. Within the same vibrant classroom and under Maralee's guidance, another student's journey highlighted the transformative power of choice. Tony, a member of Cyrus's group with reading challenges, is another testament to the efficacy of Maralee's approach. Given the freedom to explore various picture books on whales, Tony's engagement skyrocketed. He not only actively participated but even clarified misconceptions about the marine mammals.

The zenith of this whale study was a student-led initiative to construct a life-sized model of a baby blue whale. Although Maralee provided guidance, the students were the ones steering the project's course. From design to presentation, every step mirrored their decisions, underscoring the profound impact of choice and agency in learning (M. Scott, personal conversation, August 14, 2023).

Building Room for Curiosity

In many ways, the energy and drive of a project-based learning classroom evoke the bustling atmosphere of a traditional newsroom, though the goals and dynamics differ in subtle but significant ways. In a newsroom, reporters are driven to investigate stories that catch their attention, while in a PBL classroom, students are encouraged to delve into subjects that resonate with their personal interests. Think of the teacher as the editor-in-chief, guiding the overarching vision, while the students, much like reporters, take the lead in their investigative learning quests.

Modeling curiosity is paramount. When a teacher poses intriguing questions or shares "I wonder" statements, it inspires students to harness their own inquisitive nature. The PBL classroom, like a newsroom, values an environment where every question is cherished, as each inquiry adds to the collective understanding.

Similar to how a reporter sifts through multiple sources to weave a story, PBL tools like mind mapping assist students in visualizing connections between ideas and prompting their questions. This questioning becomes an empowered form of learning reminiscent of how reporters feel in pursuit of a groundbreaking story. Yet, the magic truly unfolds when students assert control over their learning, selecting the best medium to showcase their discoveries, be it writing, visuals, or other channels. Here, the PBL classroom borrows from the diversity in journalistic styles, recognizing the spectrum of students' learning methods. Howard Gardner's theory of multiple intelligences (Marenus, 2023) further accentuates this by highlighting that students may excel in areas such as linguistic, spatial, or musical intelligence, to name a few. In championing their choice of expression, PBL recognizes and nurtures these myriad intelligences, leading to a more holistic learning milieu.

For a deeper examination of Howard Gardner's multiple intelligences, scan this QR code.

Just as every role within a newspaper room amalgamates to birth a comprehensive edition, PBL celebrates each student's individuality, resulting in an academic experience that treasures their unique insights and strengths.

However, it's crucial to remember that while a PBL classroom and a newsroom might share similarities in structure and spirit, their functions are distinct. Students aren't traditional reporters. Their explorative journey should center around their innate curiosities. The essence of curiosity is its unpredictability; hence, strategies that don't allow for genuine student agency can sometimes miss the mark. After all, curiosity is an organic entity needing space to meander, grow, and occasionally surprise.

This led to a moment of self-reckoning for me, which took the form of a seemingly simple query from a peer: "Are all the questions provided? Or can they add questions that they are curious about?" It was the nudge I needed to reconsider the architecture of curiosity in my classroom. Would it be a fortress built of my questions and criteria, or could it be more of a collaborative sketch, where students actively participate in drafting the lines and contours? This pivotal moment set the stage for a significant transformation in how mind mapping and research would be conducted in my classroom.

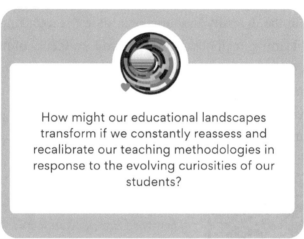

How might our educational landscapes transform if we constantly reassess and recalibrate our teaching methodologies in response to the evolving curiosities of our students?

Journaling Your Journey

Use the space below to reflect on this question.

_____

_____

_____

_____

_____

_____

_____

_____

_____

_____

From Pedagogy to Practice: Natural Wonder

As I noted, mind mapping is a successful strategy for engaging students in building and nurturing curiosity in your classroom. Before mind mapping, I used to provide my students with the essential questions (open-ended questions that require students to engage in higher-order thinking and lead to deeper understandings about a unit of study or specific subject area) and a series of driving questions from each lesson within the unit. My goal was to get students researching so that when they started a unit, they went into it knowing that they knew something about the content. I felt this would give them more confidence and increase their buy-in because they already knew where the unit was headed and knew pieces and parts.

In theory, that research process should have worked, but it didn't. The research was still boring, and students were stuck at their desks copying and pasting questions and whatever Google summary was provided at the top of their search. Students weren't engaging with the process, and it wasn't time well spent.

I will never forget the day I unrolled a sheet of white butcher paper on a table in the center of the room. Immediately, the students' curiosity was kindled. I explained that research was evolving and would no longer be a solitary task; they'd collaborate in teams. Handing each team a uniquely colored pencil, I was eager to see their individual contributions. Placing the essential question in the center of the paper, I then branched out to the lessons' driving questions. The students' task was to uncover the details to answer those questions. See Figure 1.

This new process enabled the students to get up and move while researching. It created an active learning scenario. Students were building off of each other's findings, and they were talking to each other as they worked to see who was finding important information and where they were accessing it. After the activity, the results of their research resembled the example seen in Figure 2.2.

Figure 2.1
Essential Question Mind Map

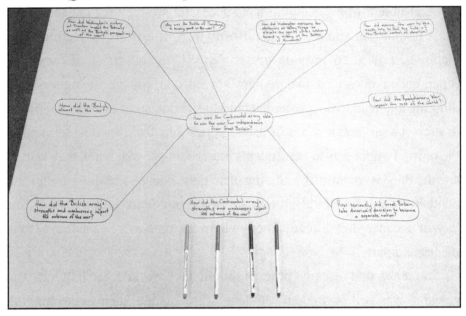

Figure 2.2
Completed Mind Map

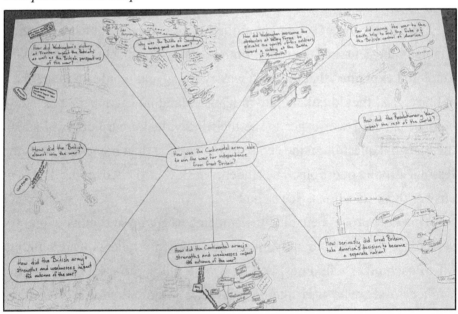

These steps signaled progress, yet there was an evident gap: the innate curiosity of students. While I was busy designing the questions, the students, in turn, were engrossed in answering them. Their natural wonder was left untapped, replaced by a need to adhere to my preset queries. It wasn't until a colleague probed about the nature of these mind maps, inquiring, "Are all the questions predefined? Or do students have the freedom to introduce their own, driven by personal curiosity?" This struck a chord.

In the back of my mind, there was always the looming structure of the curriculum guiding what I believed students needed to learn and seek in their research. The idea of giving them the reins to formulate their own questions seemed risky and unconventional. Yet, this perspective was shortsighted. It dawned on me that just because students were actively participating didn't imply the learning was genuinely student-centric. They might have been engaged, but their engagement was on a predefined path, not one forged from their own curiosity and interests.

True student-centered active learning hinges on granting students the autonomy to shape their learning experiences. This isn't about forsaking the curriculum but rather weaving it with their natural inquisitiveness. The two can coexist, with students' questions acting as supplementary, not contradictory, to the core curriculum.

Embracing this philosophy, I overhauled the mind-mapping activity. It transitioned from being a mere exercise to a platform where students could blend their wonder with the established curriculum, making learning more organic and engaging. Using Genially, an online tool that allows users to create interactive digital content such as presentations, infographics, gamifications, images, and other content, I created the mind map on the next page.

Access this Genially mind map and then manipulate it for your unit by scanning the QR code.

Figure 2.3

Genially Mind Map

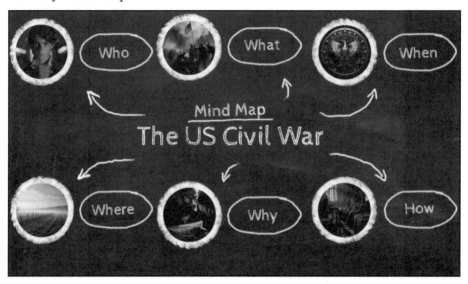

While mind-mapping began changing how students engaged with content, it was clear that the overall classroom environment also played a pivotal role. This led to a focus on effective classroom routines.

From Chaos to Calm:
Creating Order through Effective Classroom Routines

One thing that everyone notices when they walk into my classroom is its calm atmosphere despite the varied activities. Students are working diligently, each on different tasks, yet all know exactly what is expected of them.

The establishment of routines not only sets a standard of what I expect but it provides students with a navigational map of the curriculum. These procedures create an environment where there is always something to do. There is no such thing as "free time" or "downtime" in the classroom. Students need to know that they can move on to the next thing. It is an empowering component of the classroom because it allows for self-pacing to exist. If a student finishes a particular activity or checkpoint (typically a short cycle assessment that provides feedback to the student regarding their understanding of the content), students are encouraged to engage in their curiosity questions. This gives them a purposeful, personal, and meaningful exploration of deepening their understanding of the content to enrich their project.

In a dynamic classroom where students are engaged in various activities, it can be challenging to keep track of their progress and hold them accountable. However, implementing micro-conversations plays a crucial role in creating calm learning environments and establishing routines.

Micro-Conversations

Micro-conversations are brief, informal exchanges between teachers and students or among students themselves that can occur at any time—before, during, or after class. Though seemingly inconsequential due to their short duration, these quick dialogues serve multiple important functions, such as providing formative assessments, offering clarifications, boosting motivation, promoting inclusion, guiding behavior, and building relationships. These interactions, whether planned or spontaneous, contribute to a more cohesive, inclusive, and effective learning environment. They align well with the concept of informal cooperative learning, which involves

> students working in small groups for a few minutes to help them process what has been taught, to think about a particular question, to assist the teacher to identify and address any misunderstandings about the content, and to quickly recap on the key points in the lesson (Gillies, 2020).

Through these brief exchanges, the classroom transforms into a dynamic space where learning is continually fostered, assessed, and refined, creating a holistic educational experience for everyone involved.

By engaging in daily check-ins with each student, teachers can stay connected and ensure that students feel supported and heard. These micro-conversations provide an opportunity to address individual needs, provide guidance, and reinforce expectations. They contribute to a sense of routine and structure, giving students a clear understanding of what is expected of them and helping them stay on track.

While the effectiveness of micro-conversations in promoting academic growth and responsibility is evident, they also play a crucial role in students' emotional well-being. Inconsistent or absent feedback can generate unnecessary anxiety among students, leading them to question their academic standing and often inhibiting their ability to focus on learning. "Am I passing your class?" is a question borne out of such uncertainties. By incorporating consistent and structured micro-conversations into classroom routines, we alleviate this emotional weight. When students know where they stand in terms of mastery, their academic anxiety diminishes. They transition from an unsettled state to a calm and receptive mindset, better prepared for both learning and personal growth.

To address challenges like lack of time or the risk of superficiality, it's vital to set aside dedicated moments for these interactions and ensure they are meaningful. Prioritizing these brief yet impactful dialogues can be achieved through time management techniques, such as incorporating them at specific junctures during the lesson or making them a structured part of project check-ins. Furthermore, while it's crucial to maintain these consistent micro-conversations, they should not completely replace deeper, more substantive discussions, especially when complex issues or academic challenges arise. Thus, by balancing micro-conversations with more in-depth interactions and making them a routine part of the educational process, we not only facilitate academic growth but also contribute to students' emotional well-being.

While micro-conversations can be a powerful tool for enhancing student engagement and accountability, it's essential to be aware of the obstacles that can hamper their effectiveness. One of the most pressing challenges is time. Teachers already operate under tightly packed schedules, making it difficult to consistently allocate time for these brief yet meaningful interactions. A workaround for this could be integrating micro-conversations into existing routines—perhaps while students work on independent activities or during transitional periods between lessons.

Consistency in these conversations is vital for empowering students to become self-reliant learners. If time constraints make daily micro-conversations difficult, consider setting a specific day or days each week dedicated to this practice. Inconsistency could dilute the benefits, as students might then perceive these interactions as arbitrary rather than a structured component of their learning.

Another pitfall is the potential for superficiality. Teachers should be prepared with pointed questions and active listening skills to make the most of these brief exchanges. If a more complex issue arises that can't be adequately addressed in a short dialogue, it's crucial to recognize the need for a more in-depth conversation at a later time. This ensures that important issues aren't glossed over due to time constraints.

Additionally, teachers should not rely solely on micro-conversations for building relationships or conveying important instructional feedback. These should be complemented by deeper discussions and varied forms of assessments to offer a more comprehensive view of student progress and needs. Workarounds for deeper conversations might include creating smaller breakout sessions within the class or allocating specific 'office hours' aimed at more extended, focused discussions.

Finally, setting and communicating clear expectations about the purpose of these micro-conversations is crucial. Teachers could discuss the intent behind these interactions during the first week of school or include them in the syllabus. Students are more likely to take them seriously if they understand how these conversations fit into their broader educational experience and growth.

While micro-conversations are a valuable tool for facilitating progress and accountability, they're not without their challenges. However, with some strategic planning and a balanced approach, these challenges can be effectively mitigated to harness the full potential of this instructional strategy.

While classroom routines and micro-conversations help in shaping the academic and emotional contours of a student's day, it's also crucial to explore methods that celebrate student achievements in a more visible way. This creates a dynamic loop of positive reinforcement that goes beyond the four walls of the classroom, extending to parents and the broader community. This is where the concept of a classroom museum, an idea I initially thought of as merely a decorative touch, profoundly changed my perspective on how to create a holistic educational experience for everyone involved. The classroom museum, I discovered, could take the essence of micro-conversations and project it onto a larger canvas, where individual achievements and interactions become part of a collective, enriching educational narrative.

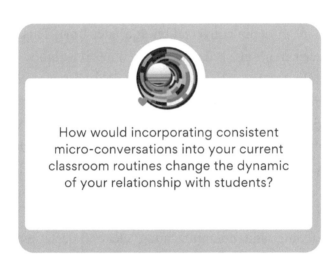

How would incorporating consistent micro-conversations into your current classroom routines change the dynamic of your relationship with students?

Journaling Your Journey

Use the space below to reflect on this question.

_____

_____

_____

_____

_____

_____

_____

_____

_____

_____

_____

_____

_____

From Pedagogy to Practice: Classroom Museum

In today's diverse educational settings, the importance of inclusivity and appreciation cannot be overstated. Showcasing and evaluating student work not only sets benchmarks for academic performance but also fosters an environment where every student feels valued and included. Research underscores the need to give students clear insights into the expected quality of their work. An effective strategy involves using exemplars, or typical examples of varying quality from past students' work. When educators mark and explain these exemplars interactively, they clarify standards and demonstrate appreciation for diverse perspectives and approaches to learning. This inclusive approach, rooted in appreciation, leads to deeper understanding and heightened engagement among students (Hendry & Jukic, 2014). Such practices pave the way for more immersive and collaborative educational experiences, echoing the transformative journey of building a classroom museum where every student's contribution is celebrated.

When I first started building my classroom museum, I thought it was merely a vibrant way to showcase my students' best work. Little did I know how impactful this corner of our room would become, not just for my students but for me as an educator as well as for the parents.

The museum began humbly as a simple bulletin board adorned with exceptional drawings and essays. As the students realized they could produce physical products—like models, crafts, and even simple machines—the bulletin board grew into shelves, then wall mounts, and eventually display cases. I remember funding some of these enhancements through local grants, and others were thrift-store finds.

But the true evolution happened when I began sharing students' work online. This digital extension allowed parents and the entire school community to view the projects in real-time, which has been nothing short of transformative. Parents shared during conferences how much they appreciated seeing the projects online, stating it helped them understand the depth of what their kids were learning. They felt more connected to the classroom and, more importantly, to their children's academic journey. Parents take pride when we teachers value what their children are doing in the classroom. It spurred conversations at home, prompting a whole new level of parental involvement in their children's education.

As for me, the museum turned into a real-time portfolio of student work, a living, breathing tapestry of educational milestones. Gone were the days when I solely relied on end-of-the-unit assessments to gauge understanding. Now, every project on display has become a focal point for reflection. What was the class collectively grasping? Where did I need to adjust my teaching strategies?

And let's not forget the students. One moment that captured the essence was when Grace, a shy but brilliant student in my class, produced a project combining her love for Harry Potter with our unit on colonial regions. Her face lit up when I told her that her project would not only feature in our classroom museum but would also be shared in our digital space. "You mean my parents and others can see it any time they want?" she asked, her eyes wide with a mix of thrill and nervous excitement. I nodded, and that was one of those moments I wish I could freeze. The sense of pride, the boost in self-esteem, and the recognition of hard work were palpable.

In the following figure, you can see the colonial region project that aligns with 8th-grade content standards and the student's passion for Harry Potter. Each wand was designed to represent the economies within the various colonial regions. The spell book contained Latin descriptions of colonial regions along with specific wand movements. The potions represented the individual colonies found within the regions. It was a truly magical connection

The classroom museum became more than just a display; it morphed into an ecosystem of learning, validation, and connection. It didn't just set standards and showcase quality work; it built a culture of collaboration and mutual appreciation among students. It didn't merely serve as a window into each student's academic journey; it acted as a bridge connecting educators, students, and parents in a synergistic relationship that transcended traditional barriers.

Figure 2.4

Harry Potter Inspired Project

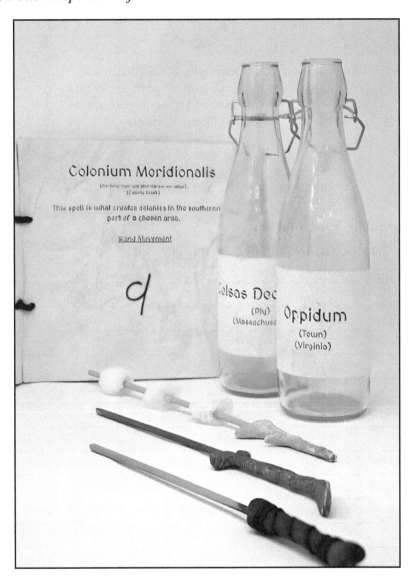

By recognizing and valuing the effort put into these projects, we were doing more than decorating a room. We were creating a supportive and inclusive atmosphere, laying the foundation for effective classroom routines, and strengthening our classroom community in ways I hadn't initially imagined.

How could you integrate a classroom museum into your current setting? What would it look like, and how do you see it impacting your students?

Journaling Your Journey

Use the space below to reflect on this question.

_____

_____

_____

_____

_____

_____

_____

_____

_____

_____

_____

_____

_____

_____

Unity in Diversity: Nurturing Inclusive Learning Spaces

In the push toward student-centered learning, recognizing and appreciating our students' diverse characteristics and needs becomes essential.

As highlighted in recent studies, "Learner diversity is an issue worth addressing in education practices across countries if inclusive societies are to be developed, promoted, and sustained" (Possi & Reginard Milinga, 2017, p. 28). Our classrooms present a variety of learning preferences, paces, backgrounds, and support systems. Rather than seeing this diversity as a challenge, we should shift our mindset to view it as an advantage. Creating a classroom culture that values each student's unique contributions requires intentionality and commitment.

As an educator, I understood that my mindset had to change to allow true inclusivity to flourish in my classroom. I recognized the need to make my teaching methods reflect the diversity I wanted my students to experience. Wishing for ideal students wasn't enough; I took active steps to support and engage with their unique needs and interests.

When teaching topics like Spain's exploration of the southwest region of North America in my history class, I deliberately included diverse perspectives. Adding indigenous viewpoints alongside dominant narratives balanced the students' understanding of history. Another example of including diverse perspectives is when my students study the beginnings of the Revolutionary War. As they explore the battles of Lexington and Concord, students read through Colonial Joseph Warren's report as well as the testimony of F. Smith, Lieutenant-Colonel 10th Foot of the British Army. There isn't a right or wrong answer in these activities. It is about presenting two perspectives and allowing students to hear a diverse narrative. I also led open and safe conversations that allowed students to connect personally with the material. These discussions shifted the focus from merely studying history to truly exploring life, fostering student empathy and understanding.

One of my 8th-grade students, Hadley, encapsulated this experience beautifully:

> The moment I walked into Mr. Jones's class, I felt like I
> was in a totally different world. He makes everyone feel
> like they can be themselves and be super creative. It's
> awesome because we all feel like we matter in his class.
> I actually look forward to going to school. We learn stuff

but also have a lot of fun. Before I came to his class, I was kinda nervous because I have dyslexia, and it's always been a big struggle for me. But with Mr. Jones, I didn't have to worry. He makes everyone feel comfortable, like it's okay to be different or have challenges. I used to be super quiet about my dyslexia, like it was something to be ashamed of. But Mr. Jones made me feel like it was okay to talk about it, and now I don't feel like I have to hide it anymore. In his class, you feel like everyone's opinion matters. So yeah, Mr. Jones doesn't just teach stuff, he changes how you feel about school and about yourself. And that's something really special.

Teachers hold a critical role in cultivating a classroom culture that celebrates diversity. "Equitable conversational practices in the classrooms between the two genders are important as a means of appreciating individual differences in the teaching and learning processes. Coupled with disability issues in the classrooms, teachers become more loaded with responsibilities" (Possi & Reginard Milinga, 2017, p. 32). Consistency matters. Clear expectations about treating, valuing, and respecting students establish a supportive and non-judgmental environment for exploring interests and passions. Setting non-negotiable rules about student interactions and communication lays the foundation for mutual respect and understanding. We must correct missteps and protect our boundaries. By upholding these expectations, we nurture learning for all students and create an inclusive environment that honors diverse experiences, perspectives, and ideas.

The willingness of a teacher to set the tone and expectations serves as the cornerstone of an inclusive, diverse classroom culture. Teachers must lay down rules for respectful interactions and communication and must also remain open to their learning and growth. As facilitators, we guide open and safe discussions, encouraging empathy and mutual understanding. In such an environment, the effectiveness of our efforts becomes clear when students, seeing the value of diverse perspectives, eagerly engage in projects and discussions with their peers.

42

This leads us to the essential point: diversity in the classroom is not just beneficial but necessary. Students bring various backgrounds and experiences into our classrooms, offering viewpoints that enrich the learning process. In the realm of project-based learning, collaboration takes center stage. When students embrace and appreciate diversity, they actively seek differing perspectives to enhance their problem-solving and solution development. A range of perspectives enriches the development of robust and well-rounded solutions. The focus shifts from a singular "right" way to valuing diverse perspectives' contributions to the table.

Promoting diversity as an asset rather than a hindrance cultivates an environment where students learn to appreciate and respect their peers' viewpoints. Students understand diversity enhances creativity, critical thinking, and a deeper global understanding. This mindset challenges their assumptions, broadens their horizons, and fosters empathy and cultural competency.

Valuing diversity in the classroom empowers students to explore diverse perspectives, collaborate effectively, and develop comprehensive solutions. Embracing the richness of student backgrounds nurtures critical thinking, empathy, and a broader understanding of the world's complexities. Further enriching this collaborative learning environment is the practice of cooperative learning, which, as highlighted,

> involves an emphasis on the diversity rather than uniformity of instruction, which means that teachers can ensure that students are given tasks that they have the potential to accomplish. It also permits greater flexibility to adjust learning objectives, as teachers can adjust tasks to meet the needs of specific students in groups"(Gillies, 2020).

Through cooperative learning, the classroom becomes a dynamic space where the collective diversity serves as a powerful tool for enhanced learning and problem-solving.

What steps have you taken or could you take to actively integrate diverse perspectives and experiences into your curriculum?

Journaling Your Journey

Use the space below to reflect on this question.

_____

_____

_____

_____

_____

_____

_____

_____

_____

_____

_____

From Pedagogy to Practice: Diverse Perspectives

Students bring diverse backgrounds and experiences to our classrooms, and recognizing this diversity's impact on their learning approach is crucial. Creating an inclusive environment that values and celebrates diversity encourages students to consider issues, classroom content, problems, and projects from multiple angles. Each perspective holds value and deserves consideration for a comprehensive understanding of the topic.

In the realm of project-based learning, collaboration takes center stage. When students embrace and appreciate diversity, they actively seek differing perspectives to enhance their problem-solving and solution development. A range of perspectives enriches the development of robust and well-rounded solutions. The focus shifts from a singular "right" way to valuing the contributions that diverse perspectives make to the table.

Promoting diversity as an asset rather than a hindrance cultivates an environment where students learn to appreciate and respect their peers' viewpoints. Students understand diversity enhances creativity, critical thinking, and a deeper global understanding. This mindset challenges their assumptions, broadens their horizons, and fosters empathy and cultural competency.

Valuing diversity in the classroom empowers students to explore diverse perspectives, collaborate effectively, and develop comprehensive solutions. Embracing the richness of student backgrounds nurtures critical thinking, empathy, and a broader understanding of the world's complexities.

Plan, Personalize, Pursue

Plan

Embracing project-based learning is akin to embarking on a journey of transformation – not just for your students but also for you as an educator. As you walk through this journey, it's important to remember that the path isn't always straight, and there will be twists and turns along the way. But that's the beauty of this journey. It's about continual learning, growing, and evolving as an educator. It begins with understanding the existing classroom culture and envisioning how it can transform to nurture a vibrant PBL environment.

It's time to bring your plans to fruition. Reflection is your navigational tool, guiding you through a deep introspection and assessment of your existing classroom culture. This journey of discovery could reveal practices that already align with your PBL goals or spotlight areas in need of enhancement. Your primary objective is to lay a sturdy foundation upon which you can confidently construct a PBL classroom culture that is nurturing, inclusive, and engaging.

Commit to putting pen to paper and record your answers to the questions presented at the outset of this chapter. The honesty you employ in your reflections will directly influence the authenticity and significance of your forthcoming steps.

Figure 2.5
Reflective Workbook

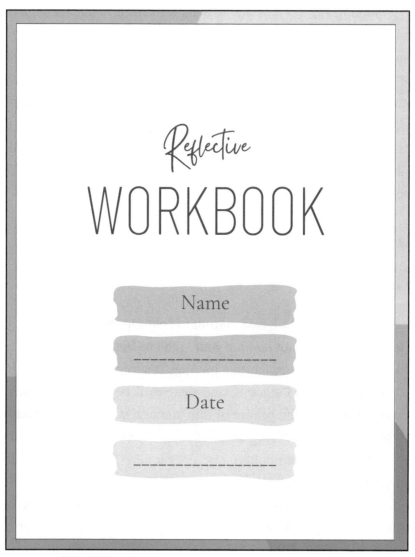

Scan the QR code to access your copy of the Reflective Workbook.

Personalize

Every classroom is a unique blend of diverse personalities and perspectives. The richness of this diversity can be harnessed to create an inclusive PBL culture that empowers every student. As you plan and implement your strategies, infuse personalization into your classroom culture, recognizing and valuing each student's uniqueness.

Your visualization of the ideal PBL classroom must reflect this diversity, allowing space for each student to contribute, grow, and thrive. The transformation process will be unique for every classroom, mirroring the distinctive mix of students who bring their backgrounds, ideas, and experiences into the learning environment.

In my classroom, I infuse student choice into every unit. Students are abe to tell me how they would like to represent their mastery of the content. This empowers each student to draw on their interests and skill sets to motivate and drive their learning. Each student is held accountable for their understanding of the content when we have micro-conversations, but how they represent that content is unique to each student. I may have a student designing a Minecraft world, one designing Hot Wheels cars using AI software, one using virtual reality to draw three-dimensionally, one making a pop-up book, and another writing a script for a short film. This diversity builds engagement and intrinsic motivation for students to own their mastery of the content.

Now that you've looked closely at your classroom and identified potential areas for enhancement, it's time to turn those observations into a concrete plan. The objective is to devise a set of actionable steps that can help foster a more inclusive, personalized learning environment that recognizes and celebrates each student's uniqueness. Perhaps you need to incorporate more differentiated instruction into your lessons, or maybe you recognize the value in implementing projects catering to different strengths and learning preferences. Consider including more culturally diverse resources in your curriculum or creating opportunities for students to share and celebrate their personal experiences and backgrounds. Whatever the specifics, the aim is to ensure that every student feels seen, heard, and valued in your PBL classroom.

As you formulate these steps, it's also important to attach a timeline to each one. Remember that meaningful change doesn't happen overnight. It's a gradual process that requires patience, consistency, and time. Therefore, set realistic timelines for implementing each of your actionable steps.

Maybe you decide to introduce one new strategy or activity each week, or perhaps you choose to focus on one area of improvement each month. This timeline is not set in stone but serves as a guideline to keep you on track and committed to your goals. You must allow yourself the flexibility to make adjustments as necessary based on your progress and the feedback received from students. This way, enhancing your classroom's inclusivity and diversity becomes a dynamic, responsive journey rather than a rigid task.

Scan the QR code to access your copy of the Classroom Culture seen in Figure 2.6.

Pursue

The implementation portion, where your planning and personalization are put into action, will involve various activities like restructuring the learning environment, reformulating lesson plans, fostering a growth mindset, promoting an open and respectful environment, and embracing diversity. You will adapt your teaching practices to prioritize curiosity, inquiry, and collaboration. The pace of implementation may differ based on individual classroom dynamics and institutional support structures.

Embracing the journey of transforming your classroom culture into a more inclusive, engaging, and dynamic learning environment also means acknowledging that it is a process, one that's likely to have its share of trials and triumphs. It's important to understand that facing challenges and experiencing setbacks is not a sign of failure but rather an inherent part of the journey.

Figure 2.6
Classroom Culture

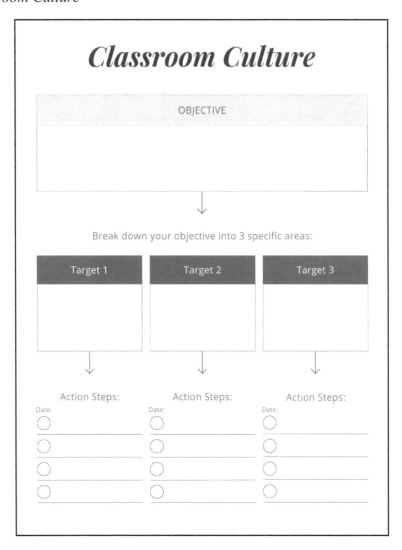

Just as we teach our students, trial and error are fundamental to learning and growth. Sometimes, a strategy you implement does not produce the desired result, or a particular approach might not resonate with your students as you expected. These instances should not be seen as failures but instead as valuable opportunities for learning and refinement.

Think of each setback as a lesson that guides your next steps. When a strategy doesn't work as planned, take the time to reflect on why it didn't and how it can be improved. Engage with your students, seek their feedback, and understand their perspectives. This open dialogue provides valuable insights for tweaking your strategies and fosters a sense of shared responsibility and community within your classroom.

As you continually apply, reflect, and adjust, you foster a culture of perseverance and resilience in yourself and your students. Remember, consistent and reflective implementation is critical to successful transformation. This cycle of trying, learning, adapting, and trying again keeps the process dynamic, ensuring your classroom is a space that continually evolves to meet the unique needs of your diverse students.

Moreover, embracing this iterative approach models an important life skill for your students - it shows them that 'failure' is not an end-point but a stepping stone towards improvement and success. This mindset encourages them to take risks, learn from their mistakes, and understand that effort and perseverance are key growth elements. In this way, the process of enhancing your classroom environment not only enriches the learning experience for your students but also imparts valuable lessons that extend beyond the classroom walls.

The Pathway

Remember Jean Piaget's insightful words – the objective of education is to enable individuals to do new things, not merely to replicate past efforts. In your endeavor to reshape your classroom culture, you are pivotal in fostering these 'doers of new things.'

How can we, as educators, transform our classrooms into nurturing and engaging environments that foster a sense of belonging, encourage a growth mindset, cultivate respect, nurture curiosity, and celebrate diversity?

Revisit this question often. Let it inspire and steer your decisions and guide your PBL practices.

The path of transformation into a PBL classroom is not a sprint but a marathon. Each stride, irrespective of its size, is valuable progress toward achieving an immersive, inclusive, and profound learning experience for your students. Remember, you are not alone on this journey. Support, guidance, and encouragement are always at hand.

How will you leverage the support, guidance, and encouragement available to you to create the classroom culture you desire for your students?

Journaling Your Journey

Use the space below to reflect on this question.

_____

_____

_____

_____

_____

_____

_____

_____

_____

_____

This chapter has illuminated the critical role of nurturing supportive classroom cultures centered around growth, diversity, and student empowerment. This cultural foundation sets the stage for the richer learning experiences explored in project-based learning. In the next chapter, we dive deeper into the nuts and bolts of effective PBL practices, from crafting compelling essential questions to designing authentic tasks and assessments. Just as a vibrant classroom environment provides fertile soil for student growth, these dynamic PBL components become the nourishing waters that sustain curiosity and fuel profound learning.

As you transition into dissecting the intricacies of impactful PBL, reflect on how these practices can be woven into the culture you envision for your classroom. What essential questions might spark wonder in your students? How can you design authentic tasks tailored to their diverse passions and skills? Let these reflections guide you as we continue building the framework needed to cultivate engaging PBL experiences.

Chapter 3
Designing Effective Practices

Interview with Jay McTighe
Writer & Educational Consultant

"It is not enough to be busy... The question is: what are we busy about?"
- Henry David Thoreau

Part One: Essential Questions

Project-based learning transcends traditional educational paradigms and deeply engages students in a process where their learning is vivid and alive. This approach, championed by education experts like Jay McTighe, weaves together the fabric of inquiry-based learning with the threads of real-world relevance and structured intellectual discovery. McTighe, who has profoundly impacted curriculum development through his Understanding by Design framework, brings a wealth of knowledge on crafting *essential questions* that provoke deep thought, creating *authentic tasks* that mirror the complexities of life, and devising *project plans* that serve as the scaffolding for student learning.

These essential questions are the sparks that ignite the flame of inquiry, prompting students to venture into uncharted intellectual territories. Authentic tasks live up to their name by providing tangible, real-world challenges that solidify students' learning experiences, giving shape to their newfound knowledge. Project planning becomes the architectural blueprint, guiding learners to construct their understanding piece by piece, ensuring a robust and coherent structure to their educational journey.

As these components synergistically come together, they do more than just animate PBL; they embed in students a profound sense of purpose and relevance, fundamental tenets McTighe emphasizes as critical for successful learning. In the following passages, we will explore the terrain of PBL with McTighe as our guide, examining how these essential elements contribute to an engaging and dynamic learning method and illuminate the path for students to find meaning and connection in their educational endeavors.

Essential Questions

In project-based learning, specific pedagogical tools are fundamental to guide and enrich the students' learning journeys. Among these tools, essential, topical, and guiding questions hold a special place (McTighe & Wiggins, 2013). While seemingly similar, each type performs distinct roles and is utilized differently in an educational setting, according to Jay McTighe and Grant Wiggins in their work *Essential Questions: Opening Doors to Student Understanding.*

For those looking to deepen their understanding of pedagogical tools like essential questions, Jay McTighe and Grant Wiggins's book, Essential Questions: Opening Doors to Student Understanding, is a seminal work worth consulting. Their methodology has become a cornerstone in modern pedagogy, especially advantageous for those implementing project-based learning environments. They demonstrate how well-crafted questions can catalyze critical thinking, interdisciplinary exploration, and student engagement. If you're an educator aiming for a more nuanced and effective teaching strategy, McTighe and Wiggins's insights offer a foundational roadmap for elevating your curriculum and student outcomes.

As we journey into project-based learning, we must acknowledge that not all questions are created equal. Within a pedagogical framework, different types of questions serve distinct purposes, helping guide students through their learning journey. Collectively, essential questions, topical questions, and guiding questions work together to foster students' critical thinking and problem-solving skills.

Figure 3.1
Essential Questions Graphic

Essential questions are the Sun in our educational cosmos—illuminating the big ideas and enduring learning themes. Topical questions are the Earth—specific landscapes of inquiry within broader subject areas. Guiding questions are the Moon—more minor, reflective prompts that illuminate the path for day-to-day learning and understanding. Each has its place in the learning journey, with the essential questions providing a broad light of understanding, topical questions giving context and depth, and guiding questions offering immediate, actionable steps for students to follow. Together, they create a harmonious system for navigating the universe of knowledge.

Essential questions encompass a broad spectrum of inquiry. In project-based learning, understanding the distinction between overarching essential questions (OEQs) and topical essential questions (TEQs) is critical. An OEQ might be, "How does technology influence society?" This broad question spans various subjects and encourages ongoing exploration and discussion.

In contrast, a TEQ is more specific, such as "What were the key causes and effects of World War II?" This question is narrower, focusing on a specific historical event and its implications, and is typically explored within a particular unit or topic (McTighe & Wiggins, 2013). As we progress, we'll dissect the nuances that distinguish OEQs from TEQs, enabling educators to leverage these questions to foster profound learning experiences.

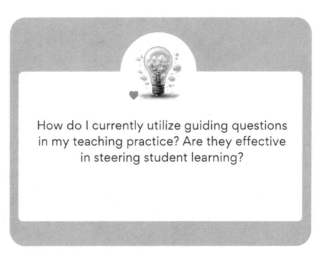

How do I currently utilize guiding questions in my teaching practice? Are they effective in steering student learning?

Journaling Your Journey

Use the space below to reflect on this question.

_____

_____

_____

_____

_____

_____

_____

_____

Let's circle back to the analogy of the Sun, the Earth, and the Moon. The dynamic nature of essential questions can be likened to the role of the Sun in our solar system, a constant force that anchors the orbits of all planets, much like how essential questions anchor topical questions within a unit. As students delve deeper into the subject matter, their understanding and responses to these essential questions expand, similar to how the Sun's gravitational pull guides the Earth's orbit.

Unlike guiding questions, which provide more straightforward answers—akin to the Moon's evident influence on Earth's tides—essential questions provoke evolving responses. These reflect the students' growth within the specific unit and their broader intellectual journey.

In the same way that the Sun's influence extends beyond anchoring Earth's orbit, affecting climate, tides, and life itself, essential questions extend beyond the unit, encouraging students to engage in higher-order thinking and continued intellectual exploration.

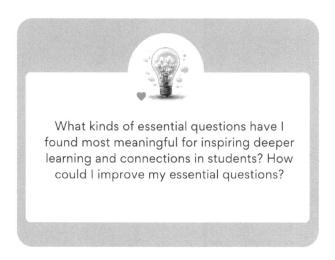

What kinds of essential questions have I found most meaningful for inspiring deeper learning and connections in students? How could I improve my essential questions?

Journaling Your Journey

Use the space below to reflect on this question.

_____

_____

_____

_____

_____

_____

_____

Overarching essential questions are broad, cross-disciplinary, and pertinent throughout a student's life.

On the other hand, topical essential questions are tied directly to a specific unit, topic, or standard being taught. They are more narrowly focused and help students grasp the significance of their learning (McTighe & Wiggins, 2013).

In a PBL environment, teachers often utilize topical essential questions as they are directly tied to specific standards or topics. They guide students' exploration and project direction in a targeted manner, ensuring academic rigor. The PBL approach involves students actively researching these topical essential questions before starting a new unit, a process known as front-loading. This active involvement from the onset sparks interest, builds confidence, and scaffolds knowledge, preparing the ground for deeper learning.

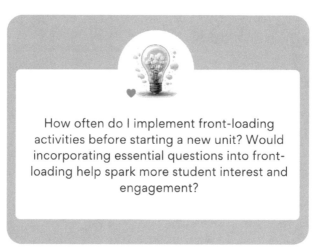

How often do I implement front-loading activities before starting a new unit? Would incorporating essential questions into front-loading help spark more student interest and engagement?

Journaling Your Journey

Use the space below to reflect on this question.

_____

_____

_____

_____

_____

_____

Examples From Various Subjects

In social studies, essential questions could be:

- What is the role of government in a democratic society? (OEQ)
- How do the government branches help create a more perfect Union? (TEQ)
- How does the judicial branch help create a more perfect union? (GQ)

- How does ancient civilization influence our modern world? (OEQ)
- How has Ancient Rome impacted your life? (TEQ)
- How does the legal system of Ancient Rome influence modern legal systems? (GQ)

- How have historical significant change and innovation periods influenced the modern world? (OEQ)
- What advancements were made during the Renaissance, and how do they impact your life today? (TEQ)
- How has Renaissance art influenced modern artistic techniques and aesthetics? (GQ)

In math:

- When and why is precision important in mathematics and everyday life? (OEQ)
- How do I know when to estimate or use exact amounts? (TEQ)
- How do rounding numbers help in making quick estimates? (GQ)

- How do we choose the right mathematical tools to solve a problem? (OEQ)
- How do you know what operations to use in a given situation? (TEQ)

- How does understanding the relationships between operations help choose the correct operation for a given problem? (GQ)

- How can mathematical principles be applied to solve real-world problems? (OEQ)

- How can we use the Pythagorean Theorem to determine the total length of the cable line around our town? (TEQ)

- What is the Pythagorean Theorem, and how is it used in geometry? (GQ)

In science:

- How do individual actions contribute to global environmental outcomes? (OEQ)

- What effect does recycling have on decreasing my environmental footprint? (TEQ)

- How does the process of recycling work, and why does it help the environment? (GQ)

- How do past geological events inform our understanding of Earth's future? (OEQ)

- How has Earth changed over time, and what does that tell us about its future? (TEQ)

- How do we study and understand changes in Earth over time? (GQ)

- How does science allow us to understand and quantify the unseen aspects of our world? (OEQ)

- How do we measure things that we cannot see? (TEQ)

- What tools and methods do scientists use to measure these unseen things? (GQ)

In reading:

- How does tailoring writing to a specific audience enhance communication and impact? (OEQ)

- Why is it important to know your audience when composing a piece of writing? (TEQ)

- What factors should be considered when identifying the target audience for a piece of writing? (GQ)

- How does exploring diverse viewpoints and experiences in literature contribute to our understanding of human nature and empathy? (OEQ)

- How can looking at literature from different perspectives help to give a greater understanding of the characters in the story? (TEQ)

- How does analyzing characters from different perspectives impact our overall story interpretation? (GQ)

- In what ways do a reader's prior knowledge and personal experiences shape their interpretation and engagement with a text? (OEQ)

- How does what I am reading influence how I should read it? (TEQ)

- How does being aware of the author's intentions and historical background impact our reading of a text? (GQ)

Creating effective essential questions requires thought and creativity. McTighe and Wiggins (2013) suggest that educators should strive to frame questions, especially topical essential questions, that resonate with students' interests, instill a sense of lifelong learning, and align with key curricular concepts. Both essential questions and guiding questions, when thoughtfully constructed, transform the classroom into an active space of intellectual exploration, making the learning process more engaging and effective.

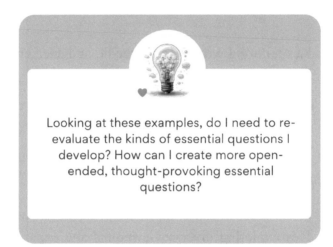

Looking at these examples, do I need to re-evaluate the kinds of essential questions I develop? How can I create more open-ended, thought-provoking essential questions?

Journaling Your Journey

Use the space below to reflect on this question.

_____

_____

_____

_____

_____

_____

_____

_____

_____

Part Two: Performance Tasks

"Learning without thought is labor lost; thought without learning is perilous."
-Confucius

In the dynamic world of project-based learning, performance tasks stand as pivotal milestones. Echoing Confucius' insights on the necessity of combining learning with critical thinking, these tasks are not just exercises in applying knowledge but critical opportunities for students to reflect on their experiences. Through this reflection, students gain a deeper understanding of the subject matter, mirroring Confucius' concept that true learning arises from thoughtful consideration of our actions. In this way, performance tasks in PBL serve as a bridge between theory and practice, fostering a reflective learning environment that Confucius advocated.

Performance tasks are designed to align with academic standards while resonating with real-world scenarios. They provide a canvas for students to apply their knowledge creatively and for educators to assess understanding comprehensively.

On a cool autumn evening, the chocolate chip cookies my wife and daughter aimed to perfect for the local street fair embodied the essence of performance tasks in project-based learning. Every ingredient paralleled a critical piece of knowledge, and their meticulous preparation mirrored the application of learned concepts. Much like the scrutiny of an assessment, the oven's heat tested their effort. The final, delicious cookies represented the successful outcome of a performance task, demonstrating knowledge, application, and skill—essential elements of the educational process. Their triumph at the fair mirrored the achievement of a PBL objective, illustrating the journey from theory to a rewarding, tangible outcome.

Performance tasks embody the essence of project-based learning by fusing authentic, real-world engagement with rigorous assessment, thereby acting as the modern educational apprenticeship. These tasks are meticulously crafted to immerse students in scenarios that resonate with the core objectives of their subject matter. Unlike conventional methods that may emphasize theory or rote memorization, performance tasks compel students to apply their knowledge practically and meaningful-ly. By plunging into the intricacies of real-world problems, students are honing their analytical and creative abilities and preparing themselves for the nuanced challenges awaiting them beyond the classroom walls.

The seamless integration of application and assessment is at the heart of performance tasks. These tasks are structured to demand a comprehen-sive synthesis and application of students' skills and knowledge. They transcend traditional evaluations by offering a holistic insight into a student's grasp of the subject matter, extending from basic comprehension to critical problem-solving abilities. Unlike separate constructs of authentic and assessment tasks, performance tasks embody a unified approach toward evaluating a student's readiness for future educational and professional endeavors.

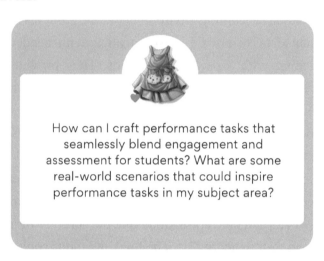

How can I craft performance tasks that seamlessly blend engagement and assessment for students? What are some real-world scenarios that could inspire performance tasks in my subject area?

Journaling Your Journey

Use the space below to reflect on this question.

_____

_____

_____

_____

_____

_____

_____

_____

_____

_____

_____

_____

_____

_____

_____

In the realm of PBL, performance tasks play an indispensable role by offering a multifaceted platform for students to demonstrate mastery of content and skills. They are meticulously designed to align with academic standards, ensuring a robust evaluation of students' understanding, progress, and achievement of learning objectives. The diverse nature of performance tasks may encompass quizzes, tests, conversations, presentations, projects, simulations, fieldwork, or community engagement; all orchestrated to resonate with real-world complexities.

The essence of performance tasks lies in their ability to provide educators and students with valuable feedback, pinpointing strengths and areas necessitating further attention or support.

Moreover, by engaging in performance tasks, students are nurtured to develop transferable skills and competencies instrumental in navigating complex, real-world scenarios. They learn to think critically, collaborate efficiently, communicate effectively, manage time, and adapt to ambiguous situations, all within a structured, evaluative framework.

 Reflect on your most recent or upcoming unit through the lens of performance tasks.

Assess how well your current approach integrates authentic engagement with rigorous assessment. Identify the harmonies and, perhaps, the dissonances, and challenge yourself to refine these components. By consciously aligning and refining these critical aspects of performance tasks, we set a robust foundation for comprehensive, impactful learning experiences that assess and prepare our students for real-world exigencies.

Assess Does Not Equal Grading

In project-based learning, the essence of performance tasks lies in fostering growth rather than just assigning grades. These tasks encourage students to engage authentically and apply their understanding in real-world scenarios, marking a shift from traditional grading to a more constructive form of assessment. This is particularly beneficial for students transitioning from conventional academic settings to the explorative nature of PBL. The focus is guiding students through ambiguity and promoting higher-level thinking without fearing a wrong answer.

Performance tasks also emphasize meaningful feedback, highlighting strengths and areas for improvement. This approach contrasts with conventional grading systems, which often inhibit creativity and risk-taking. Instead, it cultivates a nurturing environment where learning and growth are prioritized over achieving specific grades.

In a PBL classroom, assessment evolves into a dynamic exchange of feedback and self-reflection. Performance tasks are crucial in guiding students through their learning journey, helping them apply their understanding in new, authentic contexts. This approach was evident in my classroom at the beginning of the academic year, where I emphasized a growth-oriented strategy over traditional grading. Students were encouraged to see assignments as opportunities for deeper understanding, shifting their focus from grades to mastering content.

This reorientation from grade-centric to growth-centric learning fosters a more enriching and engaging educational experience. In PBL settings, the goal of assessment is to champion students' development, valuing their learning journey and the application of knowledge. By centering assessment within performance tasks, educators create a vibrant atmosphere that supports curiosity, exploration, and risk-taking, ensuring all students are prepared to meet challenges and reach their potential.

The transition to growth-oriented learning in PBL naturally leads us to embrace authentic tasks, with mind mapping emerging as a standout example. Mind mapping embodies the essence of authentic tasks by closely mirroring real-life problem-solving processes. It engages students in organizing and connecting ideas in a way that reflects genuine intellectual activities beyond the confines of traditional classroom tasks. This method encourages students to not only visualize but also critically analyze and synthesize information, making their learning process more reflective of real-world applications. As such, mind mapping exemplifies an authentic task, bridging academic concepts with practical skills and serving as an ideal segue into its application in a K-12 setting.

Do my current assessments focus more on grades or on providing meaningful feedback? How can I shift towards prioritizing growth and constructive feedback?

Journaling Your Journey

Use the space below to reflect on this question.

_____

_____

_____

_____

_____

_____

_____

_____

_____

_____

_____

_____

_____

_____

_____

Authentic Tasks

Mind Maps

In the context of mind mapping as an authentic task, the use of a topical essential question can be particularly effective. A topical essential question focuses on a specific area of study or unit theme, providing students with a clear and concentrated point of exploration. When creating a mind map, this question is the central node or starting point. From there, students can branch out to explore various aspects of the topic ("Who, What, Where, When, Why, and How"), connecting their thoughts and findings back to this central question. This approach aligns well with performance tasks, encouraging deep exploration of a specific subject and promoting thorough understanding and meaningful application of knowledge.

Branching out from this topical essential question, the "**Who**" segment identifies key stakeholders or individuals linked to the problem, thereby mapping the human aspect of the scenario. The "**What**" component delves into the specifics of the problem, encapsulating its scope, key elements, and impacts.

The "**Where**" segment pinpoints the location of the occurrence, be it a physical place or a more abstract location such as a specific industry. Meanwhile, the "**When**" section establishes a timeline, helping learners understand the problem's origins and the key moments of its manifestation.

The "**Why**" branch serves as the root cause analysis, dissecting the underlying causes and the mechanics of the problem. And finally, the "**How**" branch creates a space for solution brainstorming and implementation strategies.

Expanding main connection points into additional branches allows learners to dive into the complexities of each aspect. It fosters a thorough comprehension of the central theme. Beyond the simple understanding of concepts, learners are engaged in integrative thinking. This type of thought process, which involves drawing connections between diverse ideas, is critical in our increasingly interconnected world of knowledge.

Mind mapping is not only flexible but also visually engaging, catering to an array of learning preferences. It has the potential to enhance information recall significantly. This is achieved through using colors, symbols, and images to emphasize key points, transforming the learning process into an engaging and memorable experience. Beyond its educational value, a mind map is a tangible testament to learners' thought processes. It captures a clear snapshot of their understanding, making it a powerful tool

Figure 3.2
Mind Mapping

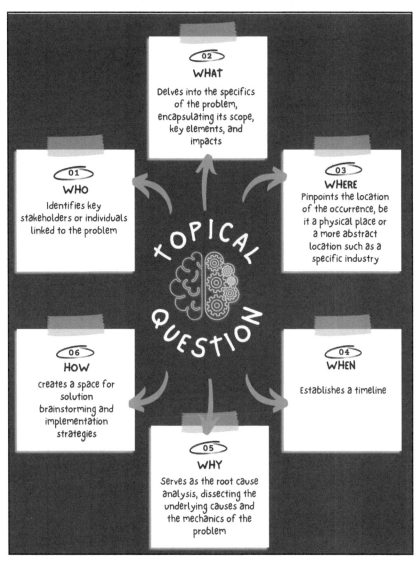

for educators to gain insights into students' thinking and provide targeted feedback. Additionally, it allows learners to carry out self-assessment, helping them identify gaps in their understanding and chart their progress over time. Ultimately, the expanded branches of a mind map facilitate profound engagement with the content and nurture critical and creative thinking skills, making mind mapping an indispensable tool in the journey of knowledge exploration and application.

Benefits

The usage of mind mapping brings a multitude of benefits to the classroom, serving as a tool for generating and connecting ideas and as a method for planning and organizing tasks. Its application in authentic tasks within project-based learning is invaluable due to its adaptability, supporting critical thinking, creativity, problem-solving, and collaboration. Mind mapping's versatility extends to the visual exploration of concepts, allowing students to integrate images that enhance comprehension and recall. This active engagement in the learning process through mind mapping fosters a deeper understanding and personalizes the learning journey (Sembiring & Harahap, 2015).

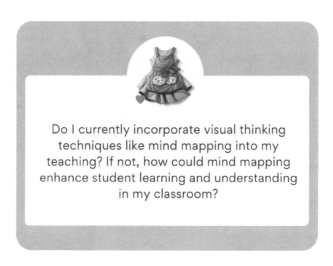

Do I currently incorporate visual thinking techniques like mind mapping into my teaching? If not, how could mind mapping enhance student learning and understanding in my classroom?

Journaling Your Journey

Use the space below to reflect on this question.

_____

_____

_____

_____

_____

_____

Discussions

As previously discussed, authentic tasks offer a significant platform for students to engage with their learning actively. They can move beyond memorization by providing them with opportunities to apply their knowledge through meaningful interactions such as classroom discussions and personal conversations with their teacher. This approach facilitates the processing and internalization of concepts, transforming the learning experience into an active, participatory process.

Such active learning can manifest in a myriad of ways, all adaptable to your classroom's specific context and your students' unique characteristics. Although these methodologies are infinitely diverse, we will explore a few examples to inspire and inform your approach to crafting authentic tasks in your classroom. These instances serve as sparks to ignite the potential for active learning and meaningful application within your unique educational environment.

Socratic seminars, grounded in the Socratic method employed by the renowned philosopher Socrates, provide an engaging platform for stimulating critical thinking and fostering rich dialogue among students. These student-led discussions revolve around a shared text, topic, or theme and allow students to probe deeper into the subject matter. While commonly used in higher education, this educational strategy can be adapted to cater to all ages, from early learners in K-3 classrooms to high school students.

In a typical Socratic seminar, students engage in a roundtable dialogue, transforming the classroom into a collaborative inquiry and discussion space. The teacher is a facilitator, steering the dialogue with thought-provoking questions and ensuring every student has a chance to contribute. For younger learners in K-5 classrooms, discussions could revolve around a beloved children's book or an engaging scientific phenomenon. This hands-on learning method sparks curiosity and makes learning an interactive experience. Here are some examples.

- **Reading Prompt:** How do the relationships between characters in *Charlotte's Web* change over the course of the story, and what do these changes tell us about friendship?

- **Social Studies Prompt:** What are some important jobs in our community, and how does each person help make our community a better place?

- **Science Prompt:** What can we learn about growth and change by observing the life cycle of a butterfly, and why is each stage important?

As the method is adapted to middle grades and high schools, Socratic seminars evolve to match the increasing complexity of the subjects and the development of analytical skills in the students. The conversations could analyze a sophisticated literary piece, a historical event, a complex scientific theory, or societal challenges. The facilitator guides students to cite evidence supporting their viewpoints, nurturing their skills in evidence-based argumentation. The students are encouraged to respect diverse viewpoints, substantiate their claims with evidence, and interrogate assumptions. Below are some examples for high school and middle school.

Middle school level:

- **Literature Prompt:** How do Harry's experiences in *Harry Potter and the Sorcerer's Stone* teach us the value of courage and friendship in facing challenges?

- **Social Studies Prompt:** What role did the Nile River play in the development of ancient Egyptian society, and how might things have been different without it?

- **Science Prompt:** Why is the water cycle important to Earth's ecosystems, and how can we protect our water resources?

High school level:

- **Literature Prompt:** What does the mockingbird symbolize in *To Kill a Mockingbird*, and how do the characters of Tom Robinson and Boo Radley fit into that symbolism?

- **History Prompt:** How did the Treaty of Versailles contribute to the outbreak of World War II, and could the war have been prevented with different diplomatic actions?

- **Science Prompt:** How might the widespread use of CRISPR technology change society, and what ethical dilemmas does it present?

At higher education levels, Socratic seminars delve into intricate theories, texts, or contemporary issues. The discussions challenge students to engage with and analyze these subjects critically. The facilitator introduces thought-provoking questions, guiding students to develop and sharpen their critical thinking and communication skills.

Regardless of the grade level or educational context, a Socratic seminar is a dynamic, student-centered approach to learning. It promotes active participation, curiosity, critical thinking, and a deep understanding of complex concepts. With appropriate facilitation, students are equipped to navigate intellectual dialogues, a skill that proves beneficial beyond the confines of the classroom.

In project-based learning, the essence of collaboration and diverse perspectives is undeniably important. But how can we enrich this collaborative experience, taking it beyond the boundaries of classroom walls? The answer lies in online discussions. Online discussions are invaluable extensions of classroom dialogue, especially in an era where remote learning and asynchronous environments are becoming increasingly prevalent. They offer an ideal space for diving deeper into project-based learning topics, fostering an inclusive environment that celebrates the diversity of student thoughts and experiences.

When facilitating online discussions within a PBL framework, it's important to consider technological barriers. Ensuring all students have access to necessary devices and reliable internet is crucial. Solutions may include school-provided devices or internet subsidies for those in need. Additionally, providing training and clear instructions on using online platforms can help mitigate challenges. Beginning these online discussions in the classroom can be a way to meet technological challenges head-on. Walking students through what it should look and sound like is essential. This also helps students learn how to navigate the platform you are having them use.

When executing online discussions within a PBL framework, several mechanics can enhance the experience. One effective approach is scaffolding the discussion posts. Start with a general discussion that invites initial thoughts and reactions to a video or prompt. In the example pictured here, you can see that two questions are provided. Students can pick one of the questions for their initial response. You are incorporating student choice into the equation by offering a few questions for students to choose from. Also, it helps bring in a more diverse and robust online conversation in the online platform. As the discussion progresses, encourage students to ask questions, critique arguments, and draw connections to the project, but you must teach students how to engage with their peers online. Be explicit in your expectations and model it for them. Talk about what is appropriate and what is not. This layering approach ensures that the discussion evolves and doesn't stagnate, capturing various perspectives that can inform the project's development.

Figure 3.3
Online Discussion

Challenges can arise in moderating online discussions, such as ensuring equitable participation or dealing with conflicting viewpoints. However, these challenges can also be turned into opportunities for learning. Teachers can use analytics tools to track participation and can offer private feedback to students who may need encouragement to engage more fully. Also, conflict can catalyze deeper discussions, especially if managed in a way that respects diverse perspectives and encourages constructive debate.

Acknowledging that not all students may have equal access to online resources is essential. Offering alternative participation methods can help include students facing technological challenges. Creating offline, print-based resources that mirror the online discussion topics allows students who face access issues to participate and stay engaged. This approach helps maintain the integrity and inclusivity of online discussions in a PBL setting. By addressing these barriers and providing inclusive solutions, online discussions can become a more effective and equitable part of the project-based learning experience.

Evaluation techniques can include a variety of metrics, such as the quality of posts, frequency of interaction, and the depth of critical thinking displayed. Rubrics that lay out expectations for meaningful engagement can also be useful in guiding students and providing transparent criteria for grading. Rubrics can contain categories such as Quality of the Initial Post, Engagement with Peers, Critical Thinking, Timeliness, and Real World Connections. The important thing to remember is that the rubric doesn't have to be a grading tool. It can be an assessment tool. Providing feedback will help students grow in how they respond and the richness of their responses. A narrative rubric is a style of rubric that focuses more on qualitative feedback rather than quantitative scoring. They provide detailed descriptions for each level of performance, emphasizing constructive feedback over numerical scores.

Empowering Online Discussions with Canvas and Google Classroom

In my journey to bring project-based learning alive, Canvas and Google Classroom have been pivotal. For instance, a project on the U.S. Constitution can be drastically transformed through the insights shared when students are given time to process a prompt and express their perspectives, thanks in large part to the rich discussions facilitated on Canvas. This experience not only brought out the students' passion for issues rooted in morality but also enhanced their collaborative and critical thinking skills. The ease with which we could navigate these platforms, creating spaces for every voice to be heard, underscores their value in today's educational landscape. Google Classroom, with its straightforward interface, allowed for the seamless sharing of ideas and resources, making the dive into online discussions an accessible step for any educator.

These platforms stand out not just for their technical capabilities, but for how they can be used to kindle the flame of inquiry and passion in students. By allowing students to explore topics that resonate with their interests and engage in meaningful dialogue, we pave the way for a more passionate, engaged learning community. I encourage educators to consider how integrating these tools into their classrooms can not only facilitate dynamic discussions but also empower students to take ownership of their learning journey.

Let's not just teach; let's inspire. Start small, perhaps with a single discussion post or project, and watch as the walls of your classroom extend into the vast, interactive world of online education. The potential for growth, connection, and passion-driven learning is immense, and it all begins with the click of a button. You can access Canvas by visiting k12. instructure.com and Google Classroom at classroom.google.com.

Scan the QR code to access your copy of the Online Discussion Rubric seen in Figures 3.4 and 3.5.

Figure 3.4
Online Discussion Rubric (Part 1)

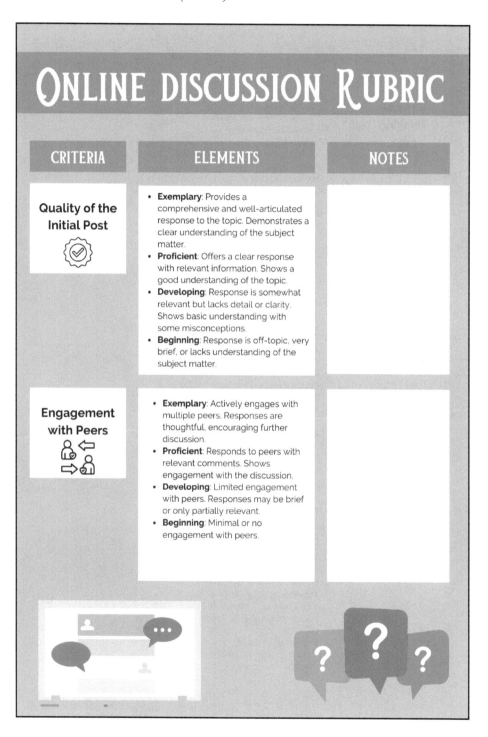

ONLINE DISCUSSION RUBRIC

CRITERIA	ELEMENTS	NOTES
Quality of the Initial Post	• **Exemplary**: Provides a comprehensive and well-articulated response to the topic. Demonstrates a clear understanding of the subject matter. • **Proficient**: Offers a clear response with relevant information. Shows a good understanding of the topic. • **Developing**: Response is somewhat relevant but lacks detail or clarity. Shows basic understanding with some misconceptions. • **Beginning**: Response is off-topic, very brief, or lacks understanding of the subject matter.	
Engagement with Peers	• **Exemplary**: Actively engages with multiple peers. Responses are thoughtful, encouraging further discussion. • **Proficient**: Responds to peers with relevant comments. Shows engagement with the discussion. • **Developing**: Limited engagement with peers. Responses may be brief or only partially relevant. • **Beginning**: Minimal or no engagement with peers.	

Figure 3.5
Online Discussion Rubric (Part 2)

CRITERIA	ELEMENTS	NOTES
Critical Thinking	• **Exemplary**: Demonstrates high-level critical thinking and connects concepts effectively. Provides insightful perspectives. • **Proficient**: Shows good critical thinking. Makes relevant connections between ideas. • **Developing**: Some evidence of critical thinking, but analysis is basic or surface-level. • **Beginning**: Lacks critical thinking. Responses are more opinion-based without supporting reasoning.	
Timeliness	• **Exemplary**: Contributes to the discussion in a timely manner, facilitating ongoing dialogue. • **Proficient**: Generally responds in a timely fashion, allowing for steady conversation flow. • **Developing**: Occasionally late in contributing, which may hinder the flow of discussion. • **Beginning**: Frequently late in responses, disrupting the discussion timeline.	
Real World Connections	• **Exemplary**: Effectively relates the topic to real-world examples or personal experiences. Enhances understanding of the subject. • **Proficient**: Makes relevant real-world connections, aiding in the comprehension of the topic. • **Developing**: Attempts to make real-world connections, but they may be tenuous or minimally relevant. • **Beginning**: Struggles to relate discussion topics to real-world situations or experiences.	

These online discussions provide an alternative platform for all students to participate and are particularly beneficial for those who feel more comfortable expressing their thoughts in writing rather than verbally in class. It grants them the time to reflect on the material, articulate their responses, and engage with their peers' ideas at their own pace.

While online discussions offer tremendous value in expanding the scope of collaboration in project-based learning, it's essential to recognize the irreplaceable benefits of in-person discussions. Face-to-face interactions foster a unique dynamic characterized by immediate feedback, nuanced understanding through verbal and non-verbal cues, and a sense of community and connection that can be harder to replicate online. In-person discussions encourage spontaneous and organic conversation, often leading to unexpected insights and deeper engagement. They also allow for more direct mentorship and guidance from educators. Balancing online and in-person discussions can create a comprehensive, multi-dimensional learning experience that leverages the strengths of both formats, ensuring students benefit from diverse interactions and perspectives.

Additionally, using real-world videos and prompts in online discussions can aid students in drawing connections between the learned content and its application in different contexts. It offers them a broader perspective, helping them understand how theoretical knowledge can be transformed into practical action. This transfer of learning is crucial in cultivating critical thinking and problem-solving skills, equipping students for real-world challenges beyond academia.

Classroom Games

Using games as authentic learning tasks offers a dynamic way to encourage collaboration, deepen comprehension, and validate understanding. Games take learning beyond traditional methods by adding elements of fun and competition. They naturally promote group discussions, where students strategize and exchange knowledge, enhancing not just the learning but also fostering empathy and community.

While navigating these educational games, students actively apply and test their knowledge. Success and challenges within the game serve as real-time feedback and learning opportunities, making it a form of active learning.

It's essential to note that the real value in these educational games lies in the learning process itself, not in extrinsic rewards like prizes or extra credit. Adding such rewards can shift the focus from learning to winning, diminishing the educational impact. Therefore, the ultimate goal should be intrinsic motivation, emphasizing that the true reward is the knowledge and skills gained.

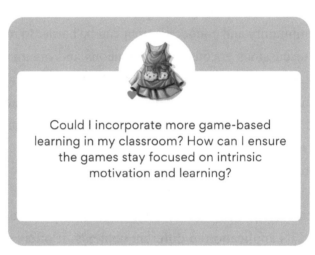

Could I incorporate more game-based learning in my classroom? How can I ensure the games stay focused on intrinsic motivation and learning?

Journaling Your Journey

Use the space below to reflect on this question.

_____

_____

_____

_____

_____

_____

_____

_____

Part Three: Project Planning and Implementation

"Planning is bringing the future into the present so that you can do something about it now."
– Alan Lakein

In a student-centric classroom, where project development is a collaborative effort led by students, the teacher's role shifts to facilitate the process. This approach aligns with bringing the future into the present by actively empowering students to engage with and shape their learning experiences. It steers away from a teacher-dominated approach, which can diminish the student-centric nature and intrinsic motivation. By prioritizing student needs, experiences, and interests, educators effectively prepare students for future challenges by involving them in the present planning and execution of their learning journey.

Building on this student-centric approach, giving students the room to exercise their curiosity about a subject and the freedom to explore it on their own terms is crucial. By encouraging them to apply their interests and passions to their projects, we create an environment that fosters not only academic growth but also personal development. However, for many students, the freedom to design their project is a novel experience, and therein lies the importance of teacher guidance. To facilitate a smooth transition into this more autonomous learning model, educators must provide intentional direction, mainly because while students may be enthusiastic about the freedom they've been given, they might also struggle with where and how to begin.

Mind mapping is an excellent starting point for sparking student interest and engagement around a specific topic or set of standards. By allowing students to freely explore and visualize their understanding, we awaken their innate curiosity and set the stage for deeper inquiry. This dynamic activity lays the foundation by encouraging students to uniquely represent the subject matter.

Figure 3.6
PBL Classroom Structure (Part 1)

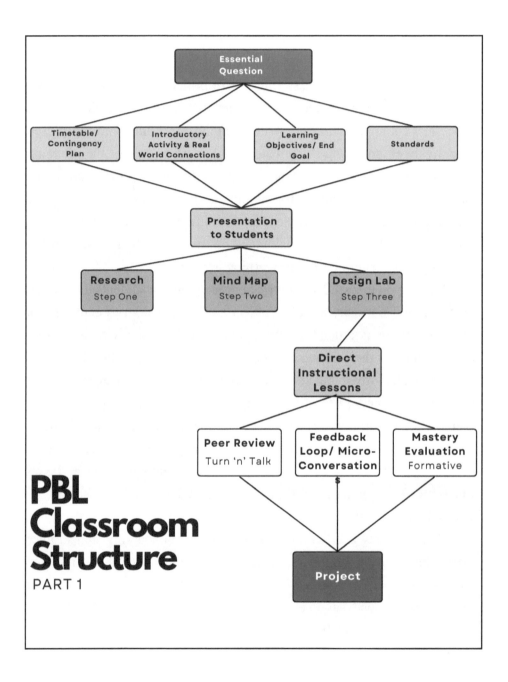

Figure 3.7
PBL Classroom Structure (Part 2)

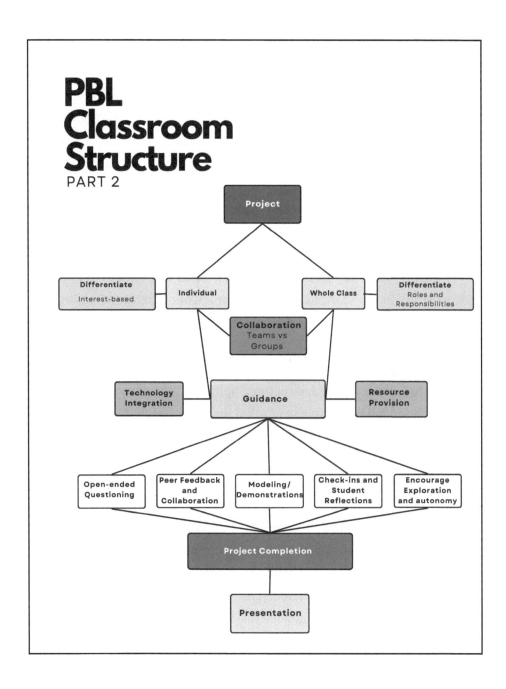

Following the burst of creativity unleashed during the mind mapping phase, where students' curiosity branches out into myriad directions, we reach a pivotal juncture in the PBL journey—the transition to structure. At this point, the PBL Classroom Structure diagram comes into play. This visual tool is not merely a guide; it embodies the scaffolded support framework that educators require to channel their students' raw enthusiasm into structured yet equally engaging learning experiences. Here, learners' free-flowing ideas are funneled through the design lab, fostering a collaborative climb through Bloom's Taxonomy from basic understanding to complex application. The diagram serves as a roadmap, charting each deliberate step in this transformative process, ensuring that the voyage from curiosity to concrete knowledge is clear, comprehensive, and captivating. Through this, the classroom metamorphoses into an incubator for innovation, where students actively construct knowledge, culminating in original project proposals that are the hallmark of authentic PBL.

However, what comes after this initial burst of curiosity and exploration? How do we scaffold a support framework that allows teachers to provide the help needed to take their students to higher levels of understanding, this raw enthusiasm into something more structured yet equally engaging? This is where we transition from the open-ended nature of mind mapping to a more focused, structured approach: the design lab.

The design lab picks up where mind mapping concludes, providing an immersive, interactive framework to guide students through ascending levels of Bloom's Taxonomy in a collaborative fashion. Through a sequenced process of peer discussions, reflections, and group analysis, learners are progressively taken from basic comprehension garnered during mind mapping to actively evaluating information, finding patterns, and translating this enhanced understanding into original project proposals. The design lab offers a structured platform for students to assimilate knowledge and refine their understanding, empowering them to design unique expressions of the subject matter. Each phase scaffolds critical thinking, building on previous steps to equip students with strategies that foster problem-solving, communication, and self-directed education. By progressing students from passive to active learners, the design lab transforms classrooms into environments where thinking becomes an engaging endeavor. Aligned with project-based learning principles and informed by frameworks like Bloom's Taxonomy, the design lab provides an immersive, interactive process to guide meaningful learning.

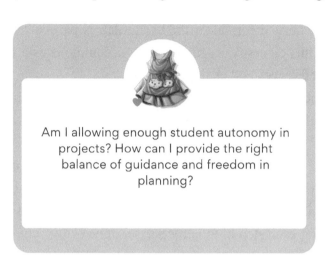

Am I allowing enough student autonomy in projects? How can I provide the right balance of guidance and freedom in planning?

Journaling Your Journey

Use the space below to reflect on this question.

_____

_____

_____

_____

_____

_____

_____

_____

_____

_____

_____

_____

_____

_____

Meeting Diverse Learning Needs

In the dynamic landscape of today's classrooms, recognizing and catering to the diverse learning needs of students is paramount, especially when implementing a structured approach like the design lab. The step-by-step, teacher-led format of the design lab is particularly effective in addressing this diversity, as it inherently accommodates a wide range of learning preferences and challenges.

The structured nature of the design lab provides a clear and predictable learning pathway, which is essential in a classroom with varied learning needs. This approach reduces potential confusion and anxiety, making the learning process more accessible and manageable for all students. It ensures that each step is understood and followed, allowing students who may need more time or different methods to grasp concepts effectively.

Modeling each step of the process is a universally beneficial strategy. It transcends various learning barriers by providing a visual and practical example of what is expected. This method is especially helpful for students who may struggle with traditional instructional methods, as it offers a concrete, observable guide to follow.

Repetition and reinforcement are key components of this approach. By revisiting each step and reinforcing the instructions, all students, particularly those who may need additional support to retain information, are given the opportunity to solidify their understanding and build confidence in their abilities.

Pacing and clarity in instruction are crucial. Adjusting the speed of delivery and using straightforward, jargon-free language can significantly enhance comprehension for all students. This careful pacing ensures that students are not overwhelmed and have adequate time to process and engage with the material.

The immediate feedback and correction provided in this teaching method are invaluable. It allows for real-time adjustment and support, ensuring that misconceptions are addressed promptly and learning is reinforced continuously.

Incorporating differentiated instruction within this framework is seamless. Teachers can adapt their language, use of visual aids, or the complexity of tasks to meet the varied needs of their students. This adaptability ensures that each student's unique learning requirements are met, fostering a more personalized and effective learning experience.

Ultimately, this method promotes an inclusive learning environment. Engaging all students in the same structured process while providing individualized support as needed underscores the principle that every student, regardless of their learning style or challenge, can participate and succeed. This inclusive approach is vital in building a classroom community where diversity in learning is not just acknowledged but embraced and valued.

In essence, the design lab's step-by-step, teacher-led approach is a powerful tool for addressing the diverse learning needs within a classroom. It offers structure, visual support, repetition, clear instruction, immediate feedback, and the flexibility for differentiation, creating an accessible and supportive learning environment for all students.

The Design Lab

The design lab, a key component of the PBL classroom, structures itself to promote higher-order thinking based on Bloom's Taxonomy principles. Drawing inspiration from Stanford University's D-School and Design Thinkers for Education, this approach adapts to a classroom setting. Each stage in the design lab has a fixed timeframe, ranging from one to ten minutes, to help students manage their time effectively. Students work individually, in pairs, and in small groups, typically comprising four students.

So, how does the design lab operate when starting with a mind-mapping activity? Since students have begun exploring the topical essential question, they can use the class-created mind map as their conversational roadmap. Some students might miss the mind mapping activity, so providing a copy to all students ensures everyone can participate in the design lab. This mind map contains all interconnected ideas, sub-topics, initial queries, and potential projects from early discussions and serves as a precursor to subsequent design lab stages.

The design lab is a highly structured session, allowing students to review their existing knowledge and gain new perspectives from their peers. Its main purpose is to let students share research findings on the topical essential question, using the initial mind map as a guide.

The interview model fosters active listening and stimulates academic discussion, helping to understand the depth and enthusiasm of peers' research on various subjects. As students collectively examine their research, they begin categorizing information, another vital function of the design lab. Frequent updates to the mind map facilitate this categorization and fuel creativity, preparing students for project design.

The structure of the design lab offers a dynamic setting, letting students move between pairs, groups, and solitary work. Though it might seem complex, the diagram clarifies the design lab's step-by-step process.

Students use a specific handout for note-taking during interviews. A grid sheet also helps them draft a rough but detailed sketch of their future project, informed by the evolving mind maps. To promote active sharing, consider setting up areas around the room with mounted paper for collective brainstorming and updating the collective mind map directly.

The design lab's approach can differ based on the audience but remains crucial in the PBL classroom, continuously providing learning and refinement opportunities. You can complete the design lab in one day or over a few days, depending on the time allocated for each lab part.

The design lab follows a preplanned trajectory, systematically progressing students from one step to the next. Even though it is timed and scripted, it demands explicit instruction. Since many students are new to this kind of conversation, they require guidance on engaging in academic dialogues. The explicit instruction during the design lab is a step-by-step process in which you tell students what is expected in each step as you go through it with them. You can even model what that conversation should look like and sound like. Traditional classrooms often prioritize silence over conversation, but the design lab reverses this trend, teaching students academic communication and providing ongoing learning and refinement opportunities.

Now, let's explore my design lab's step-by-step process. These time frames are merely suggestions. Keeping times short helps students stay focused, and a displayed timer shows the elapsed time, preventing any stage from overextending.

You can find the handout I use to guide students through this journey by scanning the QR code.

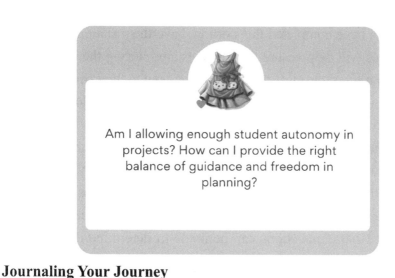

Am I allowing enough student autonomy in projects? How can I provide the right balance of guidance and freedom in planning?

Journaling Your Journey

Use the space below to reflect on this question.

_____

_____

_____

_____

_____

_____

_____

Step One (each student has 3 minutes: a total of 6 minutes for the pair)

The process initiates with students examining a copy of the mind map, presenting them with the chance to delve into their *Worthy of Wonder* (W.O.W.) moments. These moments signify particular points that spark their interest. For instance, a student might express surprise about an unknown event in a specific context, share excitement about upcoming learning topics, or ponder the connections between seemingly disparate elements.

Upon pinpointing their W.O.W. moments, students will share the insights that particularly caught their attention with a partner. Subsequently, they will attentively listen to the intriguing moments highlighted by their partner. Once students have completed this portion, have them share their W.O.W. moments. This will help ensure that students are meeting the objectives of this step, and it gives the class to see what stood out to their peers.

Students in this portion of the design lab engage in the lower level of Bloom's Taxonomy: *understanding*. When students identify their Worthy of Wonder moments, they're interpreting the material from the mind map in a way that's personally meaningful to them. When they share those moments with a partner, they have to summarize their ideas and explain why those pieces stood out. At this point in the process, students are trying to figure out what connections can be made to determine the degree to which they understand the ideas presented. They also get to hear how their peer is processing the information. Students can gain insight into different perspectives regarding the same material by engaging in this dialogue.

Figure 3.8
Design Lab Step One

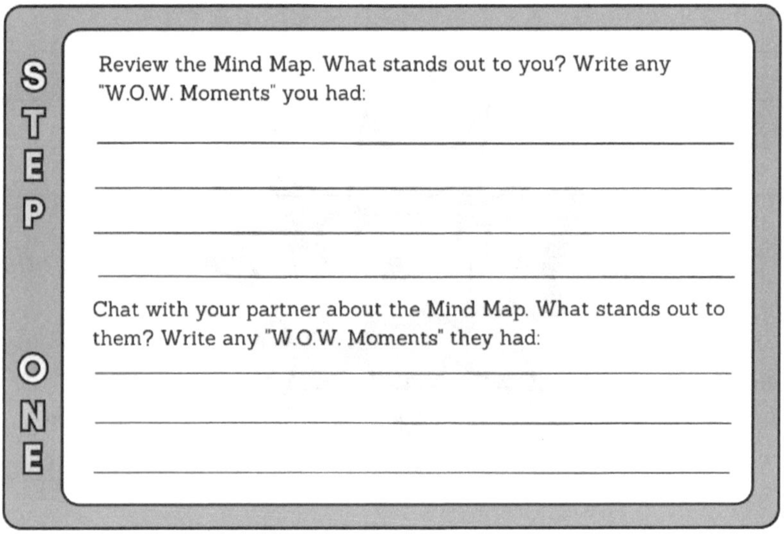

STEP	Review the Mind Map. What stands out to you? Write any "W.O.W. Moments" you had:
ONE	Chat with your partner about the Mind Map. What stands out to them? Write any "W.O.W. Moments" they had:

Step Two (each student has 3 minutes: a total of 6 minutes for the pair)

The second step in the design lab is to clarify any confusing information. At this point, students are asked to identify content from the mind map that was confusing or lacked context. Once they have identified their points of confusion, students invite their partners to share what they found confusing. This step makes it okay to have questions and to express a desire to learn more about a particular area of the mind map. During this dialogue, students can answer each other's questions or clarify certain aspects of the mind map. Again, when this step is complete, have students share what they found confusing. This is an excellent opportunity to address misconceptions and confusion so that as students move forward, they have a solid foundation to build upon.

Figure 3.9
Design Lab Step Two

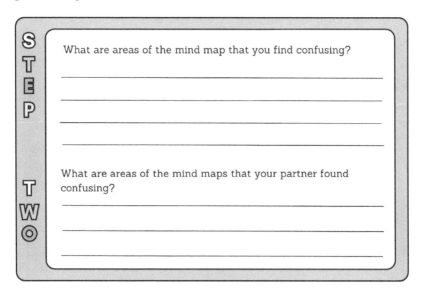

When looking at how this step aligns with Bloom's Taxonomy, it engages a few different areas. Students must *evaluate* what they understand and what they don't. Expressing confusion means that they have attempted to comprehend or interpret the material. Acknowledging areas of difficulty is a part of the comprehension process and is a step towards a deeper understanding of the material. By recognizing and articulating what they don't understand, students *analyze* and break down the information into parts, figuring out how the aspects relate to one another and the overall structure or purpose. This reflective analysis helps identify areas for further clarification or study. Evaluating occurs when students judge the clarity of the mind map, in this case, acknowledging that certain parts are confusing or unclear. This process helps them to think critically about the information presented.

Step Three (3 minutes)

Step three allows students to process the mind map. This step asks them to summarize their W.O.W. moments and any other connections they could make. Summarizing encourages students to process the information more deeply and understand it more nuancedly. By condensing their W.O.W. moments and the connections they found, they reframe the knowledge in their own words, which enhances understanding and improves memory retention. This process helps students identify areas they may not understand as well. If they struggle to summarize or make connections, they realize their comprehension may be lacking, prompting further questions and exploration. As students write their summaries, it is essential to circulate throughout the room and read what students are writing. This will help ensure that students are summarizing their understanding.

Figure 3.10
Design Lab Step 3

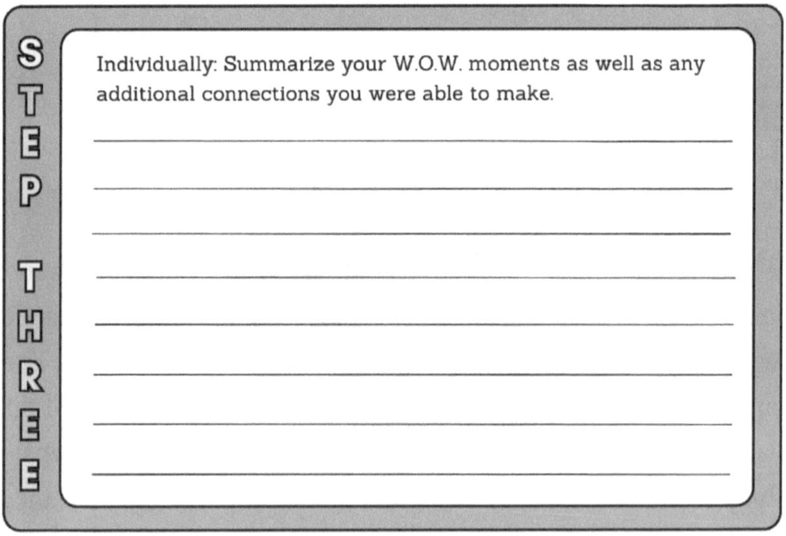

S
T
E
P

T
H
R
E
E

Individually: Summarize your W.O.W. moments as well as any additional connections you were able to make.

_____

_____

_____

_____

_____

_____

_____

When students are tasked with summarizing, they engage with various stages of Bloom's Taxonomy. Initially, they exercise the *understanding* stage by interpreting the information from the mind map, translating complex ideas into simpler, personal language. This also extends to the *analyzing* stage, where they dissect the mind map, examining how different elements interrelate to form a cohesive whole. As they write down these connections, they implicitly evaluate their comprehension of the topic.

Moreover, deciding what is noteworthy enough to write down enables them to evaluate their understanding, thereby determining the significance of various pieces of information. Through these steps, students deepen their comprehension, apply their knowledge, and hone their critical thinking skills.

Step Four (each student has 1 minute: a total of 4 minutes for the group)

Step four, where students collectively identify patterns, relationships, or connections among the ideas in the mind map, plays a critical role in the learning process. This collaborative analysis fosters deeper understanding by encouraging students to view the subject from multiple perspectives. By examining how various ideas interlink, students can discern underlying patterns and relationships that might not be immediately apparent. Moreover, this group activity also nurtures critical thinking and communication skills, as students must articulate their thoughts and negotiate different viewpoints. Ultimately, this step not only aids in cementing the knowledge gained but also cultivates the higher-order thinking skills required in real-world problem-solving and decision-making. Upon completing this portion, you can chart out the connections students made on the whiteboard. This will help ensure that everyone contributes and sees the connections, patterns, and relationships within the content.

At this point, we see students begin to engage in the upper levels of Bloom's Taxonomy. When students work as a group to identify patterns, relationships, or connections among the ideas, they engage in the *analysis* level. They are breaking down complex information into parts and understanding how these parts interrelate. The collaborative nature of the task also taps into the *evaluation* level of Bloom's Taxonomy. Students assess each other's understanding and arguments, critique the ideas presented, and negotiate which connections or patterns are most relevant or significant.

Figure 3.11
Design Lab Step 4

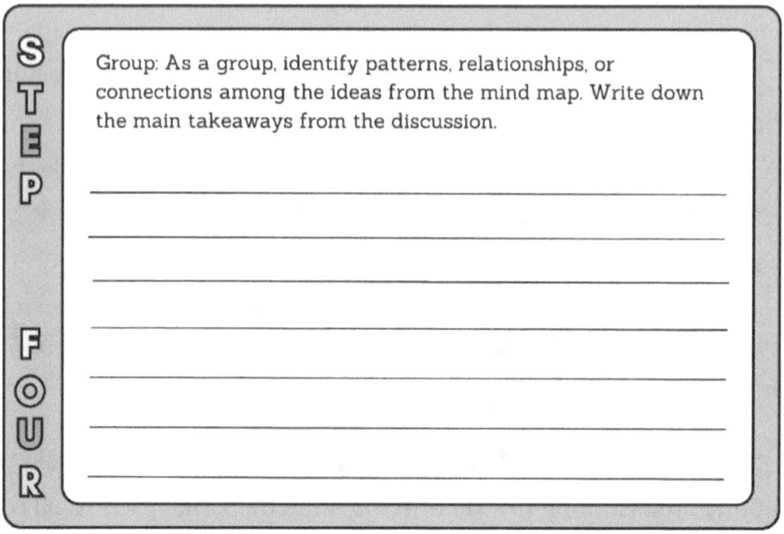

STEP FOUR

Group: As a group, identify patterns, relationships, or connections among the ideas from the mind map. Write down the main takeaways from the discussion.

Step Five (7-10 minutes for brainstorming)

The fifth step is central to fostering students' engagement and creativity. This stage is grounded in PBL principles, where the objective is not for the educator to dictate a specific project but to allow students to take ownership of their learning. They are given the liberty to devise, design, and develop their projects in ways that align with their understanding of the content and link with their passions and interests.

In this step, students contemplate the most effective way to represent their understanding of the subject matter. The process encourages students to take the reins, and it caters to diverse learning preferences and personal inclinations. It builds the intrinsic motivation for the project because it is "their project." Circulate the room and have conversations with students. Let them share their idea with you. If a student struggles to think through how they would like to represent content, this is a great opportunity for you to help get them on an exciting and creative path.

Figure 3.12
Design Lab Step 5

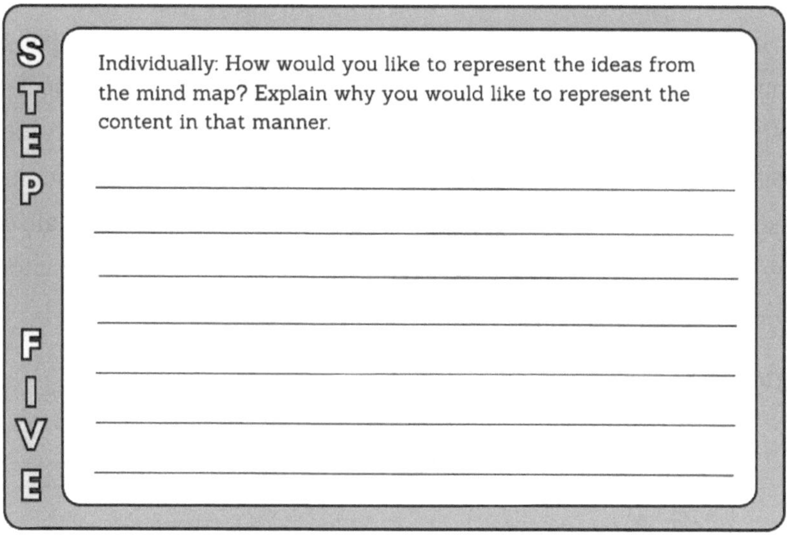

In this fifth step of the process, students commence their journey into the upper levels of Bloom's Taxonomy. They are not merely applying and analyzing information but also taking steps toward creating based on their newfound knowledge. Here, students use their understanding of the content to conceptualize a personalized project, an exercise that involves the application of learned theories to tangible ideas. Subsequently, they embark on the *analysis* process, dissecting the information they've gathered and gaining insight into relationships and connections among various elements. This analysis process lays the groundwork for determining the most meaningful way to represent their understanding of the subject matter. Upon choosing their approach, they are ready to engage in Bloom's highest level, *creation*. They transition from passive receivers of knowledge to active creators as they design and develop their projects. They merge fragments of knowledge into a unique and meaningful whole, directly corresponding to their interests and understanding of the content. By this stage, the students have navigated from lower-order cognitive to higher-order thinking skills, setting the stage for defending their ideas.

Step Six (each student has 2 minutes: a total of 4 minutes for the pair)

In the sixth step, students are encouraged to delve deeper into the dynamics of collaboration and peer review, an essential aspect of project-based learning. They pair up and share their unique project ideas, explaining the specifics of what they intend to create and articulating the reasons behind their choice. This peer discussion provides an opportunity for students to effectively communicate their comprehension of the subject matter and promotes active listening.

Figure 3.13
Design Lab Step 6

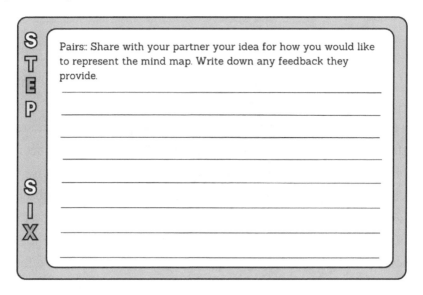

Embracing a growth mindset is key at this juncture, as it allows students to view the feedback they receive not as criticism but as a valuable tool for growth and improvement. By perceiving feedback as a means to expand their understanding, students become more open to revising their initial ideas and exploring alternative perspectives. It fosters resilience and adaptability, vital qualities for the evolving nature of project work. Moreover, it encourages students to strive for continual learning, reinforcing that knowledge and understanding are not static but grow over time. Therefore, this step deepens students' comprehension of the subject matter and cultivates an important life skill: the ability to learn from feedback and maintain a growth mindset.

By engaging in dialogue, students receive feedback on their project, a process that aids in refining and improving their initial ideas. This constructive critique helps students refine their projects further and ensures they effectively represent their understanding of the content. This step strengthens the metacognitive process as students listen to alternative perspectives and, consequently, reassess and consolidate their own understanding and learning strategies.

In the sixth step of the project, students interact with the upper levels of Bloom's Taxonomy, primarily in *evaluating* and *creating*. The process necessitates students to critically evaluate their understanding and the suitability of their proposed project for effectively conveying their comprehension. This evaluation process promotes introspective thinking and self-assessment of their grasp on the subject matter. At the same time, they engage with the concept of "evaluation" in another sense as they receive and consider feedback from their peers. They need to determine the relevance and utility of this feedback, deciding if and how they should integrate it into their project. In doing so, they must assess their peers' suggestions compared to their original project design. This process underscores the necessity of critical thinking and assessment skills in effective learning.

Step 7 (7-10 minutes)

In the seventh step, students translate their theoretical concepts into tangible form, marking the transition from abstract ideas to concrete plans. This stage necessitates that students draw a visual sketch of their proposed project to provide a clear depiction of how they wish to represent their comprehension of the content. Graph paper facilitates this creative process, encouraging students to think through their projects in meticulous detail. Students are reminded that their design can evolve as the unit progresses, promoting a growth mindset and the acceptance of revision as part of the learning process. However, the goal is to design as many aspects of the project as possible, such as layout, game pieces, card designs, and tokens. This task not only aids visualization but also helps students foresee potential challenges and devise suitable solutions. As students work on their designs, circulate throughout and check in to see how they are doing with the development of their ideas. Encourage students to use online images as references to develop their ideas. This design is something that students will keep throughout their project development. They are able to revise it as they learn new information.

Figure 3.14
Design Lab Step 7

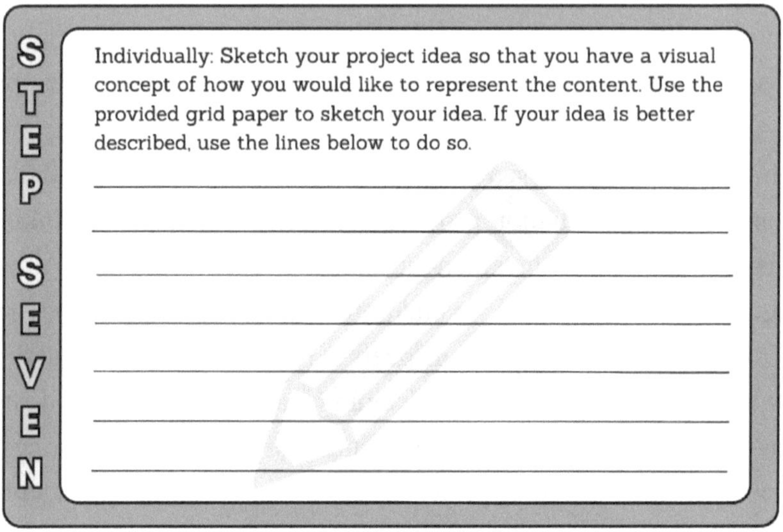

This seventh step aligns with the highest level of Bloom's Taxonomy, *creating*. When students draft a visual representation of their projects, they are synthesizing the information they've learned, integrating it into their existing knowledge, and using it to create something new. This process involves not only an application of their understanding but also requires higher-order thinking to innovate and design a relevant and meaningful project. They are creating a new product or point of view using the skills and knowledge they have acquired. Moreover, as they sketch and plan their project, they're compelled to make strategic decisions about representing their learning best, calling upon the evaluation and analysis skills they've developed in the earlier stages of the process. This level of intellectual behavior involves the development of new patterns or ideas and requires students to be creative and original.

Step 8 (each student has 3 minutes to share plus 3 minutes to listen to feedback: a total of 12 minutes)

This stage of the design process is incredibly beneficial as it allows each student to share their project concept with a classmate. Students must describe their project in great detail while their peer silently listens, jotting down notes, suggestions, and queries. It is important to explain to students the difference between constructive and destructive criticism. I have found that providing examples of constructive criticism shifts the focus from telling their partner what is "wrong" with the project to ways to "improve" the project. Once both students have presented their ideas, they discuss each other's projects, pose questions, and propose possible improvements. Students must document any recommendations received and spend time contemplating these new insights. By promoting this level of communication and reflection, we ensure that every idea is thoroughly examined and optimized. It is so important to monitor these discussions. You will want to redirect as necessary and affirm when you hear things going well.

As students present their ideas to their peers, they learn to communicate in a way that invites feedback and further reflection. I often frame this as presenting a proposal, encouraging them to think deeply about their project's design and purpose. This approach often leads to insightful moments of realization and learning. For instance, during a session on a project about the thirteen colonies in America, one student proposed creating a mobile. At first, her idea seemed simple, but it opened the door for deeper exploration. When I asked her, "Why a mobile?" she initially responded, "I don't know." I saw this as an opportunity to encourage her and deepen her understanding and connection to the project. Probing further, I asked where we typically see mobiles. Her reply, "In nurseries, I guess," set the stage for a moment of clarity. As she connected the dots, her eyes lit up. "A mobile is perfect, Mr. Jones because we are looking at the birth of our nation." This breakthrough moment exemplified how project-based learning not only fosters creativity but also guides students to make meaningful connections, enhancing their engagement with the content.

Figure 3.15
Design Lab Step 8

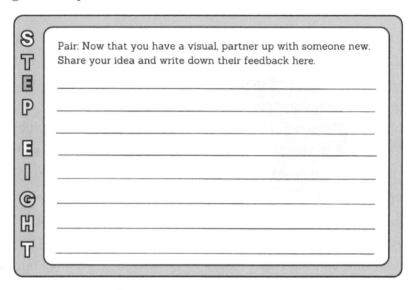

The eighth step of the design process is instrumental in aligning with the *evaluating* stage of Bloom's Taxonomy. As students articulate their project ideas to their peers and incorporate the feedback they receive, they are actively engaged in critical evaluation. They must assess their understanding of the content and their approach to representing it. This peer-to-peer exchange encourages students to critically evaluate not only their work but also their peers' ideas, thus reinforcing the evaluative skills central to Bloom's Taxonomy. Furthermore, their ability to accept and integrate constructive criticism into their projects demonstrates the crucial role of evaluation in learning. The case of the student planning to create a mobile about the thirteen colonies in America illustrates the transformative power of evaluation. Initially conceived with a basic understanding, her project evolved into a profound metaphor for the birth of the nation through questioning and reevaluation. This instance showcases how the evaluative stage of Bloom's Taxonomy is vital in enhancing the depth of understanding and enriching the learning experience in project-based learning.

Step Nine (10+ minutes)

The ninth step in the design lab is a whole class activity where students share aspects that stood out to them in their peers' projects, as well as what they are excited about moving forward. This exercise serves a pivotal role in enhancing students' learning experience. Not only does it promote a sense of shared understanding and community, it also cultivates an environment of mutual recognition and respect for each individual's ideas and work. This peer-to-peer interaction fosters a constructive dialogue, enabling the students to learn from each other's strengths and innovative approaches.

Figure 3.16
Design Lab Step 9

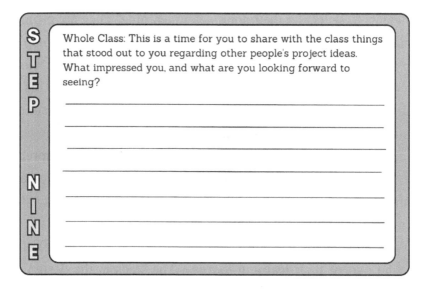

STEP NINE

Whole Class: This is a time for you to share with the class things that stood out to you regarding other people's project ideas. What impressed you, and what are you looking forward to seeing?

Moreover, this step significantly contributes to building intrinsic motivation. By publicly acknowledging the distinctive elements of each project, students gain a greater appreciation for their contributions and can see how their work positively impacts the learning environment. This sense of purpose can motivate students to delve deeper into their projects. Similarly, expressing their anticipation for future developments can stimulate excitement and curiosity, further driving engagement and a desire to progress.

This process also underscores that learning is a communal and social activity that can foster a sense of belonging and shared purpose. By actively participating in this group discussion, students can bolster their confidence and mastery over their projects, enhancing their intrinsic motivation to succeed and learn. Ultimately, this step energizes the classroom atmosphere, motivating students to persist through challenges and strive for excellence in their projects.

Step 10 (5-7 minutes)

Step ten of the design process involves a comprehensive self-reflection phase, where students assess not only their areas of interest but also how they have interacted with the learning process. This stage goes beyond merely identifying engaging topics on the mind map; it encourages students to reflect on their approach to learning. They are prompted to consider questions such as, "How has working with the mind map altered your approach to complex subjects?" and "Which strategies employed during this activity were most effective for you, and why?" This deeper level of reflection allows students to evaluate their problem-solving techniques, adaptability, and resilience in their learning journey. It's not just about what they learn but how they learn, fostering a comprehensive understanding of their personal learning preferences and strategies. This enhanced self-awareness is crucial for effective learning and contributes to a more meaningful and satisfying educational experience.

Walking students through the different stages of Bloom's Taxonomy is a vital part of their learning journey. The steps in the design lab are crafted to align with Bloom's hierarchy, gradually moving students from lower-level cognitive tasks to higher-order thinking. This intentional progression helps students build a solid understanding of the material before they are asked to analyze, evaluate, and create, which are tasks requiring more complex cognitive abilities.

This progression through Bloom's Taxonomy prepares students to navigate the unit at various cognitive levels. By scaffolding the learning experience in this way, students can better absorb, understand, analyze, evaluate, and ultimately create something that reflects their understanding of the material. This process empowers students to engage with the content actively, resulting in a more enriching learning experience and a deeper, lasting comprehension of the subject matter.

Figure 3.17
Design Lab Step 10

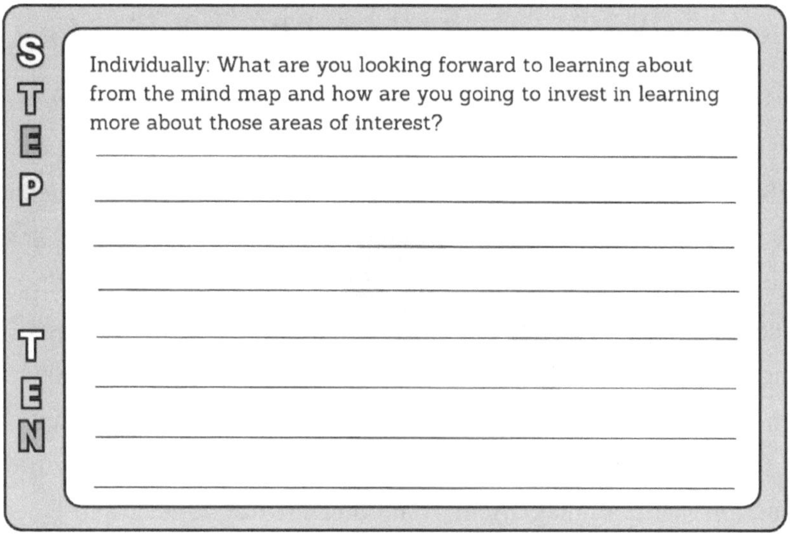

S T E P   T E N

Individually: What are you looking forward to learning about from the mind map and how are you going to invest in learning more about those areas of interest?

_____
_____
_____
_____
_____
_____
_____
_____

An important note: The design lab process can be completed in one day, or it can take a couple of days, depending on how much time you give to each portion of the lab.

Plan, Personalize, Pursue

Hint

To effectively utilize QR codes and Google Sheets in setting up your PBL unit, here's a simplified guide. QR codes are square barcodes that, when scanned with a smartphone camera, redirect to online content. Simply open your camera app, point it at the QR code, and tap the notification that appears to access the linked resource. Google Sheets, an online spreadsheet tool, can be accessed via these QR codes. Once opened, you can view and if signed in with a Google account, edit or add to the sheet.

This is particularly useful for the activities list available under the "6th-8th grade" tab in the provided sheet. You can download the sheet for offline use in formats like Excel or PDF. These tools are integrated into the PBL setup process for planning, personalizing with a range of activities, and pursuing detailed planning with downloadable worksheets.

Potential Challenges and Mistakes When Setting Up a Unit

When setting up a project-based learning unit, educators often encounter several challenges. A common mistake is beginning with the project itself rather than formulating an engaging, open-ended question that drives the project. It's essential to have clear objectives for what students should learn; otherwise, projects can lose focus. Incorporating student voice and choice is vital for engagement, so offering options in project topics and methods is beneficial. Assessment shouldn't be overlooked; both formative and summative assessments should be integrated throughout the project, coupled with continuous feedback and opportunities for reflection. Time management is another critical aspect, as PBL requires careful planning to allocate sufficient time for research, discussion, project development, and presentation. Ensuring access to necessary resources is crucial, as a lack of materials or information can impede project progress. Additionally, group dynamics play a significant role in PBL. Teaching and monitoring collaboration skills, including conflict resolution and effective communication, are essential for group projects. Finally, linking projects to real-world issues enhances their relevance, thereby motivating students and deepening their learning. Regular reflection and feedback from students can guide educators in refining the PBL process, making it more effective and engaging.

When planning the initial steps of setting up your PBL unit, use this poster as a guide.

Download a copy of the following graphic by scanning this QR code.

Figure 3.18
Developing a PBL Unit

DEVELOPING A PBL UNIT
Steps for setting up a successful PBL Unit

Essential Question

Begin by determining the question you want students to answer by the end of the unit. Students will revisit this question throughout the unit as they build their understanding of the content.

Mind Map

Students engage in active research that explores the Topical Essential Question in the realms of Who, What, Where, When, Why, and How.

Design Lab

Step-by-step process of guiding students through the various levels of Bloom's Taxonomy as they design their project.

Classroom Games

A dynamic and engaging approach to learning, fostering an environment of collaboration, discussion, and comprehension validation.

Discussions

Moving beyond rote memorization, conversations aid in processing and internalization of concepts, transforming the learning experience into an active, participatory process.

Plan

When selecting a unit of study for your class, whether it's a current, future, or past unit, it's crucial to consider the main themes and learning objectives. A guiding question for a PBL unit should be overarching and open-ended, stimulating critical thinking and deep exploration of the unit's themes. For instance, if the unit is about environmental science, a guiding question could be, "How can we develop sustainable practices to reduce our local community's environmental footprint?" For a history unit on ancient civilizations, consider, "What can the rise and fall of ancient empires teach us about modern society?" In a mathematics unit focused on geometry, a question like, "How can understanding geometric principles help us solve real-world problems in architecture and design?" would be appropriate. What overarching, open-ended question could serve to guide students' learning throughout the unit? This question should encourage critical thinking and exploration of the unit's main themes.

Personalize

When developing a series of authentic tasks to deepen students' understanding of your unit's topics, it's crucial to design activities that engage students in active learning and real-world applications. To determine if a game is the right fit for your unit, start by aligning the game's objectives with your unit's learning goals. Consider the interests and age group of your students, and select games that enable them to apply skills and knowledge relevant to the unit. Choose games that provide real-world context, ensuring they are practical and feasible for your classroom environment. The games should also allow for post-activity reflection and discussion to reinforce learning objectives. Review the section on authentic tasks for guidance and refer to the provided list of games and activities, which includes images, videos, materials needed, and playing instructions. Remember to adapt these games as needed to effectively support your unit's topics.

Please scan the QR code and navigate to the tab labeled "6th-8th." On that tab, you'll find a list of games that I use with my students. Feel free to explore the games and see if any would be suitable for your class, regardless of the grade level. This is a Google Spreadsheet, and you are welcome to contribute by adding your own content.

Pursue

As you make this process your own, use the following worksheet to aid in your planning.

Figure 3.19
Essential Questions Guide Cover

Figure 3.20
Essential Questions Guide (Page 1)

PLANNING
Task

ESSENTIAL QUESTIONS

What is the overarching theme or idea you want your students to learn?

_____

_____

_____

_____

_____

What are some real-world issues, challenges, or scenarios connected to your theme or idea?

- - - - - - - - - - - - - - - - -

- - - - - - - - - - - - - - - - -

- - - - - - - - - - - - - - - - -

- - - - - - - - - - - - - - - - -

- - - - - - - - - - - - - - - - -

How could this theme or idea be covered in unique ways?

_____

_____

Figure 3.21
Essential Questions Guide (Page 2)

PERSONALIZE
Task

Craft your essential question:

_____
_____
_____
_____
_____
_____
_____

How could this question be explored in other content areas?

- -
- -
- -
- -
- -
- -
- -

How does your question support the lessons included within the unit?

_____
_____

Figure 3.22
Essential Questions Guide (Page 3)

PERSONALIZE
Task

Identify key topics within the unit:

1. _____

   _____

2. _____

   _____

3. _____

   _____

4. _____

   _____

How do these topics build upon each other in a way that supports the Essential Question?

Design a topical essential question that promotes a deep understanding and encourages students to go beyond surface-level.

_____

_____

Figure 3.23
Essential Questions Guide (Page 4)

PURSUE
Task

How has this exercise changed how you use questions?

_____

_____

_____

_____

_____

_____

_____

How do you see essential questions impacting your classroom?

_____

_____

_____

_____

_____

_____

_____

Find a peer that you can share your questions with. Write their constructive feedback here.

_____

_____

Download a copy Essential Questions handout by scanning this QR code.

Download a copy of the Design Lab handout by scanning this QR code.

This chapter has unpacked the intricacies of effective PBL practices, from thoughtful questioning to authentic tasks and thoughtful assessments. As we now transition into our next chapter on Igniting learners' passions, we explore the pivotal role passion plays in catalyzing PBL's transformational potential. Just as the dynamic components of PBL set the stage for impactful learning, igniting individual student passions provides the spark that brings this framework to life.

Reflect on the diverse passions, interests, and dreams that motivate your students. How can you transform your classrooms into environments where these innate flames are nurtured rather than extinguished? Let these reflections guide you as we delve into passion-based learning.

Chapter 4
Igniting Learner's Passions

 **Interview with Dr. Eric Anderman**
Writer and Professor of Educational Psychology
at The Ohio State University

"Passion is the driver of achievement in all fields. Some people love doing things they don't feel they're good at. That may be because they underestimate their talents or overestimate what they need to do, so they're constantly striving to meet some standard that inspires them. But passion is the key. If you're doing something you love, an hour feels like five minutes."
- Sir Ken Robinson

Sir Ken Robinson, an influential voice in the world of education, has long championed a radical rethinking of our school systems. Renowned for his persuasive talks on developing creativity and innovation in teaching, Robinson's insights have inspired educators worldwide to cultivate environments that foster students' innate passions. His philosophy underscores the importance of passion as a central component of learning, suggesting that when students connect with their interests, their educational journey becomes tolerable and invigorating. It was with this understanding that I began to reflect on my practices in the classroom.

A pivotal moment in my teaching career, still fresh in my memory, marked a turning point. As I surveyed my students—some with their heads down, some blankly gazing out the window, and others conversing privately—a variety of emotions surged within me: anger, sadness, frustration, and a profound sense of being unappreciated. When I asked a student a question, I received a defiant stare. The following student mimicked the same silent rebellion. I had incorporated technology, projects, and even film into my teaching methods, but the lack of progress made me question my competence and the future of education.

This internal conflict led me to a crossroads: continue down the path of traditional methods or forge a new one that could rekindle the joy of learning in my classroom. In response to my frustrations, my administrators suggested exploring new ways to cater to the students' needs. However, my disillusionment had grown so deep that I considered quitting teaching unless I found something groundbreaking.

In the midst of my search for a solution, I stumbled upon a concept that resonated with my yearning for change. While scouring articles, websites, and videos for inspiration, I realized my classroom lacked student-centeredness. My teaching style had been too authoritarian, creating resistance rather than fostering interest. The question arose, "How do I remedy this?" The answer was simple—ask the students how they wished to demonstrate their learning.

The pathway to this new educational philosophy was Project-Based Learning, but not just any PBL—the kind that integrates students' passions with their projects. This approach amplifies intrinsic motivation by leveraging students' interests. Daniel Pink, a well-known author and speaker, echoes this sentiment,

> At some level, PBL is an ideal structure for fostering autonomy, mastery, and purpose in students. For instance, if students choose their project — rather than its subject and its form foisted on them, as in many education settings — that confers a fundamental sense of autonomy. That has knock-on effects, of course (personal communication, June 20, 2023).

It was clear that igniting learners' passions could be the key to transforming my classroom and, perhaps, the future of education itself.

Drawing upon the principles of Expectancy-Value Theory (EVT), articulated by researchers such as Eccles and Wigfield, the anticipation of success (expectancy) and the perceived importance or relevance of the task (value) play crucial roles in driving student motivation. EVT posits that students' expectancies for success and task values are two critical factors impacting their motivation, academic performance, and choice of activities (Rosenzweig et al., 2019). Similarly, Project-Based Learning and Passion-Based Learning (PsBL) hinge on aligning tasks with students' interests and perceived values, fostering a conducive environment for enhancing intrinsic motivation.

In her article *The 4 Essential Elements of Passion-based Learning*, Jill Badalamenti further illustrates this point. She describes passion-based learning as harnessing a student's interests to aid their learning, allowing them to feel valued, and transforming a teacher-centric classroom into a student-centric one.

While passion-based Learning is an embedded element within PBL that enhances student involvement, it parallels the foundations of EVT, where the perceived value and expectancies of success in tasks significantly influence students' motivation and engagement. The correlation between EVT and PsBL underscores the importance of personal relevance and perceived success in fostering a conducive learning environment.

The beauty of passion-based learning is its ability to enrich the learning experience regardless of the teaching method. By selecting projects or problems that align with their passions, students can integrate these interests into various PBL frameworks, leading to more profound learning outcomes.

Passion-based learning fosters a more holistic, student-centric educational approach by aligning academic content with personal interests. It stimulates creativity, intrinsic motivation, and a sense of ownership, helping students develop self-directed learning, research, communication, and problem-solving skills. It leverages the power of students' passions, offering a more personalized, engaging learning experience that promotes a profound understanding of the content.

Intrinsic motivation is pivotal in passion-based learning, boosting student engagement and performance. It's important to acknowledge that not every subject will spark passion in every student. However, the magic happens when we identify those unique areas that captivate a student's interest. By providing daily opportunities for students to delve into their passions, we cultivate a rich, diverse learning experience.

Passion-based learning isn't just about allowing students to learn what they want. It's about discovering their passions and integrating them into the required curriculum, shifting grading to reward mastery and risk-taking, and fostering an environment that encourages the pursuit of passions. This aligns well with the tenets of EVT, which emphasizes the significance of perceived value and expectancy in enhancing motivation, engagement, and, ultimately, academic success (Wang & Xue, 2022).

When I first implemented a teaching strategy that involved tapping into students' passions, I noticed increased engagement and enthusiasm. At that time, I was unaware that this pedagogical approach had a specific terminology. Only later did I discover it was referred to as passion-based learning. Importantly, this approach is more than merely anecdotal or intuitive. A substantial body of academic research underscores the pivotal role of passion in enhancing the educational process, validating the effectiveness of the approach I had instinctively adopted.

In their research titled *Motivation and Engagement in Student Assignments: The Role of Choice and Relevancy*, Dabrowski and Tanji (2018) delve into how student interest and emotional investment significantly impact learning outcomes. They argue that motivation leads to deeper engagement, where students are actively immersed in their learning process.

The research identifies three crucial factors for enhancing student motivation and engagement: the content's usefulness, its ability to intrigue students, and the trustworthiness of the person presenting it. Assignments that encourage inquiry and revolve around significant themes or 'big ideas' help students develop critical skills necessary for academic and professional success. Integrating real-world materials into assignments makes them more relatable and interesting for students.

Dabrowski and Tanji also emphasize the importance of choice in assignments. Allowing students to make decisions regarding content, products, or processes fosters a sense of ownership, vital for sustained engagement and high-level achievement (Dabrowski & Tanji, 2018).

I had the opportunity to meet with Dr. Eric Anderman, interim Dean and Director at The Ohio State University. He is the co-author of *Classroom Motivation: Linking Research to Teacher Practice.* In our conversation, he expressed the importance of knowing your students. He said students fall into one of four quadrants with any given lesson, which you can see in the following graphic.

Figure 4.1
Quadrants of Motivation

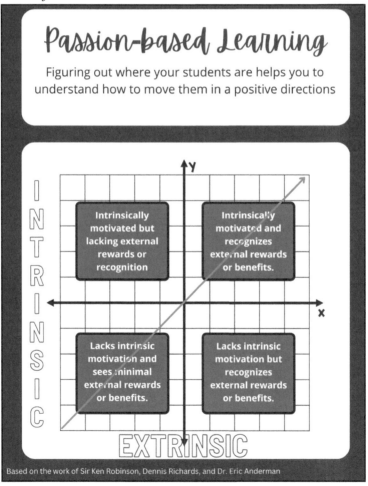

Dr. Anderman acknowledged that not every student will find every lesson engaging, but they might recognize its practical value. Students might think, "While I don't particularly enjoy this topic, I understand its utility and can appreciate its future relevance." This perspective allows students to make connections to the topic's future applications, even if they aren't passionate about it.

During our discussion about the intrinsic and extrinsic motivation chart, I asked Dr. Anderman about strategies for engaging students who don't feel intrinsically motivated about the subject nor see its value. He suggested that such students require extrinsic motivation. However, he warned against fostering a dependency on such motivation. The goal is to initiate momentum in the student's learning process, and if a reward can stimulate this, it's a step in the right direction.

Dr. Anderman stressed that extrinsic motivation should not be a punishment. Threats of negative consequences, such as calling home or failing the student if an assignment isn't completed, won't foster "continuing motivation" (2021, p. 48-49). He emphasized that sustainable motivation cannot be built on avoiding negative outcomes.

I was fortunate to communicate with Daniel Pink about engaging students who are apathetic and fall into the category Dr. Anderman described. I asked him what educators should do when it seems impossible to foster intrinsic motivation. He said,

> Look for it in other places — then reverse engineer! Take teenagers. Yes, they seem apathetic on some dimensions — especially inside a traditional classroom. But look at them in the marching band theater on a sports team or a school newspaper. They're the opposite of apathetic — alive, alert, engaged, and self-directed. The question is why. And by examining these domains, we can find missing features in classrooms. For starters, all places where students are engaged are freely chosen. Nobody forced them to play basketball or join the marching band. Second, they're typically collaborative. Your performance — on the playing field, on the stage, or in the school orchestra — affects

other people's performance, and your performance affects theirs. That can be challenging, but it's often exhilarating (not to mention great preparation for the rest of life.) Third, all those domains are outward-facing in ways that most school assignments are not. Somebody watches the baseball game. Somebody reads the school paper. It's real in ways that many classroom exercises are not (personal communication, June 20, 2023).

"The problem is that our current education systems were conceived, organized, and implemented at the height of the Industrial Revolution in the 19th century, and they are modeled on the principles and procedures of industrial production. They are based on conformity, compliance, and linearity. The problem is life is diverse, creative, and organic."
-Sir Ken Robinson, co(lab) summit 2013

The research paper *Passion-Based Learning for 21st Century: A Way to Promote Creativity in Language Classroom* by Mas'ud et al. (2019) narrates an innovative journey in the realm of English education. It advocates a shift towards passion-based learning, especially for secondary school students. This approach recognizes students' diverse interests, empowering them to select topics and skills they are passionate about. The teacher's role evolves into that of a facilitator, guiding students to apply their chosen skills to solve real-life problems, making the learning process more engaging and effective.

Highlighting the significance of creativity in education, the research references Balkin (1990), who contends that creativity is not only teachable but essential for fostering an innovative classroom environment. The paper recommends discovery, inquiry, and problem-solving methodologies to enhance creativity.

Specifically, in improving reading skills in English classrooms, passion-based learning encourages students to choose reading material that aligns with their interests, enhancing engagement and comprehension (Mas'ud et al., 2019). The paper also draws upon Zion & Mendelovici's

119

(2012) study which demonstrates that passion-driven learning leads to deeper engagement in problem-solving and decision-making processes, fostering critical and logical thinking and nurturing a sense of ownership and responsibility in students.

Furthermore, the research incorporates insights from Treffinger (1980) and Widarsa (2013) on the necessity of creative learning and how the educational system can be leveraged to support this. It also utilizes Csikszentmihalyi's (2013) five steps for achieving creativity in the class-room – preparation, incubation, insight, evaluation, and elaboration – as outlined by Avila (2015). These steps serve as a framework for teachers seeking to cultivate creativity and innovation in their teaching practices.

Promoting passion-based learning in secondary school and possibly in higher education could help improve creativity in the English classroom. This method can help students understand the subject well because they focus on their passion, leading to more effective learning. The research's findings, supported by a wealth of specific details and references to other studies, provide a strong foundation for the role of passion-based learning in promoting creativity in the classroom (Mas'ud et al., 2019).

Integrating passion into a project-based learning environment involves navigating certain challenges while embracing the potential for profound educational transformation. One primary challenge is aligning individual student passions with the broader curriculum. To address this, educators can allow students to develop projects. This allows for greater person-alization within the curriculum's framework, ensuring students explore their interests while meeting educational standards.

Another challenge lies in ensuring equitable access to diverse resourc-es. Teachers can overcome this by providing various resources catering to different interests and learning preferences, including digital tools, books, community resources, and expert talks. Within my classroom, I have a maker's space. I have used grant money each year to get supplies for students. I have also worked with the cafeteria and custodial staff to get cardboard for the classroom. These resources ensure that all students have equal access to materials for projects.

In passion-based learning, balancing individual pursuits with the crucial aspect of collaborative learning in project-based learning can be challenging. To avoid overemphasizing solitary endeavors, educators should foster a teamwork approach distinct from mere group work. Teamwork emphasizes cohesive project development where each member's contribution complements the others, ensuring every student engages with the entire content. This contrasts with typical group work, where tasks are often divided, leading to uneven engagement and contribution levels. A common pitfall in group work is the unequal distribution of workload, resulting in situations where one student might do most of the work while others contribute minimally, yet all receive the same grade.

Teamwork, however, necessitates that each team member completes a comprehensive portion of the project that harmonizes with their peers' contributions.

Figure 4.2
Student Project on American Colonies

An illustrative example of this is a project I assigned to two students on early American colonial regions. They chose to create a tea set to represent their topic. Their creative idea was to link the English origins of the colonies with the concept of England "pouring out" itself to establish these colonies. One student crafted all the saucers, while the other made the tea cups. In this manner, both students covered all aspects of the content through their pieces, which, when combined, formed a cohesive and complementary whole. This approach ensures that while individual exploration is valued, it is seamlessly integrated into a collective learning experience, which is vital in PBL.

Moreover, continuous assessment and adjustment of the learning process based on student feedback and progress are vital. This approach ensures that learning remains relevant and engaging for all students. Supporting this, a study on designing PBL experiences using motivation theory suggests that educators should scaffold learning by integrating diverse activities, emphasizing personal relevance, and ensuring project authenticity to keep students engaged and motivated (Cooper, 2022).

Lastly, the successful implementation of this approach requires ongoing professional development for educators. This involves training, resource sharing, and collaboration with fellow educators to integrate passion-based learning within the PBL framework effectively. The study further highlights the importance of faculty roles, authentic project contexts, and integrating client and service elements in PBL to enhance student motivation and learning outcomes (Cooper, 2022).

By understanding these challenges and proactively seeking solutions, educators can create a learning environment that not only fosters individual student passions but also upholds the collaborative, comprehensive essence of PBL. This alignment paves the way for a more engaging, effective, and personally fulfilling student educational experience.

Solutions for Building Intrinsic Motivation to Ignite Learner Passions

The framework, originally conceived by Joyce Epstein, focused on fostering school, family, and community partnerships, as elaborated in her work *School/Family/Community Partnerships: Caring for the Children We Share* (Epstein, 2010). Carole Ames later adapted this framework, now known as the TARGET framework, to address motivation within the educational setting. Ames's adaptation is a robust model educators can employ to nurture a classroom environment conducive to mastery goals and building intrinsic motivation (Ames, 1992). The acronym TARGET stands for Task, Authority, Recognition, Grouping, Evaluation, and Time, each representing a critical element in the learning process. Each element of the framework uniquely contributes to this goal:

Task: By creating meaningful, engaging, and moderately challenging tasks, students are more likely to be intrinsically motivated to learn. These tasks should promote understanding and mastery rather than rote memorization. When students see the value in what they are learning and feel challenged but capable, they are more likely to be motivated to learn for understanding rather than for external rewards.

Authority: Giving students autonomy and control over their learning process can foster intrinsic motivation. When students feel they have a say in their learning, they are more likely to take ownership of it and be motivated to succeed.

Recognition: Recognition in the classroom should be based on individual improvement and effort rather than comparison with others. This helps to foster a mastery orientation rather than a performance orientation. When students feel that their efforts and improvements are recognized and valued, they are more likely to be motivated to continue learning and improving.

Grouping: This framework advocates for flexible grouping strategies, avoiding rigid ability grouping or tracking to enhance students' intrinsic motivation. Students interact with a diverse cohort by fostering a dynamic, adaptable grouping environment, promoting a growth mindset, and enriching learning experiences. This approach aligns with differentiated instruction, enabling tailored teaching to meet varied student needs, thereby creating a more personalized and motivating learning environment. Through flexible grouping based on interests, goals, or tasks, students engage actively, take ownership of their learning, and contribute to positive interdependence and individual accountability, essential for boosting intrinsic motivation and achieving mastery goals.

Evaluation: Criterion-referenced evaluation, where students are evaluated based on their improvement and mastery of learning objectives rather than their performance relative to others, can foster intrinsic motivation. When students see that their progress and learning are valued more than their grades or ranking, they are more likely to be motivated to learn and improve.

Time: Allowing students to work independently can also foster intrinsic motivation. When students feel they have sufficient time to understand and master the material, they are less likely to feel pressured and more likely to be motivated to learn (Ames, 1992).

The traditional classroom often emphasizes external rewards, competition, and a one-size-fits-all approach. However, research shows fostering intrinsic motivation and a mastery mindset is crucial for long-term student learning and growth. This is where the TARGET framework, adapted by Carole Ames, becomes invaluable. Ames's model provides robust strategies for nurturing an environment conducive to mastery goals and building intrinsic drive. By addressing the key elements of Task, Authority, Recognition, Grouping, Evaluation, and Time, TARGET empowers students to own their learning journey. It values individual progress over ranking, aligns with psychological needs, and cultivates an authentic love for learning. Grounded in extensive motivation research, TARGET's comprehensive approach overcomes the limitations of extrinsically driven classrooms. Its strategies enable student autonomy, mastery orientation, and an engaging atmosphere tailored to diverse learners. The implementation and specific strategies of the TARGET framework will be explored in greater depth later in this chapter.

Challenges Within the TARGET Framework

In addressing the challenges within the TARGET framework in a project-based learning environment, educators can implement various strategies. First, teachers can involve students in the **task** creation process to counter the limitation of over-reliance on teacher-designed tasks in the task element. This can be achieved through class discussions, surveys, or allowing students to propose project ideas, aligning tasks more closely with individual interests and learning preferences.

For the **authority** component, balancing autonomy with structure is crucial. Educators can offer structured choices to students, providing a range of options in learning activities, assessment methods, or project topics while maintaining a guided framework. This approach ensures student ownership within a supportive structure.

In the aspect of **recognition**, it's important to focus on acknowledging effort and progress rather than just achievement. This approach ensures recognition fosters a growth mindset and intrinsic motivation rather than shifting the focus towards external rewards.

Addressing the **grouping** challenge involves implementing effective group dynamics strategies, such as defining clear roles and conflict resolution protocols. This ensures that flexible grouping leads to positive interdependence and individual accountability.

For **evaluation**, adopting a portfolio approach allows for a more comprehensive view of a student's learning journey, addressing the varying interpretations of mastery. This method evaluates students based on their improvement and mastery over time.

Lastly, in the **time** aspect, blended learning strategies can allow students to progress at their own pace while keeping within a structured timeline. This approach helps manage different pacing needs among students.

The TARGET framework aligns perfectly with the principles of a PBL classroom, making it an essential model for promoting intrinsic motivation and passion-based learning. By implementing the TARGET strategies, teachers can create a classroom environment that supports mastery goals, encourages student engagement, and promotes a love of learning. These elements are fundamental to the success of PBL and are vividly brought to life through student experiences.

Student Stories

High school teacher Steve Martinez recounts how passion-based learning transformed the life of one of his students.

In Steve Martinez's 12th-grade economics class, the integration of the TARGET framework, though subtle and unnamed, clearly indicates how teachers often naturally embed these motivational principles in their teaching practices. This is exemplified in how Steve interacted with his students at the beginning of the school year. He would initiate conversations, inquiring about their passions and desired career paths. This approach, aligning with the **authority** component of TARGET, provided students with a sense of ownership and autonomy in their learning journey.

One student, aspiring to be a science teacher, revealed her uncertainty about her motivations and her "why" for choosing this path. Steve viewed his class as an ideal environment for students to explore and clarify their motivations, potentially finding a trajectory for their lives. This aspect of his teaching aligns with fostering intrinsic motivation, a key element in the TARGET framework.

The "Local Econ Project" that Steve introduced in the spring is a direct application of the **task** element of TARGET. By encouraging students to identify and address a local economic issue, the project provided a meaningful and engaging learning experience that promoted understanding and mastery. This student focused on student poverty and homelessness in her local school districts, a project that allowed her to connect her educational journey to real-world problems.

Through her action research, she gained a deep understanding of these issues, leading to a transformative shift in her perspective on why she wanted to pursue education. This outcome aligns with the **recognition** and **evaluation** aspects of TARGET, where the focus is on individual improvement and personal growth.

Steve's approach to grouping, although not detailed, suggests an environment where students could benefit from diverse interactions, reflecting the **grouping** strategy in TARGET. The project's nature implies a dynamic learning atmosphere conducive to a growth mindset.

Lastly, the ample time given for the project reflects the **time** component of the framework, allowing students to deeply engage with complex issues at their own pace.

In Steve's class, placing passion at the forefront of addressing real-world problems demonstrates how motivational strategies, akin to those in the TARGET framework, can powerfully direct students' learning.

Passion, as Steve observed, is not just about what makes students happy but also what drives them to empathize and support others, showcasing the profound impact of integrating motivational theory in education.

Wesley Renton, a primary teacher at Stirling Primary School in East London, South Africa, has created a dynamic and engaging unit called "What's for Lunch?"

Imagine a bustling Grade 6 classroom, alive with the energy of eager young minds embarking on a journey unlike any other. This journey, titled "What's for Lunch?" isn't just another school project; it's an adventure that perfectly encapsulates the essence of the TARGET framework, a beacon guiding students toward a more engaging, meaningful form of learning.

The mission is clear yet challenging: to reinvent the school tuckshop menu. This isn't just about choosing dishes; it's about diving into nutrition, budgeting, and culinary creativity. Here, each student becomes a young nutritionist, an economist, and a chef rolled into one. The **task**, deeply rooted in real-world applications, transcends the confines of traditional classroom walls, inviting students to explore, experiment, and ultimately master many concepts.

As the project unfolds, a sense of ownership blossoms within each student. They are not just participants but decision-makers, steering the course of their learning journey. From crafting surveys to analyzing data, their choices shape the project's trajectory. This autonomy, a crucial element of the **authority** aspect of the TARGET framework, fosters a rich environment where students feel empowered and invested in their educational journey.

Amidst the flurry of activities, each effort, big or small, is recognized and celebrated. Whether it's a keen insight during the survey analysis or a creative twist in a meal plan, every contribution is acknowledged. This culture of **recognition** nurtures a growth mindset, encouraging students to strive for progress and cherish every step of their learning journey.

Collaboration is the heartbeat of this project. Students cluster in **groups**, pooling their ideas, sharing findings, and crafting menus together. This group work, reflective of the grouping principle, turns the classroom into a vibrant community of learners, each benefiting from the shared knowledge and diverse perspectives of their peers.

As the project nears its culmination, diverse evaluation forms come into play. From meticulously crafted written reports to the aroma of cooking presentations, each form of assessment is a thread in the rich tapestry of learning. This aligns with the **evaluation** aspect of the framework, where feedback and self-reflection are valued over grades and ranks, encouraging a holistic understanding of the subject matter.

Throughout this journey, time is a gift. Spread over several weeks, the project allows students to delve deeply into each aspect, fostering a learning experience that is rich and unrushed. This adherence to the **time** element ensures that learning is not just a fleeting moment but an enduring process, allowing concepts to take root and flourish within each student.

As the journey of "What's for Lunch?" comes to a close, it leaves behind a legacy of inspired, motivated learners. This is a testament to the transformative power of the TARGET framework in action. Here, within the walls of a Grade 6 classroom, lies a microcosm of what education can and should be - a journey of discovery, empowerment, and deep, lasting learning.

You can access the "What's for Lunch?" activity by scanning the QR code.

Plan, Personalize, and Pursue

Plan

Reflecting on your current classroom practices is essential to chart a path forward. We'll utilize the TARGET strategy to guide strategic classroom modifications.

Figure 4.3
Self Reflection (Page 1)

Self-Reflection TARGET

STAR RATING

To what degree is Passion-Based
Learning implemented in your
classroom or school?

FEELING

Do you feel like you can
implement the change you want
to see?

Currently

TASK

the importance of
creating meaningful,
engaging, and
moderately challenging
tasks for students

Changes

Currently

AUTHORITY

the need for students to
have some degree of
autonomy and control
over their learning
process

Changes

Currently

RECOGNITION

the classroom should be
based on individual
improvement and effort
rather than comparison
with others

Changes

Figure 4.4
Self Reflection (Page 2)

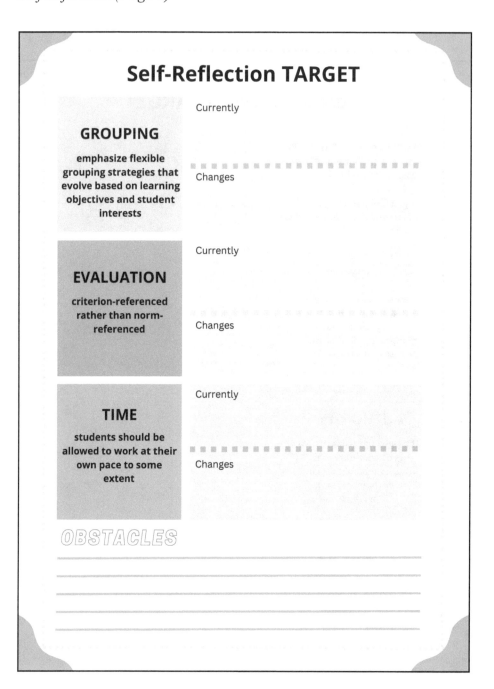

Scan the provided QR code to print the previous worksheets.

Task

Central to fostering intrinsic motivation in students is the design and structuring of tasks they engage with. The task element in the TARGET framework underscores the importance of creating meaningful, engaging, and moderately challenging tasks that stimulate students' curiosity and promote a deeper understanding and mastery over rote memorization. When the tasks are relevant to students' lives, aligned with their interests, and challenging them to stretch their abilities without overwhelming them, a conducive environment for intrinsic motivation is created.

Creating meaningful tasks entails aligning the learning activities with real-world applications and contexts that students can relate to. This relevance enhances the perceived value of the tasks, igniting an intrinsic desire to engage with the material and explore the subject matter further.

Engagement is fostered when tasks are interactive and thought-provoking and encourages students to question, analyze, and synthesize information. Engaging tasks captivate students' attention, fuel their enthusiasm for learning, and provide a platform for them to apply their knowledge in practical, creative, and meaningful ways.

The level of challenge in tasks is a delicate balance that requires careful consideration. Moderately challenging tasks should encourage students to step out of their comfort zones, yet be attainable with effort and perseverance. These tasks should promote a growth mindset, where students view challenges as opportunities for growth rather than threats to their ability.

Furthermore, a supportive feedback mechanism is crucial in guiding students through challenging tasks, providing constructive feedback that not only acknowledges their efforts but also directs them toward improvement and mastery.

By carefully crafting tasks that embody these principles, educators can significantly contribute to building a classroom environment that nurtures intrinsic motivation, encourages a love for learning, and propels students toward achieving mastery goals. Through such thoughtful task design, the foundation for a vibrant, inquiry-driven, and student-centered learning environment is established, promoting a culture where students are excited to learn, explore, and excel.

Authority

It's pivotal within the educational realm to empower students with a sense of autonomy and control over their learning journey. The element of authority in the TARGET framework resonates with this principle, advocating for an environment where students are seen as active participants rather than passive recipients in the learning process. When students are granted a degree of authority over their learning, such as having a say in setting their learning goals, choosing the methods they learn, or even contributing to the assessment criteria, they are more likely to take ownership of their education and become intrinsically motivated.

Providing students with choices, be it in the selection of topics, the mode of information presentation, or the means of assessment, allows them to align their learning experiences with their interests, needs, and individual learning preferences. This autonomy fosters a sense of relevance and personal connection to the educational material, thereby encouraging a deeper engagement and a genuine desire to learn.

Furthermore, when students are entrusted with the authority to make decisions about their learning, it instills a sense of responsibility and self-efficacy. They become more invested in the outcomes of their educational pursuits and are driven to achieve mastery out of an inherent interest rather than external pressures.

By establishing a classroom environment that values students' voices, encourages their active involvement in the learning process, and provides opportunities for autonomous decision-making, educators can significantly enhance intrinsic motivation. This approach not only enriches the learning experience but also nurtures a culture of self-directed, passionate learners who are prepared to navigate the complexities of the educational landscape with confidence and curiosity.

Recognition

It's essential to pivot the focus towards recognizing students' efforts and achievements in the learning journey to foster intrinsic motivation. Recognition in the classroom should be tailored to highlight individual improvement and effort rather than merely comparing students with one another. By celebrating the small wins, acknowledging the struggles, and appreciating the perseverance, teachers can cultivate a mastery orientation among students. This approach aligns with the principles of promoting intrinsic motivation, where learners are driven by their personal growth and the sense of accomplishment that comes with it. Recognition should be authentic and constructive, providing students with meaningful feedback that encourages them to continue learning. It's not merely about the end goal; it's about valuing the process and the effort to achieve mastery. This recognition underscores the significance of every student's unique learning journey and fosters a genuine love for learning.

Furthermore, the culture of recognition should extend beyond the classroom, involving parents and the broader school community in celebrating students' efforts and achievements. This community-wide recognition can be a powerful motivator, reinforcing the student's intrinsic motivation to learn and excel.

Grouping

The concept of grouping within the TARGET framework emphasizes flexible grouping strategies that circumvent rigid ability grouping or tracking, which could potentially hinder the intrinsic motivation of students. In a classroom, grouping should be fluid and adaptable to cater to the diverse learning needs, interests, and paces of students. Avoiding fixed ability groups helps promote a growth mindset, where students are not confined to a predetermined track but have the opportunity to interact with a diverse cohort, thereby enhancing their learning experiences and intrinsic motivation.

Flexible grouping encourages students to work with different peers in varying contexts, promoting a broader understanding and appreciation for diverse abilities and perspectives. It cultivates a sense of community and inclusivity, where every student can contribute, learn, and grow. When students are grouped in various configurations, be it based on their interests, goals, or the task at hand, they are more likely to engage actively and take ownership of their learning.

Furthermore, flexible grouping strategies support differentiated instruction, allowing teachers to tailor their teaching to meet the varied needs and aptitudes of students, fostering a more personalized and motivating learning environment. This approach aligns with the principles of promoting mastery and intrinsic motivation, as students are provided with a supportive yet challenging environment that respects their individuality and encourages continuous growth and development. Through thoughtful and flexible grouping, teachers can create a classroom atmosphere conducive to fostering intrinsic motivation, promoting a love for learning, and achieving mastery goals.

Personalize

Evaluation

The evaluation process is a cornerstone in understanding and enhancing students' intrinsic motivation and engagement in the learning process. In alignment with the TARGET framework, evaluation should shift towards a criterion-referenced approach, focusing on students' personal improvement and mastery of learning objectives rather than comparative performance. Here are some approaches to evaluate the changes:

1. **Student Reflections**: Encouraging students to reflect on their learning experiences, challenges faced, and the strategies they found beneficial can provide valuable insights. This can be facilitated through structured reflection sheets or guided discussions.

2. **Peer Feedback:** Establish a culture of constructive peer feedback where students can learn from each other's perspectives, understand

different approaches to tasks, and appreciate the process of continuous improvement.

3. **Performance Assessments:** Design assessments that gauge students' understanding, application, and mastery of the material rather than rote memorization. Include formative assessments that provide timely and constructive feedback, aiding learning.

4. **Student Surveys:** Conduct anonymous surveys to gather students' opinions on the learning environment, the tasks provided, and the evaluation methods employed. Their feedback can shed light on areas of improvement and the impact of changes on their motivation and learning.

Pursue

Time

In the pursuit to foster intrinsic motivation, the aspect of time is fundamental. It's essential to create a learning environment where students can work at their own pace to some extent, ensuring they have sufficient time to grasp and master the material. A structured timetable that delineates the pacing of learning activities, assessment timelines, and periods for reflection and feedback can be immensely beneficial.

The timetable should be flexible to accommodate the diverse learning needs and paces of students, providing them with the opportunity to engage deeply with the material, explore their interests, and achieve mastery without feeling rushed. The transition from a focus on extrinsic rewards to intrinsic motivation should be gradual and well-structured, with clear objectives, checkpoints for feedback, and opportunities for adjustments based on evaluating students' progress and feedback.

Moreover, allocating time for collaborative activities, individual exploration, and feedback sessions can create a conducive environment for intrinsic motivation. Through thoughtful time management and a supportive learning atmosphere, students can experience the joy of learning, explore their passions, and work towards mastery, thus fostering a genuine intrinsic motivation towards education.

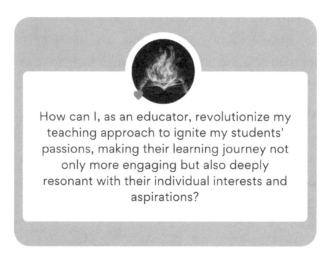

How can I, as an educator, revolutionize my teaching approach to ignite my students' passions, making their learning journey not only more engaging but also deeply resonant with their individual interests and aspirations?

Journaling Your Journey

Use the space below to reflect on this question.

_____

_____

_____

_____

_____

_____

_____

_____

_____

_____

_____

_____

_____

_____

_____

_____

Throughout this chapter, we delved into the transformative power of integrating passion into PBL, highlighting how aligning students' intrinsic interests with their educational journey enhances engagement and leads to more meaningful learning outcomes. This chapter underscored the shift towards a student-centric model, where education is not just about knowledge transmission but nurturing individual passions. As we transition into the next chapter, "Crafting Immersive Learning Practices," we will explore how these passion-infused approaches can be further enhanced by immersive learning experiences, providing practical insights and strategies to create deeper, more engaging educational environments that resonate with students' real-world experiences and aspirations. What role can educators play as change agents who model creative, student-centric, and passion-driven learning? How might our ripples inspire waves of innovation in our schools and communities? Let these reflections guide you as we explore tools for sustainable innovation that can spread the light of passion-based learning.

Chapter 5
Crafting Immersive Learning Practices

 Interview with Dr. Catlin Tucker
Education Expert, Author, and Speaker

"I never teach my pupils, I only attempt to provide the conditions in which they can learn."
- Albert Einstein

Albert Einstein's timeless words resonate profoundly with the evolving ethos of education. This sentiment echoes the core philosophy of modern educational practices, where the role of the educator extends beyond mere instruction to fostering a deep, participatory learning experience. The modern educator navigates a complex tapestry of pedagogical strategies, technologies, and evolving classroom dynamics. Amid these intricacies, one term has managed to captivate our collective imagination: immersion. Immersion points to the idea of becoming completely involved or engaged in an experience. In an educational context, immersive learning refers to classroom approaches and techniques that fully engage students in the content and skills being taught. The goal is to create dynamic learning environments where students don't just passively receive information but actively participate, inquire, apply, and take ownership of their learning experience. Immersive learning catalyzes students' innate curiosity, empowering them with agency over the learning process. When implemented effectively, these approaches can transform classrooms from mere physical spaces into vibrant landscapes for academic and personal discovery. As we delve into immersive practices, we will explore the multidimensional nature they possess in learning and provide insights into how educators can craft truly transformational experiences for their students. The aim is to dive below the surface and illuminate the immense potential immersive learning has for genuine understanding and growth. So let us immerse ourselves in this fascinating journey! This subject transcends the boundaries of technology and traditional instruction, offering a blueprint for heightened student engagement and enhanced understanding.

How can I, as an educator, revolutionize my teaching approach to ignite my students' passions, making their learning journey not only more engaging but also deeply resonant with their individual interests and aspirations?

Journaling Your Journey

Use the space below to reflect on this question.

_____

_____

_____

_____

_____

_____

_____

_____

"Immersion" often evokes images of virtual reality headsets, holographic projections, and digitally rendered 3D environments. While the advancements in augmented reality (AR) and virtual reality (VR) have been remarkable, it's crucial to understand that these tools are not prerequisites for creating an immersive learning experience. The heart of immersion lies not in the sophistication of the tools we use but in the depth of engagement and understanding we foster.

The notion of immersion in education can be dissected into two core elements: immersing students in content and using immersive technology. Both are valuable but operate on different spectrums of accessibility and impact.

Immersing Students in Content

Before the dawn of interactive whiteboards and online learning platforms, masterful teachers have crafted immersive experiences for centuries. Whether through storytelling, hands-on activities, field trips, or intricate class discussions, educators have various tools to make subjects come alive. Dr. Catlin Tucker reflects on this, stating, "The whole idea is that in the classroom, students are frequently asked to tackle questions or find solutions to problems they have never truly encountered or explored" (Tucker, C., personal communication, November 27, 2023). Immersion in content means creating an environment where students are so engaged that they become part of the learning material. They're not merely passive receivers of information; they actively interact, question, and connect with the subject matter. It's important to remember that immersive learning is not about the tools but about the experience.

In the quest for impactful education, teachers often seek strategies that dive deeper than the textbook. The reality is that irrespective of the subject area, students benefit from active and immersive learning experiences, which don't necessarily demand intricate technology or resources but a thoughtful approach to planning.

Take *mathematics*, for instance. Typically viewed as abstract and challenging, this subject becomes tangibly relatable when students physically act out story problems. It's a transformative experience to see a word

140

problem about dividing apples among friends come alive as students, with real apples in hand, distribute them and visualize the mathematical concept of division. This physical act makes abstract concepts concrete, aiding in identifying and processing relevant information.

With its rich tapestry of interconnected principles, *science* thrives on mind maps. Consider students grappling with the water cycle can represent every step - from evaporation to precipitation - delineating their connections. Couple this with field trips, like a visit to a local marsh, and scientific concepts leap off the pages and into the world they inhabit, rendering the complexity of ecosystems palpable.

On the other hand, *history* and *social studies* gain depth when students debate the motivations behind historical events during Socratic seminars or step into the shoes of historical figures during role plays. Imagine the depth of understanding a student achieves when they're not just reading about Julius Caesar but are debating the implications of his assassination or reenacting the Senate's tensions.

Figure 5.1
Images From a Titanic Experience

Angel Vega, a 4th grade teacher in Mansfield, Ohio, orchestrates an immersive culminating activity for her class by constructing a paper and desk replica of the Titanic. Each student receives a boarding pass and the identity of an actual Titanic passenger. Angel guides them through the intricacies of setting a formal dining table, followed by a high tea on board their classroom Titanic. Embracing the theme, the students use refined English accents and demonstrate their best manners while sipping tea and enjoying scones and biscuits. The experience reaches its poignant climax when the fate of each assigned passenger is revealed, allowing the students to discover whether their passenger survived the sinking. This revelation deeply affects the students, highlighting the significant loss of life and the impact of social class on survival. The immersive experience leaves a lasting impression, sparking a sustained interest and curiosity in the students, who continue to research and explore the topic long after the unit concludes, driven by their personal investment in the experience.

Recently, during our study of the events leading up to the American Revolution, I engaged my students in a unique Boston Tea Party experience. While we didn't actually throw tea off a ship, each student had the chance to taste the different types of tea that the Patriots famously discarded. Accompanying these tastings, each student received a card detailing the characteristics of each tea variety.

Figure 5.2

Tea, Welcome Card, and Historical Figures Card for Boston Tea Party

Furthermore, I distributed cards representing individuals involved in the actual Boston Tea Party on December 16, 1773. The students learned about the roles their historical figures played that night, along with intriguing facts about their subsequent lives. Tasting the same varieties of tea that were thrown from the ship centuries ago truly brought this pivotal moment in history to life. The words from their research transformed into a tangible, memorable experience.

To enhance this educational journey, we collaborated with a local tea brewing company. Their involvement not only supported our lesson but also provided an authentic tea brewing experience, further immersing the students in the historical context. This partnership not only enriched our learning but also connected us with our community, making the lesson even more impactful and memorable.

Language arts, a domain brimming with narratives and layered meanings, finds resonance in Socratic discussions on literary interpretations and role plays of poignant scenes from novels. It's one thing to read about the dramatic atmosphere of *Wuthering Heights*, and another to feel it while visiting the moors. Such experiences change students' perspectives, making literary elements more relatable.

One unforgettable morning, I entered my freshman English class not as Mr. Jones but as Grumpy, the beloved dwarf from the fairy tales we were studying. This transformation wasn't a sudden whim but was inspired by a captivating trip to a Renaissance festival. There, amidst jesters and jousters, I stumbled upon a booth selling latex masks so lifelike that they seamlessly melded with one's facial features, moving perfectly with every grimace and grin.

Donning this mask, complemented by a flowing grey beard and wig, my identity evaporated. The mirror no longer showed the familiar face of a second-year teacher but rather the scowling visage of Snow White's curmudgeonly companion. Determined to bring this immersive experience to my classroom, I crafted a persona around this mask. Ragged clothes draped my body, shoes were strapped to my knees to give the illusion of short stature, and my legs were cleverly concealed beneath the draped cloth.

As my students filtered into the room, their expressions ranged from bewilderment to amusement. In place of their predictable teacher was this dwarf, acting every bit as disgruntled as his name suggested. "Mr. Jones dared to pull me from my routine to entertain children," I grumbled in character, feigning annoyance. All the while, I narrated Snow White's enchanting story. The room was electric. Any slight murmur from a student was met with an exaggerated, grumpy retort, igniting giggles and even keener attention.

The real magic of that day? Most students only realized at the very end that the irate dwarf was, in fact, their very own Mr. Jones. This playful ruse brought a fairy tale to life and left an indelible memory, proving that learning, with a touch of creativity, can truly be an enchanting experience. Reflecting on the role of the educator in these contexts, Tucker noted that teachers aren't just facilitators; they're the architects of these learning experiences. They provide the scaffolding that helps students climb higher (Tucker, C., personal communication, November 27, 2023).

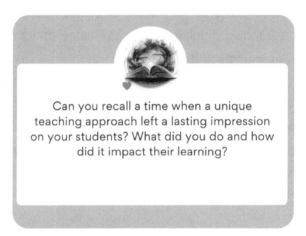

Can you recall a time when a unique teaching approach left a lasting impression on your students? What did you do and how did it impact their learning?

Journaling Your Journey

Use the space below to reflect on this question.

_____

_____

_____

_____

_____

_____

_____

At the heart of these strategies is the fundamental idea: engagement. It's about rendering subjects palpable, breaking walls between the classroom and the real world. Dr. Catlin Tucker emphasizes this concept in her interview, noting the importance of transforming textbook concepts into tangible, real experiences for students. Her perspective highlights the need to make learning more relatable and interactive, effectively bringing theoretical ideas to life. And while these immersive techniques might seem daunting at first, their successful implementation often rests on well-thought-out planning rather than intricate complications. Tucker goes on to discuss that the magic of immersive teaching isn't in complexity; it's in the planning, in the thought put into how to make these experiences resonate with students (Tucker, C., personal communication, November 27, 2023). By integrating these methods into the curriculum, educators have the potential to redefine learning experiences, creating lasting impressions on young minds.

Yet, while these strategies are invaluable in bridging the gap between learning and real-life experiences, technology has unlocked even more possibilities for immersion. In our discussion, Tucker elaborates on the transformative role of technology in education. She describes it as more than just an add-on, viewing it as a gateway to a world where learning becomes a dynamic, interactive journey (Tucker, C., personal communication, November 27, 2023). Let's delve into how technological advancements are further revolutionizing classroom engagement.

While traditional immersive teaching methods have laid a solid foundation for engaging and effective education, the advent of immersive technology in the classroom heralds a new era of learning. This technological integration promises to elevate the educational experience, blending the physical and digital worlds to create a more dynamic, interactive, and personalized learning environment. As we step into this future, the potential of VR, AR, and MR in education opens up exciting possibilities, transforming the way students interact with and understand their subjects. This transition not only enriches the learning process but also prepares students for a future increasingly intertwined with technology, marking a pivotal moment in the evolution of educational methodologies.

Figure 5.3
Immersive Education

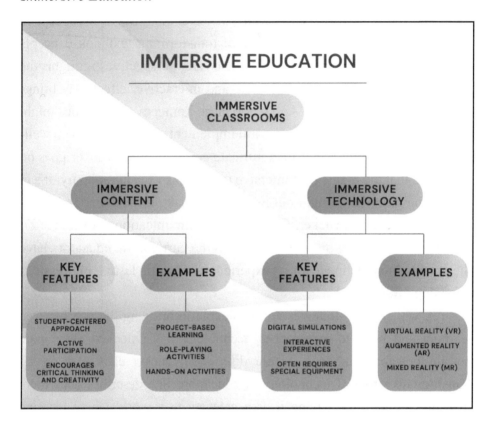

Immersive Technology in the Classroom

The digital age has revolutionized educational approaches, introducing tools that cater to diverse learning needs across various age groups. Delving into these tools offers insights into their applicability and versatility across subjects, from science to the arts.

MindMeister, suitable for middle and high school students, provides a platform to connect ideas visually. In science, learners might map photosynthesis, while social studies students trace historical timelines. For English, literary enthusiasts could plot narrative structures, while in math, concepts are organized hierarchically. Even art and music classes benefit; students outline an art movement's progression or a music genre's evolution.

Pairing **Google Earth & Google Docs** delivers the magic of exploration, ideal for elementary to high school students. Science enthusiasts explore global biomes, and social studies students virtually visit world heritage sites, supplemented by Google Docs's rich context. I created a Google Doc that has links to Google Earth coordinates embedded. The students explore the coordinates and record their reflections in the Google Doc. You can access the Google Doc as an example.

Scan the QR code to access the Google Doc with links to Google Earth coordinates.

Literature settings come alive, while math classes confront real-world geometric challenges. Art and music pupils virtually explore renowned museums or historic venues.

For sharing insights post-exploration, **Padlet**, apt for mid-elementary through high school students, serves as a digital canvas. Whether sharing science hypotheses, curating historical sources, posting book reviews, solving math problems, or showcasing student art, Padlet's platform is invaluable.

Slack, which is more suited for high school and advanced middle school students due to its complexity, offers dedicated channels for fostering dialogues. Whether debating scientific theories, role-playing historical events, discussing literature themes, collaborating on math problems, or critiquing arts and music, Slack engenders vibrant interactions. This aligns with the strategies discussed in Chapter 3 regarding online discussions.

ClickUp is excellent for visual learners from upper elementary onward. Whether visualizing the plant life cycle in science, connecting historical events, storyboarding in English, visualizing fractions in cooking, or sketching art designs, ClickUp's interactive canvas is critical.

Lastly, **Flip**, versatile for all ages but incredibly impactful from middle school onward, becomes a platform for reflective expression. Be it sharing scientific conclusions, historical reflections, oral summaries, math explanations, or art and music pieces, Flip amplifies student voices. In the context of project-based learning, as Dr. Catlin Tucker notes, Flip emerges as a valuable tool for facilitating asynchronous feedback and peer interactions. Students engaging in diverse projects, like creating websites and podcasts, or advocating for important issues, greatly benefit from Flip's capability to host and share their ideas and prototypes. This platform allows for asynchronous yet interactive peer feedback, essential for groups at different stages of their projects. Particularly noteworthy is how Flip aids in cross-grade collaborations, such as sharing a Flip wall between 9th and 10th graders with 11th and 12th-grade STEM students for feedback. This not only enhances the learning experience by offering diverse perspectives but also relieves the pressure of real-time responses, making it a perfect tool for reflective and constructive student engagement.

If you had access to any technological tool for your classroom, what would it be and how would you use it to create an immersive learning experience?

Journaling Your Journey

Use the space below to reflect on this question.

_____

_____

_____

_____

_____

_____

_____

Incorporating these age-appropriate tools effectively can transcend conventional teaching methods, offering students a dynamic, immersive journey through their academic exploration.

While digital collaboration tools offer revolutionary ways to engage and educate, they come with challenges, especially when participants can freely edit and manipulate shared content. Central to navigating these challenges is a deep understanding of one's students. Each learner comes with a unique set of experiences, capabilities, and readiness levels. Recognizing these differences, especially in terms of maturity, can significantly influence the success of a tool or method in the classroom. Some students might be technologically adept but need to be more mature to use a tool responsibly, while others might need more time and guidance to feel comfortable in digital spaces. Therefore, it's essential to refrain from rushing the introduction of these tools but to phase them in gradually, providing ample opportunities for students to learn and adapt. Moreover, educators should resist the urge to simply tell students to "go" without first teaching them the how and why of a tool's use. Gauging where each student stands helps in tailoring the learning experience, establishing trust, and ensuring a more productive and safe digital learning environment.

As we progress further along the continuum of immersion, we arrive at the pinnacle of technology-enhanced experiences: AR and VR. According to Meta Quest 3's Safety and Warranty Guide, "Use of Meta Quest requires an account and is subject to requirements that include a minimum age of 10 (requirements may vary by country)" (Meta Platforms Technologies, LLC, n.d., p. 5). These tools take engagement to a new dimension, literally and figuratively. Historical eras, scientific wonders, or abstract mathematical concepts suddenly become tangible and interactively accessible. The allure they offer is distinct, expanding the boundaries of traditional learning methodologies.

Use the following graphic to help evaluate which tool(s) would best fit your classroom.

Scan the QR code to access the Immersive Technology Tool Evaluation.

Figure 5.4

Immersive Technology Tool Evaluation Form

Immersive Technology Tool Evaluation

Tech Tool	I can see this tool enhancing student engagement	This tool will help my students to understand content at new depths	The tool creates an intuitive experience	My students are mature enough to handle the collaboration aspect
Mindmeister				
Google Earth + Google Docs				
Padlet				
Slack				
Flip				

Which tool would you introduce first and what steps would you take to help your students get the most out of the tool?

As McGraw-Hill Education notes, "Augmented and Virtual Reality (AR and VR) provide deeper engagement, opportunities for collaboration, and hands-on learning that places newly acquired knowledge and skills in context" (2023). In my classroom, leveraging the power of the HTC Vive VR headset has transformed the learning experience. We're not just discussing the picturesque streets of Florence or the historical landscape of Jamestown; we're immersively exploring them. This is more than using a device; it's opening a gateway to transformative learning. Research by Zhao, Ren, & Cheah (2023) supports this approach when citing Zarantonello & Schmitt (2023), thus demonstrating "learning benefits when comparing the usage of VR to conventional approaches." Moreover, Zhang et al. (2022) found that 'students who experimented with virtual environments as part of their lessons had more positive sentiments' than those who did not. Additionally, Verner et al. (2022) observed that "adding a 3D Virtual Reality Learning Environment increased female students' physics performance" compared to a 2D environment. Furthermore, these technologies "assist students in understanding people's unique circumstances all over the globe" (Zarantonello & Schmitt, 2023), offering immersive experiences that regular classrooms cannot replicate. However, it is crucial to consider the psychological impact, as Bucea-Manea-Țoniș et al. (2022) recommend that "technology should be utilized sparingly and under tight supervision in educational settings to guarantee beneficial student outcomes" (Zhao, Ren, & Cheah, 2023, p. 3).

Figure 5.5
Student Using an HTC Vive

The Middle Ground

This chapter delves into that space, straddling the realms of high-tech and traditional methods. Here, we'll navigate the avenues that empower educators to cultivate profound engagement, reminding ourselves that the ultimate objective is enriched comprehension. Whether you're guiding students through a virtual realm or passionately illustrating concepts with basic classroom tools, this can be achieved.

As we unravel the layers of immersive learning practices, it's essential to remember that the tools and technologies are merely facilitators. The real magic happens when a student's eyes light up with understanding, when the pieces of a complex problem suddenly click, or when a quiet classroom bursts into a lively debate.

In the world of PBL, the distinction between learner and doer blurs. Students transition from being mere spectators waiting for information to becoming investigators, collaborators, and creators. Dr. Catlin Tucker highlights the transformative power of projects, saying,

> When we consider engagement, the more active a role students have in their learning process, the more likely they are to be motivated and engaged. Yet, often, they don't experience this in school. I believe projects can be a wonderful pathway to change that (Tucker, C., personal communication, November 27, 2023).

This shift from passive to active learning is vital for deep comprehension and long-term retention. Mario Buljan (2022) reinforces this idea, noting, "Immersive learning allows students to learn more naturally. Sensory learning helps students better connect with the material they are studying." Active learning, especially in immersive settings, ensures that learners move beyond shallow retention of information to truly understanding and applying their knowledge. As Buljan elaborates, "When learners are forced to figure out how to solve a problem within a given context, they learn better than simply providing memorized answers."

So what does crafting an immersive learning experience within the PBL framework entail? How can teachers ensure that students participate actively and engage deeply, connect meaningfully, and invest wholeheart-edly in their projects? How does this deep immersion advance PBL's objectives, enhancing collaboration, inquiry, and critical thinking? Let's take a look.

Effective Facilitation Strategies for Guiding Students

Sometimes, PBL is perceived as too open-ended, and lacking the structure or academic rigor of more traditional educational models. This notion is quickly dispelled when considering how seamlessly PBL can fit into a defined curriculum. Tools like mind maps and design labs are not mere add-ons but essential scaffolding. Educators can use these tools to provide a well-defined roadmap for students' educational journeys, effec-tively integrating PBL into a structured curriculum.

The Role of Guiding Questions

Three critical elements for seamlessly integrating PBL into a struc-tured curriculum are guiding questions, formative assessments, and meaningful activities. Guiding questions are anchors that direct students' inquiry and focus on the project, aligning it with key educational ob-jectives. For instance, when students start a new unit, their initial mind maps often encompass a wide range of concepts, theories, and poten-tial avenues for exploration. These mind maps capture the richness of a subject, but guiding questions help to narrow the focus, directing students toward crucial aspects most relevant to the unit's learning objectives and real-world applications. These guiding questions refine the expansive content within a mind map into a focused, coherent narrative, channeling students' curiosity toward meaningful objectives.

The Dynamics of Formative Assessments

Formative assessments serve as checkpoints, offering timely in-sights into students' understanding. These assessments allow teachers to adjust their teaching strategies and provide students with valuable feedback, helping to shape the learning process in a responsive and dynamic way. As students integrate guiding questions into their mind maps, formative assessments play a crucial role in monitoring their understanding and progress, ensuring that their exploration stays aligned with the educational goals.

The Power of Meaningful Activities

Meaningful activities, as the core of the PBL experience, provide real-world contexts for students to explore problems, develop skills, and synthesize knowledge. They enable students to apply the concepts they have learned in practical situations, making the learning process more engaging and impactful. These activities, when combined with guiding questions and formative assessments, create a comprehensive and immersive learning experience where students can truly understand and apply their knowledge in meaningful ways.

Formative assessments in the context of immersive PBL classrooms stand apart from traditional assessment methods, serving a distinct and pivotal role. They function not merely as tools for assigning grades but as compasses that consistently direct and refine the learning process.

In traditional educational settings, assessments are often equated with grades. A quiz, test, or assignment is given, students respond, and scores are subsequently entered into a grade book. This grade-centric approach, while straightforward, can sometimes obscure the deeper purpose of education: genuine understanding and growth. Dr. Catlin Tucker addresses this issue, saying,

> People often say, 'If you don't grade students' work, they won't put in much effort.' But I counter that if students have a real audience for their work, they will indeed invest time and effort. It's not just about the grades; it's about the journey and the authentic engagement in their learning (personal communication, November 17, 2023).

This perspective shifts the focus from mere scoring to creating learning experiences that are meaningful and impactful for students.

As you think about your next unit, how might you refine or develop guiding questions to further enhance the depth of understanding and active knowledge construction of your students?

Journaling Your Journey

Use the space below to reflect on this question.

_____

_____

_____

_____

_____

_____

_____

_____

_____

_____

Formative assessments are not primarily about tallying scores for grade books. Instead, they are about capturing a living snapshot of student comprehension, skills, and attitudes at any given moment. The primary objective is to gauge student understanding and to provide timely, constructive feedback that helps students evolve in their learning journey.

In this immersive context, formative assessments can manifest in various ways: journal entries detailing thought processes, peer feedback during group projects, teacher-student dialogues about challenges and approaches, self-assessment rubrics, or even hands-on prototypes that evidence applied understanding. These diverse assessment methods offer rich, multidimensional insights into how students grapple with and internalize the material.

The beauty of formative assessments in PBL settings lies in their adaptability and immediacy. Since PBL projects often encompass complex, multifaceted tasks, these assessments can be tailored to target specific aspects or phases of a project. If a challenge emerges in a student's understanding or approach, it is swiftly identified, allowing educators to intervene with relevant support or resources. This dynamic feedback loop ensures that students don't just move forward but move forward with clarity, purpose, and depth.

Furthermore, because these assessments prioritize feedback over grades, students are encouraged to view mistakes or misunderstandings not as failures but as opportunities for growth and deeper understanding. This nurtures a growth mindset, where the focus shifts from "What grade did I get?" to "What can I learn from this?"

In essence, formative assessments in immersive PBL classrooms transform the learning landscape. They bridge the gap between teaching and understanding, making education a dynamic interplay of instruction, feedback, reflection, and growth. In doing so, they reaffirm that the true measure of education is not in grades but in genuine, deep-rooted understanding and the capacity for continuous learning.

As we transition into the next critical element of an immersive PBL experience — meaningful activities — remember the complementary relationship between these activities and various forms of formative assessments. Helping students navigate their mastery through non-threatening, supportive, and immediate feedback acts as the threads that connect and reinforce the structure. This approach validates the inquiries prompted by guiding questions and sets the stage for meaningful, real-world activities. These small yet impactful interactions ensure that the activities and the overall learning experience are student-centered, focused, and effective. Integrating these with other pedagogical strategies allows educators to compose a harmonious educational symphony, where each element is enhanced by insightful formative assessments, contributing to an enriching, immersive, and student-success-focused learning environment.

As you think about your next unit, how might you refine or develop guiding questions to further enhance the depth of understanding and active knowledge construction of your students?

Journaling Your Journey

Use the space below to reflect on this question.

_____
_____
_____
_____
_____
_____
_____
_____
_____
_____
_____
_____
_____
_____
_____
_____
_____
_____
_____
_____

Socratic Seminar

The Socratic seminar stands out as an exceptionally effective form of formative assessment in the realm of project-based learning. This method not only academically challenges students but also equips them with crucial real-world skills. By delving deep into the material, students engage in structured discussions that foster critical thinking and analytical skills. These seminars are characterized by their focus on evidence-based reasoning and robust argumentation, encouraging in-depth engagement with core issues. Such an environment actively involves students in their learning journey, ensuring they are not just passive recipients of information.

Furthermore, the Socratic seminar's emphasis on analyzing different viewpoints and adapting arguments to new information mirrors real-world problem-solving scenarios. In professional settings, solutions often require a balanced consideration of diverse perspectives and a flexible approach to information. By participating in these seminars, students develop the ability to think critically and solve problems effectively, skills that are invaluable in any field.

However, conducting a successful Socratic seminar also requires proactive strategies from educators to ensure robust participation and engagement. Navigating the intricacies of student participation, particularly in moments of silence or hesitation, is crucial to maintaining the seminar's effectiveness and relevance. Ultimately, this form of formative assessment does more than test knowledge; it prepares students for the complexities of real-world decision-making and problem-solving, making it a cornerstone of immersive learning experiences.

Tips for a Successful Socratic Seminar:

- **Begin with Accessible Questions:** To dispel initial apprehension, start with relatable, "ice-breaker" questions that still relate to the main topic. These can bridge personal reflections to academic insights, easing students into more complex inquiries.

- **Rephrase and Redirect:** If students seem stuck, consider rewording the question or pointing to specific passages from the text that might inspire thought or debate.

- **Foster a Supportive Environment:** Set ground rules emphasizing mutual respect and open-mindedness. Celebrate diverse perspectives and encourage students to value each contribution.

- **Engage Directly:** Make use of the circle seating arrangement. Prompt students to engage with one another directly by responding to or paraphrasing a peer's previous comment, fostering a sense of collective inquiry.

- **Provide Multiple Entry Points:** Have backup questions approaching the topic from various angles. This ensures that there's always another avenue for discussion if one path seems blocked.

- **Build on Past Discussions:** Reference previous sessions or related discussions. By drawing parallels or contrasts to past conversations, you can reignite the dialogue and give students a foundation to build.

- **Celebrate Peer-to-Peer Affirmations:** Encourage students to acknowledge and expand upon their classmates' insights. Such positive feedback loops can energize the discussion and reinforce a collaborative spirit.

The Socratic seminar is a shared journey of discovery. While students are the explorers charting the terrain of ideas, educators serve as guides, equipped with tools to ensure the expedition's success. With patience, preparation, and responsiveness, these seminars can become a transformative cornerstone of immersive learning.

Summaries, Journals, and Learning Logs

Summaries, journals, and learning logs are vital introspective tools in the educational landscape, particularly spotlighting the reflective aspect of learning. These activities not only facilitate a deeper understanding for students by allowing them to articulate and process their thoughts, but they also offer educators a window into each student's cognitive and emotional journey. The act of writing, whether it's summarizing information, journaling experiences, or logging learning progress, aids in cementing knowledge, fostering critical thinking, and enhancing self-awareness. These benefits are predominantly reaped by the students themselves, as these tools are primarily intended for self-reflection.

Moreover, these introspective activities extend beyond the confines of academic learning. They enhance students' ability to synthesize complex information, a skill that is highly valued in various professional careers. This process of reflection and documentation not only deepens students' grasp of the subject matter but also bolsters skills like adaptability and self-awareness, which are crucial in navigating the ever-changing demands of the modern workplace.

Despite their apparent benefits, a challenge arises in the prac-tical implementation of these tools, especially with the increasing student-to-teacher ratios in many educational institutions. The question of how teachers can feasibly review the journals or learning logs of a large number of students is pertinent. However, it's essential to remem-ber that the primary value of these tools lies in the act of reflection and self-examination they foster in students rather than in the assessment of these reflections by teachers. Thus, while these tools provide valuable insights for teachers, their greatest impact is in enhancing the student's own understanding and development.

For educators, strategic approaches can be employed to manage the volume:

- **Rotating Reviews:** Instead of reading every journal after each entry, teachers can rotate and read several journals each week. This ensures that every student's journal gets attention over a month or a quarter.

- **Focused Prompts:** Teachers can streamline their review process by providing specific prompts or questions for students to address, quickly identifying key insights or misconceptions.

- **Peer Reviews:** Occasionally, students can be paired to read and provide feedback on each other's journals. This not only lessens the review load for the teacher but also fosters collaborative learning among students.

- **Spot Checks:** Rather than thorough assessments, teachers can perform spot checks, skimming for depth, understanding, and engagement. Over time, patterns of student engagement (or lack thereof) will emerge, allowing for targeted intervention.

- **Digital Tools:** Leveraging digital journaling platforms can streamline the process. Features like keyword searches can help teachers quickly identify common themes or misconceptions.

- **Class Discussions:** Sometimes, a group reflection can substitute individual journal reviews. After journaling, a few students can be selected randomly to share their insights, providing a collective understanding of the class's progress.

Educators need to remember that the primary value of journals and learning logs is the reflective process they instigate in students. While reviewing these can provide invaluable insights, the students' engagement with the process holds the most significant educational value. Teachers can and should find a balance that maintains the integrity of this practice while respecting their time constraints.

Think-Pair-Share

The think-pair-share strategy, while straightforward in structure, has profound implications for both student engagement in the classroom and the development of critical real-world skills. This method embodies the essence of progressive learning, transitioning seamlessly from individual reflection to collaborative dialogue and culminating in collective sharing.

In the *think* phase, students engage independently with a concept, question, or problem. This solitary introspection is crucial for developing personal understanding and viewpoints. It provides students with the space to process information, form initial opinions, and identify uncertainties, which is essential for solidifying their perspectives. This phase of introspection not only aids in academic understanding but also in fostering individual critical thinking skills, a vital component in problem-solving and decision-making in professional and personal contexts.

The subsequent *pair* phase introduces the element of collaboration. Here, students discuss their thoughts with peers, compare understandings, and challenge or support each other's viewpoints. This interaction is key to developing soft skills such as active listening, constructive feedback, and effective communication — skills that are highly sought after in the workplace and in community settings. This phase allows students to understand and appreciate diverse perspectives, bridging the gap between personal insight and communal understanding.

Finally, the *share* phase expands the discussion to the entire class or group, allowing for a collective exchange of ideas. This broader discussion not only enriches the academic experience but also simulates real-world scenarios where ideas and solutions are shared and refined in group settings. It provides a platform for every student, including those who are typically quieter, to voice their thoughts, fostering a sense of inclusion and community.

Through the structured yet dynamic nature of think-pair-share, students not only engage deeply with academic content but also develop essential life skills. They learn to process information critically, collaborate effectively, and communicate their ideas confidently. This strategy, therefore, transcends the boundaries of a mere classroom discussion technique, evolving into a holistic approach that nurtures introspection, collaboration, and community building, all integral to a comprehensive, immersive learning experience.

Games

Building upon the discussion of using games as engaging instructional tools in the previous chapter, games have evolved to become a powerful bridge between content and the learner in the diverse world of teaching methodologies. Far from being mere entertainment, they have become strategic tools in an educator's arsenal, transcending the traditional model of learning. Whether rooted in tradition or emerging from the digital age, games tap into students' natural curiosity and competitiveness, creating an optimal environment for immersive learning.

When students engage in a game related to their curriculum, they transform from detached observers to active participants. This shift is crucial as they navigate through problem-solving, strategic planning, and critical thinking - all skills that are not only essential in the classroom but also invaluable in real-world situations. Through games, students learn to process and assimilate knowledge in a profound and enduring manner.

Consider the example of the game of Spoons adapted for an educational setting. In this version, students must quickly process information about colonial regions, making connections to gather related cards before grabbing a spoon. This adaptation not only tests their reflexes and comprehension of the material but also their ability to draw connections between related facts, a skill highly relevant in professional and everyday contexts.

These gaming experiences are immersive in multiple ways. Students mentally sort and categorize information swiftly while also remaining attentive to the physical aspects of the game. Each playthrough reinforces their memory and understanding, with the competitive element maintaining high engagement. Such active participation in learning mirrors real-life scenarios where quick, informed decision-making is crucial.

Moreover, games foster peer interaction and collaborative learning. As students discuss, negotiate, and challenge each other based on the game's content, they engage in a form of social learning. This interaction not only reinforces their understanding of the material but also hones their communication, negotiation, and teamwork skills - competencies that are essential in the workforce and community engagements.

Incorporating games like Spoons into the curriculum demonstrates the potential of traditional games as immersive educational tools. They make learning not just effective but also engaging, memorable, and enjoyable while simultaneously equipping students with practical skills that extend far beyond the classroom walls.

Micro-Conversations

Micro-conversations, though often underappreciated, play a highly effective role in the formative assessment process, especially within project-based learning environments. These brief, yet focused interactions between educators and students, or among peers, are vital for maintaining both alignment with educational goals and immersion in the learning experience. In PBL settings, where learning paths are fluid and responsive, micro-conversations seamlessly weave into the educational tapestry, acting as unobtrusive yet insightful checkpoints. They provide educators with real-time snapshots of students' cognitive and emotional states, allowing for timely adaptation of instruction and activities.

Beyond their immediate educational value, micro-conversations also hold significant importance in developing real-world skills. These interactions foster a classroom environment where intellectual risk-taking is valued and where assessments are viewed not as high-pressure tests but as constructive, informative elements of the learning journey. This approach reduces the pressure often associated with traditional assessments, creating a more relaxed and receptive atmosphere for learning.

Furthermore, micro-conversations are instrumental in developing students' communication skills, critical thinking, and emotional intelligence. The ability to articulate thoughts concisely, respond to feedback, and engage in thoughtful dialogue are skills that are highly valued in professional and social contexts. By encouraging students to engage in these brief but meaningful exchanges, educators are not only aligning their teaching methods with the dynamic nature of PBL but are also equipping students with essential life skills. These skills include the ability to quickly process information, communicate effectively, and adapt to changing scenarios — all crucial for success in a rapidly evolving world.

These interactions also offer psychological benefits: they lower the stakes of the assessment, encouraging a more relaxed environment where intellectual risk-taking is valued. By weaving these dialogues, scenarios, and engagement opportunities naturally into the classroom, educators foster a PBL environment where students see assessments not as high-pressure, make-or-break moments but as constructive, informative elements of their learning journey.

164

As you think about your next unit, how might you refine or develop guiding questions to further enhance the depth of understanding and active knowledge construction of your students?

Journaling Your Journey

Use the space below to reflect on this question.

_____

_____

_____

_____

_____

_____

_____

_____

_____

_____

_____

_____

_____

_____

_____

_____

_____

_____

_____

_____

Determining Effectiveness of Immersive Activities

In the PBL environment, evaluating the effectiveness of immersive experiences requires a nuanced approach. Beyond the traditional assessment tools, PBL thrives on real-world application, collaboration, and critical thinking. Therefore, when assessing the effectiveness of an immersive experience, consider the following specific to the PBL context:

- **Student Outcomes and Mastery:** At the core of PBL is the end product or solution to a real-world problem. If students effectively address the project's goals and showcase a deep understanding of the subject, it signals the efficacy of your immersive technique. I encourage you to focus on the process over the final product. The processes and methodologies students adopt to arrive at a certain point are constantly developed throughout the unit. The end product does not equate to the degree of mastery from the immersive experiences along the way.

- **Engagement and Collaboration:** A cornerstone of PBL, active participation and teamwork indicate that students are deeply involved. This is an area in which observation will play a key role. Be on the lookout to see if students were actively discussing, problem-solving, and building upon each other's ideas within the immersive environment. This can easily be assessed as you walk around the room. Listen to the conversations that are occurring. Redirect as necessary and affirm students when you hear connections being made. Don't be afraid to ask a group a question. Celebrate with them if they can answer it correctly, and if they can't, it becomes a great segue into how they can navigate misconceptions and find their way back to logical solutions.

- **Application in Authentic Situations:** PBL is all about real-world application. A practical immersive experience in PBL should empower students to apply their knowledge in varied, real-world contexts outside the classroom or the immediate project. You are developing true 21st-century skills that enable students to understand the question, "Why are we doing this?" Whatever skills are being developed or used should be ones that can be carried forward into later applications.

- **Student Reflections:** Reflections are a crucial component of project-based learning, providing deep insights into students' learning experiences. These reflections, which can take the form of journals, discussions, or presentations, enable students to introspect and articulate their learning journey. For instance, after completing a unit on European exploration, I employed a structured approach by having students reflect on their projects, time management, presentations, and activities through emails or a more organized Google Form. This approach, inspired by Dr. Catlin Tucker's methodology, involves regular self-assessment against a rubric encompassing both academic and soft skills. Students use these assessments to gauge their proficiency in various skills, identifying areas where they excel or require further support. The transparency and honesty in these reflections were remarkable, providing a clear window into their developmental process and learning experiences. Such practices not only encourage self-awareness among students but also facilitate a more personalized and responsive educational approach (Tucker, C., personal communication, November 27, 2023).

- **Feedback Loops:** Continuous feedback from peers and educators can provide real-time insights into the effectiveness of immersive techniques. In PBL, where iterations are common, this feedback becomes crucial to guide project direction and enhance learning. Quiet PBL classrooms are not normal. There should be conversations occurring. It is funny how often I remind students that they are allowed to talk. Feedback becomes a much more natural component when conversations are encouraged and welcomed. Also, it makes conversations non-threatening. You are just talking to them because they need to be redirected. You are talking to them because you are invested in their learning.

- **Self-Reflection for Educators:** Being a reflective practitioner in a

PBL environment is crucial. Post-project, take a moment to assess what went well and what could be improved. Did the immersive techniques enhance the project, or were they just an added layer? Is the activity something that can be used again? Your insights as an educator, especially within the PBL framework, are invaluable in refining future endeavors.

- **Adaptability and Inclusiveness:** Given the diverse learning needs in any classroom, the effectiveness of an immersive technique in PBL can also be gauged by its adaptability. Was it accessible and beneficial for students from varied backgrounds and learning profiles? It's vital to understand that immersive experiences can significantly enhance the PBL environment but come with challenges. Some students might struggle due to factors like maturity, learning disabilities, or an initial unwillingness to participate. Tailoring the experience to cater to these diverse needs is essential.

Moreover, if an immersive experience doesn't resonate with a few students or a particular group, it doesn't render the technique ineffective. As Dr. Catlin Tucker observes, one of the most significant challenges in immersing PBL is "logistically giving students the time and space to immerse themselves in the whole experience." Even with enthusiasm for blending online and offline elements, educators often face pressure to move through the curriculum, leading to a rushed and superficial project experience. This can prevent students from fully engaging in each aspect of the process, from information gathering to design. Tucker emphasizes the need to give students "the time or space or opportunity to engage in the messiness that is a project" to ensure deeper learning and more meaningful outcomes (Tucker, C., personal communication, November 27, 2023). Adaptability and continuous growth are the hallmarks of effective teaching, especially in PBL. Combining the above strategies and consistently reflecting upon and adapting your methods will ensure that your immersive techniques align well with your PBL objectives and create meaningful, lasting learning experiences.

Project-based learning embodies the spirit of immersive classroom experiences and magnifies its impact. By intertwining PBL's hands-on, student-centered philosophy with a range of immersive techniques, from the simple act of role-playing to the sophisticated realms of VR, educators can drive deeper engagement and foster genuine comprehension. This synergy bridges the often-felt gap between theoretical knowledge and its tangible real-world application. However, like any innovative approach, the path has challenges. Some students might be resistant, and accessibility can vary. Plus, the learning curves associated with new tools can be steep. Yet, with adaptability, patience, and reflection, educators can consistently fine-tune their methods. It's a journey not just of immersion but of harnessing its transformative potential in tandem with PBL, sculpting classroom environments where students are not mere participants but dynamic agents of their learning odyssey.

Plan, Personalize, and Pursue

Plan

Embarking on creating an immersive classroom experience starts with meticulous planning. Establish a clear vision of your desired learning outcomes, aligning with content standards and targeted skills. However, flexibility is key. Know your resources—technological tools, supplies, and classroom space—and understand potential constraints. These factors will shape your approach to immersive lessons. While brainstorming techniques like role-playing, simulations, or digital explorations, also consider potential challenges, such as technology access or varying student engagement levels. In your planning, integrate guiding questions and formative assessments to keep students on track. Remember, pacing is essential; blend active learning with opportunities for reflection and adjustment based on real-time observations.

Personalize

With your blueprint ready, focus on personalization. Recognize the diversity in your classroom; each student brings unique backgrounds, challenges, motivations, and learning preferences. Tailoring the experience to resonate with each student involves more than just adapting approaches—it's about ensuring relevance and connection to their lives. Consider how immersive experiences can cater to different learning preferences and cultural backgrounds. Remember, personalization also involves being prepared to pivot your strategies in response to student feedback or observed engagement levels during the course.

Pursue

After implementing your plan, the pursuit of excellence lies in reflection and collaboration. Reflect on the effectiveness of your immersive approach, using both introspection and student feedback. This feedback is crucial for understanding the impact of your methods and for identifying areas for refinement. Embrace each experience as an opportunity for professional growth, regardless of its immediate success. Sharing insights with your peers is equally important. Collaborative sharing fosters a community of practice, enhancing the broader implementation of immersive techniques. Encourage peer observations, joint planning sessions, or even co-teaching experiences to broaden the impact and understanding of immersive learning strategies.

The transformative potential of immersive experiences in project-based learning is vast and multidimensional. Incorporating practices like Socratic seminars and reflective self-assessments, educators enable students to engage deeply, fostering an environment that cultivates critical thinking, creativity, and a genuine sense of inquiry. Immersive PBL goes beyond mere knowledge transfer; it inspires a lifelong pursuit of learning and discovery.

Scan the QR code to access the following Immersive Activity Plan.

Figure 5.6

Immersive Activity Plan (Page 1)

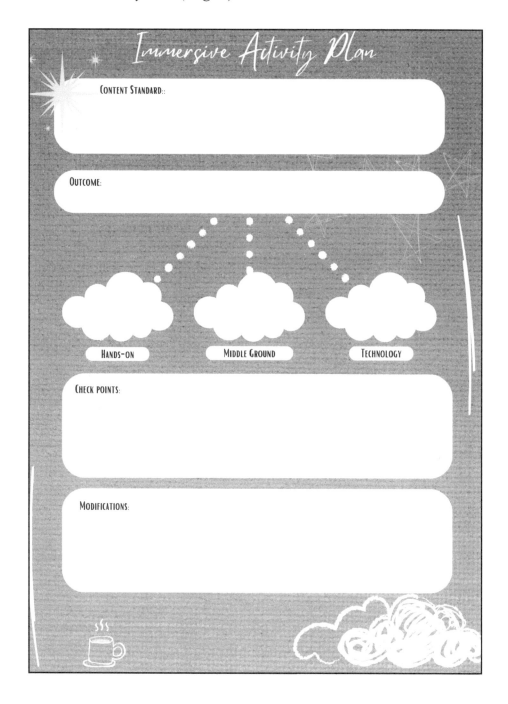

Figure 5.7
Immersive Activity Plan (Page 2)

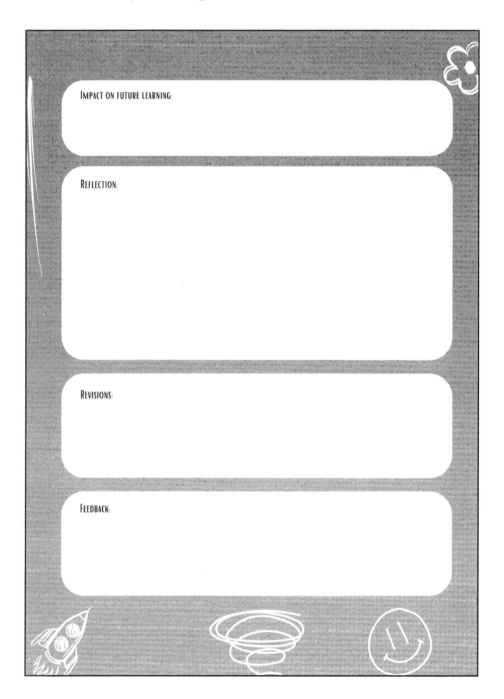

IMPACT ON FUTURE LEARNING:

REFLECTION:

REVISIONS:

FEEDBACK:

In this vibrant confluence of student-centered activities and dynamic engagements, we sculpt not just informed students but empowered thinkers and problem-solvers for an ever-evolving world.

As we turn the page from crafting immersive learning practices, we embark on an equally crucial aspect of PBL in the next chapter: "The Art of Guiding Classroom Projects." Here, we will explore the nuanced role of educators in shaping and steering students' project journeys. Building on the foundations laid in immersive experiences, this chapter will explore how educators can effectively guide and nurture students' project-based explorations, ensuring their immersive learning experiences are brought to successful and meaningful fruition.

Chapter 6
The Art of Guiding Classroom Projects

 Interview with Ron Berger
Education Expert, Author, and Speaker

One of the most nuanced aspects of project-based learning is the art of guiding classroom projects. What becomes your role as the teacher once the planning is done and the project has launched? You will morph from a planner and initiator to a guide and facilitator.

Figure 6.1
Teacher Involvement in PBL

Guidance in PBL is often misunderstood. Some educators, new to the PBL paradigm, believe their role is minimal—setting the stage and stepping back entirely to let the students navigate their learning. Others may err on the side of over-involvement, steering the project so rigidly that it undermines the very essence of student autonomy and exploration that PBL aims to foster. The truth, as you may have guessed, lies somewhere in between. Finding the right balance in guiding a project is key: you'll need to be involved but not too controlling, helping students when needed while also letting them learn independently.

Envision a carefully planned dinner, where the meal to be prepared is meant to satisfy the various appetites at the table. It's designed to engage the diners visually, dance across their taste buds, nourish their health, and satisfy their souls. As the host, you've meticulously chosen a menu akin to an educator planning a curriculum that caters to your students' diverse interests and learning needs, ensuring each student's passion is acknowledged and nurtured.

Initially, you take on the role of a planner and initiator, carefully selecting the ingredients and setting the stage for a culinary journey. The recipes are your roadmap; they outline the path to a delightful meal yet are flexible enough to allow for some improvisation based on preferences and discoveries. In a classroom setting where the curriculum serves as a roadmap, a good educator guides the students through the project, facilitating exploration and personal investment in the learning process, akin to guiding guests through cooking techniques and traditions.

As the guests arrive and the cooking begins, your role transitions from a meticulous planner to a guide and facilitator. You introduce your guests to various techniques, flavors, and culinary traditions, encouraging them to explore, taste, adjust the seasoning, and make their dishes. The kitchen buzzes with the excitement of discovery, the joy of collaboration, and the thrill of creation. Similarly, in the PBL classroom, students are not mere spectators but active participants, where their passion drives their engagement and growth in the learning journey.

The feast, they realize, is not just about the satiating dishes on the table but about the wealth of understanding and skills they've acquired, ready to be applied to future culinary endeavors. This mirrors the lifelong learning skills your students hone in a PBL environment, preparing them for real-world challenges beyond the classroom walls.

You cannot eat this meal for them, nor should you spoon-feed them. They must feel the texture of the ingredients between their fingers, experience the transformation of flavors, and navigate the delicate balance of spices. Each bite they take is a step towards a deeper appreciation and understanding; each challenge faced and solved is a recipe for growing resilience and self-efficacy. Though subtle and evolving, your role has been instrumental in preparing a meal and nurturing a room full of burgeoning chefs, akin to nurturing independent, critical thinkers in a PBL classroom, ready to explore with a sharpened palette and a toolkit of refined skills.

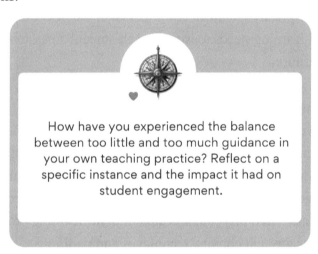

How have you experienced the balance between too little and too much guidance in your own teaching practice? Reflect on a specific instance and the impact it had on student engagement.

Journaling Your Journey

Use the space below to reflect on this question.

_____

_____

_____

_____

_____

_____

Reflecting on my early experiences with PBL, I clung to the traditional teaching methods I had learned, which cast the teacher as the primary model. I meticulously crafted a project template for students to emulate, dictating the layout to the placement of text and images. Though well-intentioned to provide structure, this approach inadvertently stifled students' creativity and led to a resentment of the learning process.

This realization sparked a pedagogical shift, much like the one illustrated by the PBL Classroom Structure diagram we first encountered in chapter 3. As we revisit this diagram, it marks the transition from my role as a directive model to that of a guide and facilitator. The diagram serves as a visual reminder of this evolution, bridging the gap between the initial planning stages and the nuanced act of facilitating student learning. It reaffirms the importance of balancing scaffolding with student autonomy, supporting learners as they navigate from curiosity to knowledge without the constraints of my early, prescriptive approach.

Today, I've learned the importance of conducting swift check-ins with every student. During these interactions, students share their notes and summaries, responding to precise questions about the lesson to gauge their understanding. I aim to ensure they have a solid grasp of the content before they delve into its application. Often, I arm myself with a checklist of tasks assigned for their initial engagement with the material. This exercise ensures they've embarked on the pathway to understanding how this newfound knowledge can be harnessed to address the core inquiry of the topic at hand. My checklist always begins with notes. Once students move through notes, I have them engage with their notes through a "Connecting the Dots" assignment. This particular assignment enables students to see how different pieces of information connect in the lesson. Finally, I have students write a summary of the notes. This process ensures that they have written, analyzed, and synthesized the information. Once the students have taken these initial steps, they meet with me for a quick conversation. Through these preliminary check-ins, I can dispel misunderstandings, setting a clear course for students as they apply their insights to their projects. This delicate balance of guiding students acts as a rudder, steering their forward movement of understanding, ensuring they navigate the waters of knowledge with a steady and informed hand.

177

Figure 6.2
PBL Classroom Structure (Part 1)

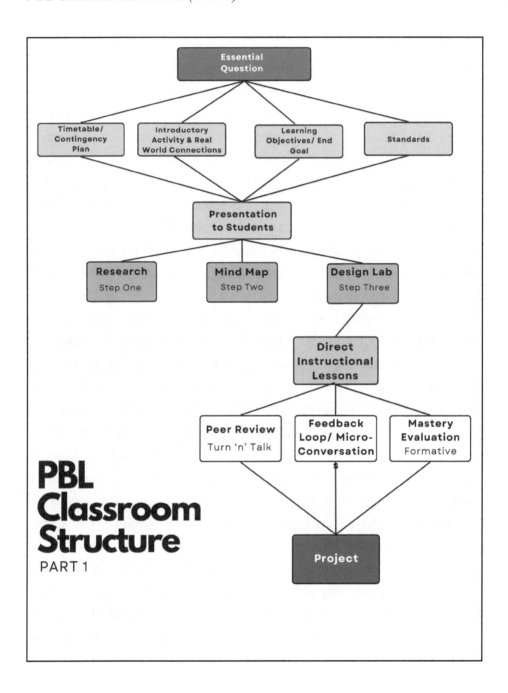

Figure 6.3
PBL Classroom Structure (Part 2)

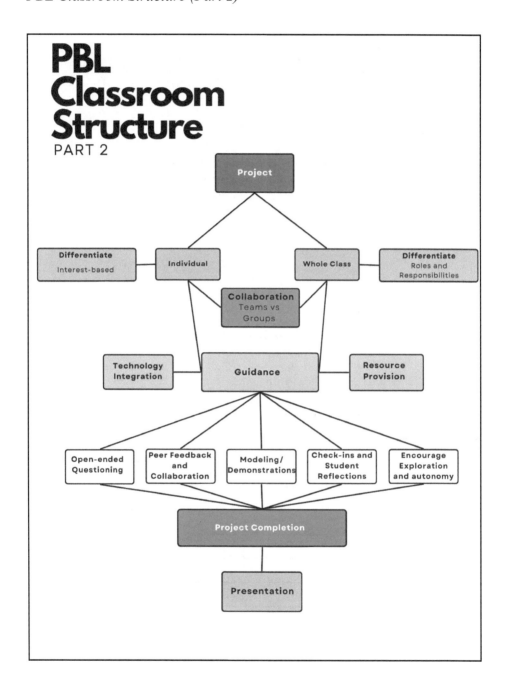

Striking the balance between student-centeredness and teacher-driven approaches is critical. It is important to ask ourselves whose project it is, and how we can support the process.

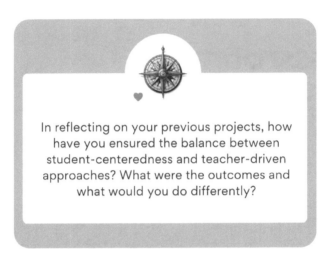

In reflecting on your previous projects, how have you ensured the balance between student-centeredness and teacher-driven approaches? What were the outcomes and what would you do differently?

Journaling Your Journey

Use the space below to reflect on this question.

The Balance Between Facilitation and Direct Instruction

The delicate balance between facilitation and direct instruction is pivotal for student-centered learning. Several key strategies emerge for navigating instruction and guidance in PBL. Ron Berger, the Chief Program Officer of EL Education, highlights the importance of starting with a "clear vision of the end goal," similar to watching a skilled soccer game or an adept guitarist, providing a "clear target to aim for" (R. Berger, personal communication, October 11, 2023). This vision sets the standard and instills a sense of quality and possibility in students.

Establishing a Clear Vision of the End Goal

1. Define the project's end goal clearly.

2. Provide students with high-quality exemplars to set a high standard.

3. Consistently remind students of this vision to maintain focus.

The transition from setting a high bar to adopting a more facilitative stance is complex, resembling a dance that responds to the rhythm of students' growth and the unfolding narrative of the project. The initial vision acts as a guiding north star. Berger's emphasis on having a "clear vision of the end goal" resonates through the project lifecycle, serving as a reminder of the standard of excellence to aspire to.

Managing Timelines and Standards Flexibly

1. Estimate the initial timeline for a project, then consider doubling it.

2. Prepare to adjust timelines in response to project progress and challenges.

3. Integrate standards from multiple disciplines for a holistic approach.

Balancing Timelines and Standards is crucial. Berger recommends a flexible timeline approach, suggesting "doubling the initially estimated timeline" to create a safety net for in-depth exploration (R. Berger, personal communication, October 11, 2023). This strategy and integrating standards from multiple disciplines foster a more realistic and engaging educational experience.

Transitioning to a Facilitative Stance

1. Start with direct instruction, then gradually shift to facilitation.

2. Adjust teaching style to fit students' evolving needs and capabilities.

3. Monitor students' growth, responding with appropriate guidance

As the project progresses, the scaffold of direct instruction gradually dismantles, giving way to a more collaborative and facilitative environment. This shift, reflecting students' increasing capabilities, underscores the essence of striking a balance between facilitation and direct instruction.

Implementing Student-Centered Guidance

1. Encourage student ownership and initiative.

2. Provide resources and support, allowing students to make decisions.

3. Guide students' learning journeys without overstepping.

The narrative of the project morphs from a teacher-led directive to a collaborative expedition, where students progressively take the reins of their learning journey, guided by the initial vision and evolving facilitation of the teacher. This fluid transition is essential in PBL.

Integrating Cross-Disciplinary Learning

1. Identify opportunities for incorporating multiple subject areas.

2. Design activities that blend different disciplines.

3. Create an environment for collaborative, interdisciplinary exploration.

Through these strategies, the initial clear vision and subsequent gradual release of responsibility harmonize with the melody of PBL, orchestrated eloquently by the educator. These steps ensure the journey towards the envisioned goal is as enriching and educative as the goal itself, embodying the dynamic and responsive nature of effective teaching within the PBL paradigm.

Student-Centered Guidance vs. Teacher-Driven Guidance

In a student-centered approach, you become a supportive architect, guiding students toward independent learning. Your role is asking probing questions, providing constructive feedback, and intervening minimally, nurturing students' creativity and decision-making.

The journey begins with questions that assess students' understanding, guided by a clear vision of the end goal, as emphasized by Ron Berger. This vision, alongside your questions, shapes a structured, exploratory learning path.

Feedback loops are central in PBL, creating a dynamic learning environment where students drive their learning. Feedback serves as a tool for refinement and improvement. Berger's "gradual release of responsibility" concept applies here, reducing guidance as students progress and fostering self-directed learning. Immediate feedback enables continuous refinement throughout the project.

As a facilitator, you offer resources and pose challenging questions, allowing students to tackle problems and learn experientially. In contrast, a teacher-driven model can stifle student engagement and creativity, reducing PBL to mere directive assignments.

PBL is more than just project completion; it's about developing lifelong skills like problem-solving and independent exploration. Student ownership of projects enhances motivation and critical thinking in real-world situations. Guide students through PBL by facilitating, not directing. Create an environment for making choices and learning from mistakes without overstepping. This approach enriches learning and embodies the essence of PBL.

Students develop critical thinking by navigating project complexities and challenges in this environment. They actively engage with information, analyzing and reconstructing it. This process transforms learning from passive absorption to active analysis, evaluation, and synthesis, showcasing PBL's power in developing discerning minds ready for real-world challenges.

How have your probing questions and feedback loops evolved in promoting a student-centered approach? Reflect on a particular project where your guidance significantly impacted the students' critical thinking and problem-solving skills.

Journaling Your Journey

Use the space below to reflect on this question.

_____

_____

_____

_____

_____

_____

_____

_____

_____

_____

_____

_____

Cultivating Critical Thinking Skills

The ultimate aim of PBL transcends the mere acquisition of subject-matter knowledge, extending to developing higher-order thinking skills such as analysis, synthesis, and evaluation. Within the PBL framework, effective facilitation is instrumental in nurturing these critical thinking skills. Students are propelled into deeper cognitive engagement by posing challenges and fostering a culture of discussion and inquiry.

Having a clear vision of the end goal is a crucial compass guiding students' inquiry and exploration, a notion that is underscored by Berger. This vision catalyzes critical thinking and sets a standard of excellence students aspire to attain. As students navigate the pathway toward achieving the project's objectives, they inherently engage in analysis, synthesis, and evaluation at each step.

The recommendation of doubling the initially estimated timeline for projects epitomizes the essence of providing a conducive space for critical thinking to flourish. By affording students ample time to delve into the intricacies of the project, there's an organic cultivation of a reflective and analytical mindset. The extended timeline isn't a mere allowance for unforeseen delays but a proactive measure to enrich the cognitive depth of students' engagement with the project.

The approach of a gradual release of responsibility from teacher to students is a cornerstone in fostering a culture of inquiry and autonomy. As students assume more control over their learning, they sharpen their ability to analyze, evaluate, and create, embodying the higher-order thinking skills that PBL aims to nurture.

Moreover, integrating standards from multiple disciplines into a single project mirrors a real-world scenario where problems are interdisciplinary (R. Berger, personal communication, October 11, 2023). Students are challenged to synthesize diverse information and evaluate complex, interconnected problems by navigating through various academic lenses. This holistic approach enhances the project's richness and significantly amplifies the scope and depth of critical thinking.

Everything we have covered in this book—mind mapping, active listening, discussions, games, reflective questioning—converge towards building critical thinking skills. These elements, woven into the fabric of PBL and reinforced by the insights from education pioneers like Ron Berger, form a robust scaffold that elevates students' critical thinking abilities while deeply engaging them in meaningful and authentic learning experiences.

How are you currently nurturing and enhancing the critical thinking skills of your students and how do you envision growing that aspect of your classroom?

Journaling Your Journey

Use the space below to reflect on this question.

_____

_____

_____

_____

_____

_____

_____

_____

_____

_____

_____

_____

Plan, Personalize, Pursue

The following journal is meticulously crafted to be a reflective tool to determine how you'll guide your students throughout the project-based learning unit. Inviting you to pre-plan your guiding strategies before the unit commences and continuously reflect and adapt these strategies as the unit unfolds promotes a dynamic and responsive approach to guidance. The sections identifying beginning and during unit guiding strategies prompt you to envision and fine-tune your guidance blueprint. As you navigate through the unit, the journal's structured reflection points at the end of each week serve as a mirror, enabling you to assess the effectiveness of your guidance, understand its impact on student engagement and learning, and make informed adjustments.

Moreover, the information gathering and differentiation sections prompt a deeper exploration of how you'll scaffold your guidance to meet varying student needs and promote active learning. The section on student choice nudges you to think creatively about empowering students, a core aspect of effective guidance in PBL. With a dedicated space to record and reflect on student feedback, the journal encourages a feedback-informed approach to guidance, ensuring your strategies align with students' evolving needs and experiences.

Furthermore, by documenting your observations, reflections, and adjustments in real time, the journal helps cultivate mindful guidance, where your actions are deliberate, informed, and reflective of the learning dynamics within your classroom. As you move from planning to personalizing and then pursuing the PBL unit, this journal acts as a critical friend, guiding your thought process, capturing your instructional journey, and helping you refine your guidance strategies to foster a rich, student-centered learning environment. Through this iterative process of planning, reflecting, and adjusting, the journal facilitates a deeper understanding and mastery of the art of guidance in PBL, ultimately enriching the learning experience for you and your students.

Scan the QR code to access the following PBL Unit Guide.

Figure 6.4
PBL Unit Guide (Part 1)

Figure 6.5
PBL Unit Guide (Part 2)

DATE: | UNIT TITLE

STANDARD(S)

END GOALS (LEARNING OUTCOMES)

ESTIMATED TIME TABLE: (START DATE) (END DATE)

GUIDING STRATEGIES:

BEGINNING

DURING

HELPING STUDENTS GATHER INFORMATION:

Figure 6.6
PBL Unit Guide (Part 3)

DIFFERENTIATION	STUDENT CHOICE OPTIONS

STUDENT FEEDBACK:

_____

_____

_____

_____

_____

◇ ◇ ◇ ◇ ◇ ◇ ◇ ◇ ◇ ◇ ◇ ◇

WEEK 1 REFLECTION:

_____

_____

_____

_____

_____

Figure 6.7
PBL Unit Guide (Part 4)

WEEK 2 REFLECTION: _____
_____
_____
_____
_____
_____

◈ ◈ ◈ ◈ ◈ ◈ ◈ ◈ ◈ ◈ ◈ ◈ ◈

SUCCESSES: _____
_____
_____
_____
_____

AREAS OF CONCERN: _____
_____
_____
_____
_____

ADJUSTMENTS: _____
_____
_____
_____
_____

Figure 6.8
PBL Unit Guide (Part 5)

ADDITIONAL NOTES:

Plan

The first step in your guiding blueprint is to chalk out a clear vision for your project-based learning unit. Begin by identifying the unit topic which should be engaging and relevant to your students. Following this, articulate the goals or learning objectives you aim for your students to achieve. These objectives should be Specific, Measurable, Achievable, Relevant, and Time-bound (SMART). An integral part of planning is estimating the timeline for your unit; pinpoint the start and end dates to have a clear timeframe. Lastly, devise your initial guiding strategies. These strategies should outline how you plan to guide your students through the project, ensuring a balance between facilitation and direct instruction to promote student autonomy and engagement.

Personalize

Personalization is pivotal in PBL to meet your students' diverse needs and interests. Start by understanding your students' needs and interests. You could gather this information through surveys, discussions, or reviewing past work. Now, with a better understanding of your students, craft personalization strategies. Differentiation is critical; plan how to adapt instructions, activities, and assessments to cater to different learning preferences and ability levels. Incorporate student choice wherever possible to boost engagement and ownership. Moreover, be prepared to adapt your guiding approach based on student feedback throughout the unit. This feedback can be invaluable in fine-tuning your instruction to better support your students

Pursue

As you move into the active phase of your PBL unit, jot down the implementation steps week by week. This should include the core activities, milestones, and check-ins you have planned. This structured approach will help maintain a clear direction as the project unfolds. Reflection is a powerful tool in PBL. At various points throughout the unit, pause and reflect on what's working well and what areas might need adjustment. Be open to tweaking your guiding strategies to better support your students' learning. Document any adjustment strategies you decide to employ. These reflections and adjustments are not only vital for the ongoing project but will also be invaluable insights for planning future PBL units.

Chapter 7
The Power of Learning with Technology

 Interview with Tanji Reed Marshall
Education Equity Champion, Author
and Keynote Speaker

"Merely incorporating technology into education doesn't make it innovative. It's about changing the way we teach and learn, powered by technology."
-George Couros

In project-based learning, integrating technology is often viewed as a hallmark of innovation. George Couros's quote is insightful and pivotal in guiding our approach to technology in PBL. Embracing this ethos, our discussion on technology in PBL is not about merely adding the latest digital tools. Instead, it is about understanding the why and how behind integrating these tools to truly transform educational experiences. In today's digital age, where new technologies emerge constantly, there is a compelling allure to adopt the latest trends. Yet, in the context of PBL, our focus shifts from this allure to a deeper examination of the reasons behind our technological choices.

Aligning the new definition of PBL, which emphasizes passion, with technology integration encourages educators to be thoughtful and intentional, ensuring that the technology ignites students' curiosity, fuels their passion, and enhances their capacity for creative problem-solving. Rather than being swayed by the novelty of new tools, I advocate for a reflective, purpose-driven technology integration. This approach enriches the learning experience and resonates with the essence of PBL - creating meaningful, engaging, and relevant learning opportunities for students.

As we explore the intersection of technology and PBL in this chapter, let us keep Couros's perspective at the forefront. We aim to delve into how technology can be harnessed not just as an add-on but as a transformative element in PBL.

It's crucial to begin this exploration of technology in the classroom by categorizing how it is employed. This initial distinction lays the groundwork for understanding the deeper why behind its use, guiding us toward more meaningful integration.

First, let's consider the **passive** use of technology. In this mode, students mainly act as consumers, absorbing content with limited interaction. This approach can be practical for introducing foundational knowledge, yet its potential to foster deeper engagement is often limited. Here, technology functions more as a one-way conduit of information, with students receiving rather than interacting or creating.

In contrast, **active** use of technology sees students as creators, collaborators, and critical thinkers. They engage dynamically with technology, using it as a tool to further their learning. This method aligns closely with the ethos of PBL, where students are encouraged to be proactive problem solvers and active participants in their educational journey.

Merely distinguishing between passive and active use isn't sufficient. The transition from recognizing these types of technology to understanding their purposeful integration is where the true essence of effective technology use in PBL lies. The purpose is the cornerstone of this integration. Rather than adopting technology for its novelty or as a symbolic nod to modernity, educators need to consider the impact of each tool or platform thoughtfully. The guiding question should always be: How does this technology enhance the PBL experience for students?

As we navigate the vast landscape of technological tools, the focus must remain on their purposeful, meaningful use. Technology should not just be a tool in the classroom but a bridge leading to deeper understanding, enhanced collaboration, and creative expression. It's about ensuring that every technological integration fosters a more prosperous, more engaging PBL environment rather than merely serving as a superficial or flashy addition.

Purposeful Integration

In the early days, technology made its tentative debut in classrooms. Bulky computers occupied dedicated corners or labs primarily serving functions like word processing and basic coding. Teachers, the trailblazers of this tech frontier, navigated these waters while students eagerly absorbed every bit. Reflecting on the past, my personal experiences with technology in education have always revolved around purpose. I vividly recall my sixth-grade excitement in 1991, marching to the computer lab lined with Apple Macintosh machines. The thrill of playing games or word processing was palpable. Two decades later, as a teacher, I saw similar setups—modernized computer labs with sleeker screens. However, one thing remained constant: each visit to this tech hub was driven by a purpose, ensuring that technology's inclusion in the lesson was meaningful.

In project-based learning, the purposeful approach to technology amplifies its importance, making its integration even more significant. PBL thrives on real-world relevance, deep inquiry, and collaboration, and technology becomes the bridge to these ambitious goals. Digital tools enable students to connect with global experts, dive deep into specialized research databases, or collaboratively map out project trajectories. The tangible products of PBL—whether a board game, podcast, or script for a sitcom—can be crafted, iterated upon, and showcased with diverse software. As educators in this PBL environment, we no longer see technology as a separate entity but as an integrated ally, facilitating each project step, from ideation to public presentation. The seamless and strategic infusion of tech tools in PBL amplifies learning experiences and mirrors the dynamic integration of technology in modern professions and daily life.

Understanding the historical context is crucial, but looking at real-world, modern-day applications for more insights is enlightening. Here's a recent personal experience that exemplifies purposeful tech integration. I recently had the privilege of interviewing Brian Eppert, the mastermind behind Noda—a cutting-edge Virtual Reality (VR) application designed to help users visualize and connect ideas in an immersive 3D environment. I was eager to discuss with him how my students have been leveraging Noda on the Meta Quest 3, a state-of-the-art VR headset renowned for its high resolution, intuitive controls, and unique "pass-through" feature that allows users to view the real world even while immersed in VR.

I detailed to Brian how my students begin each lesson by creating individual mind maps on paper, a strategy that aids them in drawing connections to the new content they encounter. This tactile exercise serves as the foundation. They then transition to the virtual realm: Using the passthrough option of the Meta Quest 3, students bring their paper designs to life, crafting a dynamic, three-dimensional representation of their mind maps and additional images within the Noda application.

Brian appreciated this two-tiered approach. He pointed out that moving from a traditional paper sketch to a VR representation is invaluable. Not only does it spotlight potential knowledge gaps as students translate their ideas into a new medium, but it also empowers them to be the authors of their learning journey, further deepening their understanding of the content (Eppert, B., personal communication, November 1, 2023).

This entire endeavor stands as a testament to the essence of the purposeful integration of technology in education. Here, technology isn't merely an accessory or a flashy add-on; it becomes a vital conduit for deeper learning. The transition from paper-based mind maps to immersive 3D visualizations is about embracing novelty and harnessing the unique affordances of the Meta Quest 3 and Noda to enrich cognitive engagement.

In a world brimming with gadgets and gizmos, it's tempting to incorporate technology merely for the sake of it, to appeal to the 'modern' or 'innovative' label. However, what sets this approach apart is the deliberate, calculated inclusion of VR. The technology doesn't overshadow or replace traditional methods. Instead, it complements and amplifies them. Students don't just use the VR headset because it's exciting; they use it because it provides an avenue to visualize, manipulate, and delve deeper into their ideas, strengthening their grasp of the content.

Furthermore, recreating their paper sketches in a virtual environment pushes students to reflect, analyze, and potentially revisit their initial thoughts. It nudges them to fill in conceptual gaps and encourages them to approach the material from various angles. This iterative process, facilitated by the technology, ensures a more holistic and nuanced understanding.

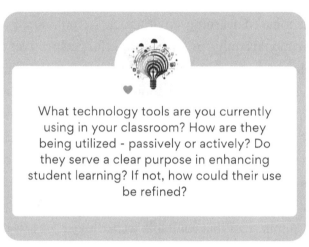

What technology tools are you currently using in your classroom? How are they being utilized - passively or actively? Do they serve a clear purpose in enhancing student learning? If not, how could their use be refined?

Journaling Your Journey

Use the space below to reflect on this question.

_____

_____

_____

_____

_____

_____

_____

_____

_____

_____

While my VR experience illustrates just one of the myriad ways technology can enhance learning, the underlying principle remains consistent. Technology, regardless of its nature, should be leveraged thoughtfully. In essence, incorporating the Meta Quest 3 and Noda in the learning process exemplifies how technology, when used with intent and strategy, can elevate education from mere knowledge acquisition to profound mastery.

Equity in Technology Integration for Project-Based Learning

Equity in technology integration is vital for creating a level playing field in project-based learning environments. Tanji Reed Marshall, an expert in educational equity, provides insightful perspectives on this issue. Marshall states, "In a project-based setting, ensuring equitable access to technology comes down to what tools are available" (Marshall, T.R., personal communication, December 5, 2023). This means examining disparities within a school district and ensuring that the least-resourced schools have access to the same level of technology as the most-resourced schools. This approach is not just fair but necessary for accountability and effective learning.

Marshall emphasizes that equitable technology access is not just about devices in the classroom but also includes reliable internet throughout a school district. She argues that shared technology, such as carts of Chromebooks, is outdated: "They have to have one-to-one access to a device in school and out of school" (Marshall, T.R., personal communication, December 5, 2023). This access is crucial for students to conduct research and effectively engage in the PBL process. Suppose teachers are asking students to complete a task that requires technology. In that case, all students must have equal access to that technology to be able to complete the assignment.

Addressing the funding disparities is another critical aspect of equity. Marshall asserts, "Inequitable spending is a choice. School districts must decide that what they say they want for every kid in their district is what they are willing to pay to make happen" (Marshall, T.R., personal communication, December 5, 2023). This statement highlights the need for a deliberate and strategic reallocation of resources to ensure equitable technology access.

Furthermore, Marshall points out the necessity of reliable, high-speed internet in schools. Suppose certain schools have better broadband capabilities due to their location or the age of the building. In that case, efforts must be made to upgrade the infrastructure in less-resourced schools. "Every single student in every building in their district [must have] reliable access to the internet" (Marshall T.R., personal communication, December 5, 2023).

However, access to technology and infrastructure is only part of the solution. Marshall also underscores the importance of adult willingness and training: "The biggest solution is making sure that the adults... have the kind of training that they need to have to implement technology beyond just entertainment" (Marshall, T.R., personal communication, December 5, 2023). This training should teach educators that technology is "part of a larger story of learning" and how to effectively use various forms of technology in the PBL context (Marshall, T.R., personal communication, December 5, 2023).

While ensuring equitable access and preparing educators through training are foundational steps, the effectiveness of these efforts is best understood through rigorous research. When we turn to empirical studies, the link between theory and practice in technology integration within project-based learning becomes evident. Research in this field validates the practical approaches and sheds light on how technology can be optimized for educational success.

The Power of Research

Research consistently shows that the thoughtful integration of technology in project-based learning can significantly enhance the learning experience. A notable meta-analysis reviewed studies on technology-infused PBL across various educational levels and content areas. It found that technologies like interactive simulations, data collection tools, and digital communication platforms led to notable improvements in content learning, collaboration skills, and student engagement in PBL settings (Lam, Cheng, & Ma, 2010).

These technologies align well with PBL's emphasis on hands-on inquiry, authentic data gathering, and collaborative teamwork. For example, interactive simulations allow students to explore and model concepts actively, while digital communication tools facilitate essential collaborative efforts central to PBL.

The application of technology in PBL is not limited to specific subjects. Research by Hernández-Ramos and De La Paz (2009) highlights its effective use in history education, demonstrating that technology-assisted PBL can deepen students' understanding and appreciation of historical content. This approach promotes disciplinary thinking and engagement, particularly when students use primary and secondary sources to engage with historical controversies or mysteries.

These findings are echoed by educators' experiences, reinforcing the idea that technology can profoundly enrich PBL across various dimensions when purposefully employed.

The Power of Purposeful Integration

While the pedagogical potential of educational technology (ed-tech) is clear, its effective integration into the dynamic PBL environment requires careful consideration. The key to success lies in maintaining a student-centered purpose, ensuring that technology enhances rather than distracts from the learning experience. The following sections will explore real-world examples of purposeful tech integration in PBL.

Challenges and Overcoming Them

As with any significant shift in pedagogical approach, integrating technology into project-based learning doesn't come without its share of hurdles. These challenges range from the tangible, such as budget constraints, to the intangible, like resistance from various stakeholders or even self-doubt among educators. Marshall (2023) states, "The biggest challenge is access and quality. And then there has to be adult willingness" (personal communication, December 5, 2023). As the digital landscape continues to evolve, so does the learning curve for teachers and students. It's essential to remember that while the road to successful tech integration in PBL might be paved with obstacles, each presents a learning opportunity to refine and better our teaching practices. In this section, we'll delve into some of the most common challenges educators encounter on this journey and offer actionable strategies to navigate and overcome them, ensuring that technology's inclusion in the PBL environment is meaningful and impactful.

I was excited when I unveiled the Meta Quest 3 to my students. I imagined wide-eyed amazement and eager hands reaching out to dive into the world of virtual reality. Instead, what echoed through the room were comments that caught me off guard: "Did you seriously drop $650 on this gadget?", "The idea alone freaks me out," and the rather straightforward, "I prefer my paper and pencil, thank you."

Their reactions were a stark contrast to the enthusiasm I had imagined. I was stumped. Why the apprehension? Why the skepticism towards a piece of technology that held such promise?

Determined not to be deterred by initial resistance, I decided to demystify the Meta Quest 3. I showcased its potential step by step, gently guiding a few brave volunteers through the process. What began as a tentative experiment became an immersive mind map that beautifully encapsulated the day's lesson.

As days turned into weeks, something transformative happened. The "weirdness" of this new technology began to fade, replaced by a growing recognition of its potential. Curiosity overcame apprehension. One by one, more students ventured into the realm of VR. They realized this wasn't just about embracing a new gadget; it was about harnessing a tool to amplify their understanding and make intricate connections within the content.

The journey with the Meta Quest 3 indicated how often innovations—though initially met with skepticism—can, over time, become powerful allies in the learning process. It reminded me that change might be gradual, but with persistence and belief in the tool's potential, we can reshape and enhance the learning landscape.

Addressing Skepticism:
From Budget Constraints to Student Safety

Navigating the ever-evolving landscape of education technology often feels like traversing a complex path laden with skepticism. Scott Will, Superintendent at the Richland School of Academic Arts, shared that technology and education have developed a synchronous relationship in modern classrooms. Everything, from our vehicles to our communication methods, incorporates technology. This ubiquity underscores its potential to positively connect content in the classroom, adapting and presenting it innovatively.

Will emphasizes the responsibility of school leaders to provide necessary tools for teachers and students, facilitating access and creativity in every lesson. However, he acknowledges the primary barrier to this integration is often cost. With its annual licenses and continual upgrades, technology represents a significant financial commitment for districts. To navigate these budgetary challenges, Will suggests looking for grants, which are plentiful at local, state, and national levels. These grants can support various technology initiatives, especially workforce development, STEM, and STEAM programming. He also advises districts to budget annually for device and technology improvements, much like they would for facility improvements (Will, S., personal communication, November 6, 2023).

Despite these strategies, there may still be cases where it's not feasible to equip every student with a device. In these scenarios, Will underscores the importance of teacher ingenuity in integrating available technology into the learning environment. He reminds us that the essence of teaching comes from the educator in the room, not the device in hand (Will, S., personal communication, November 6, 2023). This perspective reinforces the importance of balancing technology with traditional teaching methods.

Financial hurdles are a significant reality in technology integration. The appeal of innovative tools in education is undeniable, but high costs can temper enthusiasm. My experience with grant writing for an instructional lab illustrates this point. The grant covered software, recording equipment, acoustic materials, and furniture costs. This resource enabled the implementation of flipped learning practices, enhancing our project-based learning environment.

As we explore the diverse avenues for integrating technology into project-based learning, it becomes clear that innovation doesn't always have to come with a high price tag. The strategic use of low-cost technology offers equally viable solutions, enabling educators to creatively and effectively enhance the PBL experience without overstretching their budgets.

Incorporating technology into project-based learning environments can be both effective and economical, thanks to resources like Open Educational Resources (OERs), Google Suite for Education, educational apps, and bring-your-own device (BYOD) policies. These tools align with budgetary constraints and enrich the PBL experience.

Open Educational Resources offer a wealth of materials that can be utilized in PBL. Websites like Khan Academy and MIT OpenCourseWare provide access to various subjects and resources, from foundational knowledge to advanced concepts. These resources can serve as the backbone for project research, offering students a broad spectrum of information and data to explore and incorporate into their projects.

Google Suite for Education facilitates collaborative PBL endeavors. Tools like Google Docs, Sheets, and Slides enable students to work together in real-time, regardless of their physical location. This collaboration is crucial in PBL, allowing students to brainstorm, design, and execute their projects collectively. Google Classroom further aids in managing PBL workflows, assisting teachers in assigning tasks, tracking progress, and providing feedback efficiently.

Educational apps such as Duolingo, Quizlet, and Kahoot offer interactive platforms that can be seamlessly integrated into PBL. These apps allow for creating engaging, subject-specific activities and quizzes, making learning more dynamic. For instance, Kahoot can conduct quick assessments or review sessions, ensuring that students have grasped key concepts necessary for their projects. Quizlet's flashcards can be an effective tool for research and study, especially in complex projects requiring a deep understanding of specific topics.

BYOD policies are particularly beneficial in PBL settings. Allowing students to use their own devices facilitates continuous learning and project development, both in and out of the classroom. Students can access project materials, collaborate with peers, and conduct research anytime, making the learning process more fluid and adaptable to their schedules.

Educators can foster a rich, interactive PBL environment by integrating these cost-effective technological solutions. These tools help manage budget constraints and support the core principles of PBL – collaboration, research, and real-world problem-solving. They ensure that the quality and depth of project-based learning experiences remain uncompromised despite financial limitations.

In this context, open dialogue among all stakeholders becomes crucial. Effective communication strategies are vital in building a supportive community around technology integration. Regular meetings, transparent updates, and inclusive forums where stakeholders can voice their opinions and concerns are instrumental. These communication channels allow for sharing experiences, strategies, and challenges, nurturing a collaborative environment.

Educators also bear the responsibility of demonstrating the value of technology in education. Marshall suggests for those just beginning to integrate technology into their PBL curriculum, "Ask your students. Lobby for your own learning. And partner with a colleague" (Marshall, T.R., personal communication, December 5, 2023). All of this requires evidence-based advocacy, showcasing tangible benefits, success stories, and relevant research. Through this, educators can link technology directly to enhanced educational outcomes and overall student success.

Ultimately, open dialogue, creative budgeting, and effective use of available resources serve as the cohesive threads that bind the diverse tapestry of stakeholders in the educational community. By fostering a culture of trust, innovation, and collaboration, educators can ensure that, as pedagogical methods evolve, the core objective remains steadfast: to promote the holistic development and safety of every student.

Plan, Personalize, Pursue

Plan

Start by gazing inward. Reflect deeply on your overarching learning objectives. Ask yourself: Where does technology fit? What role can it play in amplifying student understanding? Begin by outlining clear, tangible goals for your tech integration. Are you hoping to foster a collaborative atmosphere, streamline the feedback process, ignite creative expression, or elevate student engagement? Determining the specific purpose technology will serve is the cornerstone of successful integration.

Moving forward, take stock of your existing resources. Understand the technological landscape you have at your disposal. Are there budget considerations that need attention? It's imperative to be realistic at this juncture—accurately appraising your resources can curtail over-extension and maintain focus.

Having solidified your goals and taken inventory of available tools, it's time to chart your course. Handpick tools and platforms that resonate with your defined purpose. Maybe you will use Padlet to instill collaboration or Flip to capture student voices. Envision this integration from the macro perspective of entire curriculums and the nuances of individual lesson plans and assessments.

Lastly, forethought is your ally. Predict potential hurdles; inequitable access, tech fluency disparities, or even reticence to change. Proactively address these through differentiated strategies like tiered activities, scaffolding, or leveraging peer-based mentoring.

Personalize

Remember, every classroom is a mosaic of unique learners. Successful technology integration is as much about these individual learners as the tech itself. Engage in active observation or even deploy anonymous surveys to understand your students' inclinations and reservations.

Couple technology with learning preferences. Interactive simulations might resonate more with students who enjoy hands-on opportunities, whereas in-depth readings or podcasts might cater to students who engage well with auditory experiences. Wherever feasible, offer a buffet of choices, which ensure that students have opportunities to engage with technology in various ways.

Rome wasn't built in a day, nor is seamless tech integration. Set an incremental pace. Begin small, acclimatizing students to new tools, emphasizing their relevance, and showcasing consistent application. This familiarization can dispel apprehensions.

However, stay malleable. Iteration is the heart of personalization. Elicit feedback, understand student experiences with the integrated tech, and pivot based on this feedback. It's a dance of meeting students in their comfort zone and gently pushing the boundaries.

Pursue

With a solid plan and a personalized approach; the stage is set for action. Begin with a narrow focus, perhaps a single lesson or project. Closely observe student engagement and interactions, looking for both sparks of enthusiasm and zones of confusion.

Make feedback an integral part of your process. Tools like anonymous digital feedback forms or old-school exit tickets can be instrumental. The insights garnered will offer a prism to refine your approach.

Remember, the path to seamless tech integration is not linear. There might be initial setbacks or unexpected reactions. Instead of viewing these as roadblocks, see them as milestones, each offering a unique learning perspective. Keep communication channels wide open, ensuring students feel part of this transformative journey.

Reflect. Reflect on successes, areas of improvement, and unexpected outcomes. Let these reflections mold your subsequent steps. After all, pursuing meaningful tech usage in the realms of PBL isn't a destination. It's a vibrant, evolving journey that enriches the learning experience with every stride.

As this chapter draws to a close, we have navigated the intricate landscape of technology's role in enhancing project-based learning. We delved into the myriad ways technology, when integrated thoughtfully, can elevate the learning experience. From the purposeful inclusion of virtual reality tools like the Meta Quest 3 to the seamless integration of digital platforms for collaboration and creation, this chapter has explored how technology can serve as more than just a tool but as a transformative agent in the realm of PBL.

As we pivot to Chapter 8, "Amplifying Learning Experiences: Flipped Learning and Technology Integration," we prepare to explore the synergistic potential of combining flipped learning with PBL. This chapter will unravel how flipped learning, a model that reallocates instructional time to maximize student engagement and participation, can be harmoniously integrated with PBL to foster deeper understanding, creativity, and student autonomy. We will examine practical strategies, real-world examples, and reflective insights to understand how this innovative instructional model can be leveraged to further amplify and enrich the project-based learning experience.

Chapter 8
Amplifying Learning Experiences:
Flipped Learning and Technology Integration

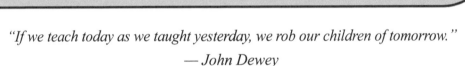

 Interview with Jon Bergmann
Flipped Learning Pioneer, Author, Speaker, and Classroom Teacher

"If we teach today as we taught yesterday, we rob our children of tomorrow."
— John Dewey

When project-based learning is combined with flipped learning, it opens up the opportunity to implement PBL effectively. Rather than asking what instructional model is the best, the key question becomes how to make the best use of face-to-face time with students. The flipped learning model grants educators the precious resource they often yearn for: time. And what does time afford us? It allows us to establish consistency and develop an instructional approach with integrity. Now, we can address the fundamental question: What meaningful activities can I engage my students in during our group interactions (in the classroom) that will deepen their understanding of the content and facilitate mastery?

My passion for education is driven by the need to engage meaningfully with students rather than merely delivering lectures from the front of the classroom. To truly involve students, they need to partake in activities that are more than just passive absorption of information. Think of flipped learning not as an isolated teaching technique but as the soil in a garden that nurtures various types of plants. In this metaphorical garden, teaching approaches like project-based learning, mastery, and inquiry are the diverse plants that thrive best in the enriched soil provided by the flipped model. This setup allows us the time and space to make the most of each educational approach, helping each "plant" reach its full potential.

By leveraging the power of flipped learning, educators can optimize their classroom experiences and create an environment where students actively participate, collaborate, and delve deep into their learning. It unlocks the potential for meaningful engagement, exploration, and application of knowledge, making the learning process more dynamic and impactful. The flipped learning model, acting as a catalyst, empowers teachers to implement various instructional strategies effectively and support students in achieving mastery. With time no longer consumed by one-way content delivery, educators can focus on facilitating meaningful interactions, guiding students' inquiries, and providing targeted support tailored to individual needs. Ultimately, flipped learning enhances the overall learning experience by creating a flexible, student-centered environment that nurtures curiosity, critical thinking, and authentic engagement.

Figure 8.1
New Version of Bloom's Taxonomy: Flipped PBL

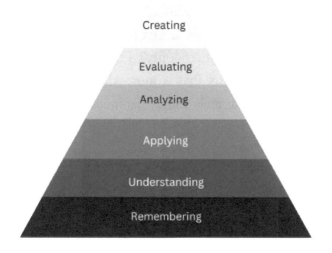

The methodology behind PBL resonates strongly with the framework of Bloom's Taxonomy. For those familiar with the conventional configuration of Bloom's Taxonomy, you might be thinking that students should first remember and understand before they even get to "apply" their knowledge. This traditional view is well-represented in Figure 8.2, which illustrates how a conventional classroom typically aligns with the classic understanding of Bloom's Taxonomy.

Figure 8.2
Traditional Classroom

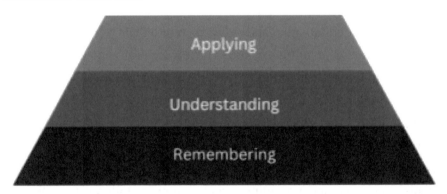

However, in traditional classroom settings, it can be challenging to progress beyond the lower-level skills due to the constraints of time and structure. This is not to say that traditional classrooms don't offer value; they offer structured learning experiences and can be effective in conveying foundational knowledge. Yet, the often-inherent time restrictions mean that advancing to the application of information, let alone the higher tiers of analyzing, evaluating, or creating, becomes a tall order.

This naturally leads us to ask a pivotal question: Does the flipped learning model flip Bloom's Taxonomy? Figure 8.3 offers an inverted version of Bloom's Taxonomy that is more aligned with a flipped PBL approach, and yet, even that feels somewhat incomplete.

Figure 8.3

Inverted Version of Bloom's Taxonomy

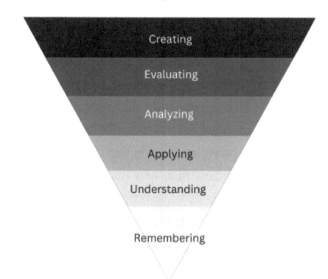

Enter Figure 8.4, the Revised Inverted PBL Bloom's Taxonomy, which presents a fluid, dynamic reimagining of how these educational strategies intersect.

Figure 8.4

Revised Inverted PBL Bloom's Taxonomy

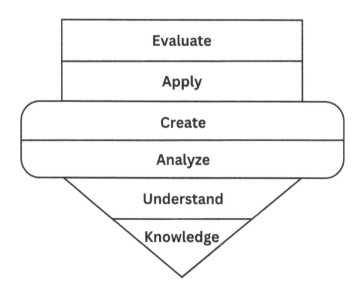

In this revised model, students first gain new knowledge through a brief video lecture or reading assignment, essentially covering the 're-member' and 'understand' categories on their own time. When they enter the group space (i.e., the classroom), they are primed to delve into deeper cognitive tasks. Together, as a class, they analyze the information, effectively progressing up the Bloom's levels. PBL activities then serve as the stage where students create, which, in this context, also means applying their newly acquired knowledge to real-world projects.

Once the application phase has been initiated through PBL, students have the opportunity to evaluate how their new understanding connects with pre-viously learned material. This iterative process of evaluation allows them to reach a level of mastery over the content, reflecting the pinnacle of Bloom's Taxonomy. Thus, flipped learning doesn't just "flip" Bloom's; it reshapes it, providing a more fitting structure for the unique demands and opportunities of PBL.

In this paradigm, whether you're a new educator taking your first steps into PBL or a seasoned veteran, integrating flipped learning and PBL provides a harmonious strategy for meeting students at every level of cognitive development. This approach is not just a theoretical construct; it is a practical solution that aligns with our overarching educational goals, preparing our students for success in an increasingly complex world.

A Better Way of Doing What I Was Already Doing

In my teaching journey, I combined two instructional methods that I was already familiar with: project-based learning and flipped learning. Incorporating flipped learning as a meta-strategy has elevated my implementation of PBL to new heights. The benefits of the flipped classroom model, as highlighted in a recent study, can be effectively translated into a PBL setting. One of the key aspects of PBL is its emphasis on collaborative problem-solving. This aligns well with the active, collaborative learning environment that the flipped classroom model fosters.

In the early years of my teaching career, I encountered a significant revelation when a student boldly declared, "I HATE YOUR PROJECTS!" At first, I was taken aback and perplexed because I believed engaging in

214

project-based activities would foster enthusiasm and a deep understanding of the content. It was only much later that I fully grasped the true meaning behind their words: "I hate YOUR projects." Despite my students participating in what I thought was PBL, they lacked choice and ownership.

The study I referred to earlier suggests that the structure of PBL, which involves students actively investigating and solving problems, can be particularly engaging for highly motivated students. The active engagement required in both PBL and flipped learning environments can thus serve to further stimulate these students, enhancing their learning experience and outcomes.

Moreover, the study indicates that many students prefer flipped learning over traditional teaching methods. This preference suggests that they may also favor the active, problem-solving approach of PBL over traditional teaching. This preference can be attributed to the active learning and engagement that both flipped learning and PBL promote, making them potentially more appealing to students.

The pivotal lesson I learned from that student's honest feedback was the importance of choice. Choice begets ownership, and ownership paves the way to mastery. This revelation propelled me to embrace a more student-centered approach, placing a strong emphasis on providing meaningful choices within PBL.

Choice is a transformative element in project-based learning for several reasons, each contributing to a more effective and engaging educational experience. When students are given choices, they naturally feel a sense of ownership over their learning, which is the first step toward mastering any subject matter.

Ownership isn't just about being accountable; it's about being invested. When students are invested, they are more likely to be motivated, and motivation is a significant predictor of academic success. The act of choosing imbues the educational experience with personal relevance, making the content more relatable and the work more enjoyable. Suddenly, the project isn't something that's imposed on students; it becomes something they "own."

In a student-centered PBL environment, choice also opens the door to creativity. Students can express themselves in ways that resonate with them personally rather than conforming to a standardized model. This autonomy often leads to more innovative solutions and approaches, fostering creativity and problem-solving skills.

Moreover, choice supports differentiation, catering to the diverse learning preferences, strengths, and interests within a classroom. This is especially beneficial in a PBL context, where projects are often complex and multidisciplinary. Offering choices allows students to engage with the content in a manner that suits their learning preferences, enhancing their understanding and retention of the material.

Integrating choice also aligns well with the flipped classroom model's emphasis on assessment as a part of the learning journey. In a flipped classroom, assessments often become learning experiences in themselves rather than just evaluative endpoints. When applied to a PBL setting, this creates a cohesive learning environment where students are assessed not just on their final product but also on their decision-making process, collaboration, and other soft skills, enhancing overall learning outcomes.

All of these elements contribute to a more dynamic and impactful educational experience. Choice transforms the classroom from a place where learning happens to students into a space where learning is something that students actively drive. This shift is not just pedagogical; it's cultural, creating an atmosphere of enthusiasm, engagement, and a deep-seated curiosity that fuels lifelong learning.

Now, I have the luxury of dedicating ample time to PBL in the manner it was always meant to be executed. I have relinquished the role of creating teacher-centered projects and instead empowered my students to design their own representations of the content, granting them agency and autonomy in their learning journey. Embracing choice as a cornerstone of PBL has transformed my classroom into a space where students actively drive their learning, develop critical skills, and embark on authentic journeys of exploration, discovery, and mastery.

Time

Time in the classroom is always at a premium, but the flipped model offers a different way to use it more effectively. Instead of adding more hours to the clock, this approach transforms classroom time into an opportunity for higher-level engagement and critical thinking. When I chatted with Bergmann, he shared that "once [teachers] hit that realization that if they move the direct instruction into the independent space, they have time to do deeper learning strategies" (Bergmann, J., personal communication, February 8, 2024).

This new use of time initially allows for a more focused and supportive teaching environment. Rather than lecturing, educators can guide students through hands-on activities, encourage discussions, and provide personalized assistance.

The extra classroom time also becomes an opportunity to nurture essential skills like problem-solving and critical analysis. With foundational knowledge acquired outside the classroom, students arrive ready to explore topics more deeply. This active, collaborative atmosphere supports a richer educational experience.

Moreover, the new time allocation supports the development of valuable life skills. Students must manage their learning outside the classroom, encouraging independence, self-regulation, and time management. This active engagement sets the stage for more insightful classroom conversations and teamwork.

When combined with project-based learning, this approach allows for more frequent and consistent implementation of PBL activities. According to Mike Gorman of the Buck Institute for Education, effective PBL is not a once-a-year event but can be integrated more regularly into the curriculum.

The flipped model makes every classroom minute count, shifting from content delivery to a more interactive, skills-based educational experience. This altered use of time magnifies the impact of each moment, contributing to deeper learning and lasting educational benefits.

How do you currently use your time for learning or teaching, and how might the Flipped Learning model alter your approach to time management? Consider the balance between acquiring foundational knowledge and engaging in higher-level thinking tasks.

Journaling Your Journey

Use the space below to reflect on this question.

_____

_____

_____

_____

_____

_____

_____

_____

_____

Taking Theory Off the Page: Practical Implementation

As educators, we often ponder how to bridge the gap between educational theories and practical implementation. The structure of a flipped project-based learning classroom presents a powerful solution, transforming abstract concepts into tangible experiences. This approach transcends geographical boundaries, resonating with educators worldwide who seek to embrace the potential of diverse instructional models. By combining the principles of PBL and the flipped model, we unlock the doors to a realm where theory seamlessly merges with practical application.

The first step is to recognize the threads of similarity that weave through every flipped PBL classroom, regardless of location. Essential or leading questions become the guiding stars, illuminating the purpose behind each learning endeavor. These questions serve as beacons, casting light on the significance of the knowledge students will acquire. Whether the classroom is in Australia, Spain, or the United States, the shared vision is to contain content within meaningful units of study, where students embark on independent research and create purposeful products. Furthermore, the integration of the community creates a web of connections that enriches the learning experience.

The magic of this approach lies in the innovative use of time. In a flipped PBL classroom, time is skillfully harnessed, redirecting the focus from content delivery to deepening student content experiences. No longer are educators confined to standing at the front of the room, lecturing about content. Instead, they become facilitators, working with students to engage in hands-on, inquiry-based projects. Students take center stage, actively participating in their own learning journey.

Stephanie Quarato, a middle school math teacher in Connecticut, designed her classroom to embody what she calls "organized chaos," a lively environment aimed at active learning. Her room is divided into four distinct areas, each serving a unique educational purpose: Mastery, In-Class Activities, Project Station, and Tutoring.

Mastery: This section is for students who feel they've grasped the day's concept. Here, they can complete exercises to demonstrate their understanding. The catch? They're only allowed one mistake. Any more, and they haven't achieved mastery.

In-Class Activities: After watching a flipped video the previous night, students come to this area to practice what they've learned. Quarato plans multiple activities, usually between three to five, for each unit. These tasks are thoughtfully designed, complete with instructions and materials lists, and can be done in any order. Quarato proactively prepares additional activities, acknowledging that students work at different paces.

Figure 8.5

Quarato's Mathematics Station Instructions Example

Section 1.1 Activity #1 Walkabout Writing Expression

Directions: Copy the chart below on your paper (there are six expressions). Flip the first card in the pile over. Write the algebraic expression, written expression, and reasoning on your chart. Once everyone in your group is done, share your answers. Be sure to check over each others' responses and have a conversation about incorrect responses, **as well as about how you got your answers**. Also, make sure you write down what your partners have written (if it is different from yours). Once you complete the first, do the same with the second, third, and so on.

Algebraic Expression	Written Expression	Reason

Materials Needed:

- Piece of paper and pencil
- Expression cards

Finished Early?! Play a game. Make a chart with four columns. Write "Addition", "Subtraction", "Multiplication", and "Division" at the top of each column. Set the timer for one minute, and write down as many words as you can for each operation. Once that minute is up, share your answers. Count how many correct answers you get. The person with the most correct words wins (make sure to write down any responses that your partners came up with that you did not write down).

Project Station: Students visit this area at least once or twice a week. It's a creative space for them to think deeply about how to apply their learning to a project. The emphasis here is on collaboration and the beginning stages of project creation.

Tutoring: This final area is for students who need extra help. It's a space where they can receive individualized attention, showcasing the advantages of a flipped, project-based learning classroom.

Each of these areas contributes to a dynamic and personalized learning environment, encouraging students to actively engage with the material.

Stephanie Quarato shared an example of how she implements this approach in her math unit. The unit outline not only starts with the essential question but also introduces an engaging hook or intro activity. Let's take a closer look.

Figure 8.6
Quarato's Mathematics Unit Introductory Activity

Composite Solids in the Real World

Essential Questions:

After completing this project, you should be able to understand and answer to following questions:

How does filling a fish tank with water help us understand the formulas for finding the volume of a three dimensional object?

How big does the fish tank have to be to hold at least 500 gallons of water?

Tanked is a reality TV-show that airs on the Animal Planet about two brothers-in-law who create unique customized aquariums for individuals.

Your task:

    (a) Watch the following video:

        http://screencast-o-matic.com/watch/cDiVFEiGoc

    (b) Discuss the following questions with your partner(s):
       (i)   Why do you think I shared this video with you? What does it have to do with composite solids?
       (ii)   In the video clip, one of the creators said there are "approximately 300 gallons" in the tank. How do you believe he came up with that number?
       (iii) In the video clip, the other creator said, "It is actually one aquarium, but it looks like three separate aquariums". What does this have to do with composite solids?

Before her students started their unit on constructing a fish tank to understand volume and composite solids, she engaged their thinking by asking her students analytical questions.

The flipped model makes the classroom more efficient and interactive. First, students learn the basics in an independent manner. This lets them move at their own pace through videos, readings, or exercises. Then, they come to class ready to dive deeper. Teachers can spend class time on one-on-one support and detailed feedback. They can also lead discussions that go beyond the basics. The result? A classroom that's alive with active learning and meaningful interactions.

Practical application also extends to the design of units and projects. Educators seize the opportunity to align curriculum with student interests. Through surveys, they gain insights into the passions that drive their students. This knowledge shapes the creation of units that spark genuine enthusiasm. By tapping into their interests, an environment is cultivated where students see learning as relevant and meaningful. I have the opportunity to walk alongside students as they are engaging with the content. This means that as students are exploring a new tool such as Canva, Genially, or MidJourney, I am able to support them in real-time. My time is spent supporting their forward momentum.

Recently, I tasked my students with creating projects about the Revolutionary War. One of my students was struggling to come up with a project idea. As I talked with her more about her interests, I began to see the project take shape. During this conversation with Addison, she expressed her fascination with movie villains. As we discussed various historical figures, she began to draw connections between them and the characters in her favorite films. Addison saw the tragedies of the Revolutionary War as if they were playing out in a movie. To help her bring her vision to life, I introduced her to Discord and showed her how to use Midjourney to combine two images and create something new. This sparked her imagination, and she quickly began designing movie covers for her horror historical movies. Suddenly, what seemed impossible before was now achievable with just a few keystrokes.

Figure 8.7

Revolutionary Horror Movie Covers

MOVIE TRAILER

JOSEPH

BENJAMIN

GEORGE

DESCRIPTION

DESCRIPTION

DESCRIPTION

Joseph is a movie that Joseph Martin stars as Chucky, the famous horror movie character. He appears to be a British troop causing problems and deaths around his colonial city.

Benjamin is a movie where Benjamin Franklin appears as Jigsaw, one of the smartest horror movie characters. He appears to be fighting in a Battle against his fellow people in his town.

George is a movie that contains George Washington himself as Joker. He appears to be in court, trying to beat a case against his own army men.

The true power of moving from theory to practical application lies in the individualization and differentiation of the learning experience. Students are given the freedom to personalize their projects, infusing them with their own interests and strengths. The result? Creativity flourishes, and lifelong learners are born. Students embark on a journey of self-discovery and expression with the guidance of routine tasks that support and hold accountable their progression through the content. Written reflections and presentations become platforms for articulating their understanding, honing their communication skills, and amplifying their voices.

In a PBL setting, it is vital that students are held accountable for their understanding so that they can apply factual and accurately interpreted information. I know that students routinely take notes by just writing words down; they don't process those words as facts or ideas, but merely as independent words that are completely unconnected. They were completing a task, not learning. As a means of holding students accountable for getting more out of the note-taking process, they are required to complete the document in Figure 8.8.

The students are also required to write a short summary of the lesson. Their summary must address the driving question for the lesson. Because I am afforded the time to support students, I am able to check in with each student each day. Students have to discuss their Connect the Dots assignment as well as their summary with me. I am able to advise students where to add more content and to go back through notes to identify missing information. By doing these steps, students are not only held accountable for their understanding, they are able to move forward with confidence as they apply their understanding to their projects.

Figure 8.8
Connect the Dots Example

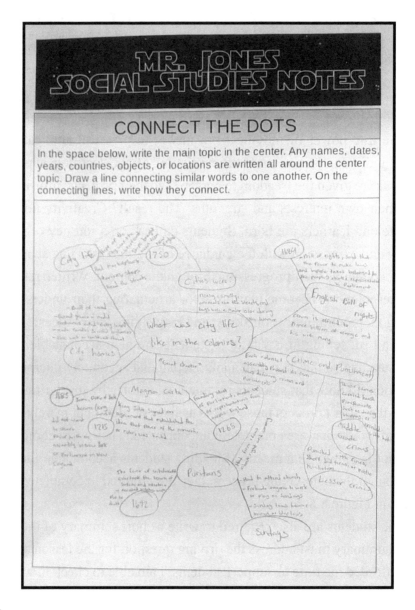

The pinnacle of practical application emerges when the learning transcends the confines of the classroom and connects with the community. By inviting community members to evaluate their projects, students witness the real-world impact of their work. The recognition and feedback they receive reinforce their belief in their ability to effect change, igniting a sense of empowerment that will guide them beyond the classroom walls.

In the flipped PBL classroom, time is no longer an elusive commodity but a tool for transformative education. The fusion of theory and practice ignites a powerful educational experience that resonates with students on a profound level. Through purposeful units, personalized projects, and community collaboration, educators embark on a journey of empowering their students to become active participants in their learning. Together, we unlock the door to a world where theory becomes reality, where learning transcends the boundaries of textbooks, and where the journey from theory to practical application transforms education into a vibrant tapestry of discovery.

Step-By-Step

In order to make this practical, it is imperative to see the step-by-step process of creating a flipped lesson so that you can truly level up or amplify your PBL classroom.

If you are an experienced teacher with existing lessons, you are already primed and ready to go. A significant difference between flipped and non-flipped classrooms is that lessons typically are not planned day to day. It is important to know where you want to go and plan backward. This enables you to have an entire unit of study ready to go before you begin lesson one. Backward Design or Understanding by Design (UbD) was developed by Jay McTighe and Grant Wiggins (1998). It

> has instructors consider the learning goals of the course first. These learning goals embody the knowledge and skills instructors want their students to have learned when they leave the course. Once the learning goals have been established, the second stage involves consideration of assessment. The backward design framework suggests that

instructors should consider these overarching learning goals and how students will be assessed prior to considering how to teach the content. For this reason, backward design is considered a much more intentional approach to course design than traditional methods of design (Bowen, 2017).

Scan this QR code to access a template created by Jay McTighe to help develop a unit of study using UbD.

The integration of flipped learning and UbD can initially appear challenging. Yet, with a structured approach, the fusion can be both intuitive and impactful.

Begin by setting a clear vision: **start with the end in mind**. Before delving into content creation for the flipped classroom, pinpoint the desired outcomes of the unit. What core understandings and skills should students master? This involves not only mapping out specific content standards but also the broader concepts they encompass.

Next, **craft essential questions**. Refer back to Chapter 3, where you created some of your own essential questions. Look to see how you would use an essential question, topical essential question, or guiding questions throughout your plan.

As you transition into the flipped learning model, **curating and creating content** becomes pivotal. Direct instruction now shifts from the group learning space to the individual space, often digitally. Whether you're curating relevant videos or crafting your own using tools like screencasting software (Screencastify or ScreenPal), ensure these resources are engaging, concise, and aligned with the essential questions and desired outcomes. Not everything has to be a video. Some students respond well to Google Slides, reading materials, or podcasts. Using a variety of content mediums helps to differentiate the lessons to meet more individual needs within your classroom.

With foundational knowledge now being built within the individual space, it's time to **plan in-class activities**. Classroom sessions should be dedicated to deeper exploration. Design activities, from collaborative projects to discussions, that allow students to apply and extend their knowledge. Here, the UbD's emphasis on authentic tasks shines brightly. In a PBL setting, students are able to work on their projects as part of the in-class activity but make sure to look back at the activities in Chapter 3.

Develop assessment strategies that go beyond traditional tests. Think of diverse ways to gauge student understanding, be it through project presentations, peer reviews, or reflective journals where students connect their in-class activities to their at-home learning. Assessments should be ongoing. Again, assessment does not equal grading. These can be mid-point check-ins to build metacognitive development throughout the unit. No student should ever get to the end of a unit and say, "I have no idea what this unit was about."

In the flipped learning environment, it's essential to **foster a feedback-rich environment**. Use digital platforms for students to ask questions about individual space content and during in-class sessions, address misconceptions. Peer feedback can also be invaluable, fostering a sense of community. A great way to do all of those things is through the use of Turn 'n' Talk cards. Turn 'n' Talk cards help to solidify the information that was presented to the students in the individual space. In my classroom, I give the students five to seven minutes to go through the questions with a partner. The beauty of this process is that it allows the students to explain content to each other, and they are able to clear up any misconceptions as well as answer each other's questions about the content. After the five to seven minutes have expired, I will gather the students together for whole class conversation. It is in this whole class grouping that students are able to ask questions that could not be answered during the TNT time. Here is an example of what I use in class.

Scan the QR code to access the template on Canva to personalize it to your classroom.

Figure 8.9
Turn 'N' Talk Template

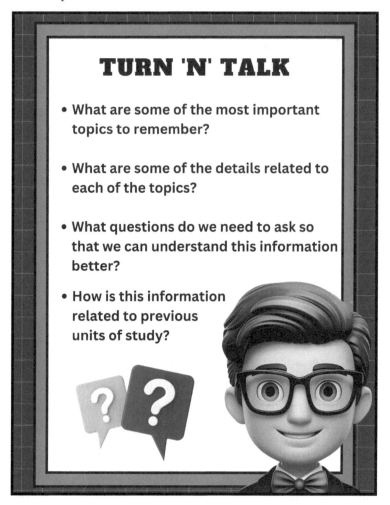

After the unit's completion, **reflect and refine**. Gather student feedback on both the individual space content and in-class activities. Assess what was effective and what areas need improvement. Use this feedback, coupled with personal reflections, to enhance the next unit.

What if Everybody Flipped?

A concern that often arises when discussing the concept of flipped classrooms is the fear of students being inundated with hours of instructional videos to watch at home. This concern, however, is based on a misunderstanding about the types of flipped classrooms. To clarify, there are two types: the traditional out-of-classroom flipped learning, where students engage with instruction outside the classroom, and the in-classroom flipped learning, where students engage with instructional materials right in the classroom, eliminating homework altogether.

For educators new to the concept of flipped learning, the in-classroom structure is a natural starting point, as it allows students to engage with instructional materials during class time. A common query often arises here: If all students are working on the same instructional material at the same time, why not just use spoken instruction?

In a recent discussion with Martha Ramirez, a professor at Universidad de los Andes, she elaborated on how combining project-based learning and in-class flipped learning can significantly enhance the learning process by creating a more student-centered educational environment. Ramirez detailed how PBL allows students to confront real-world problems with a self-guided, hands-on approach. She further emphasized how in-class flipped learning can support PBL by offering a flexible and effective instructional method.

Key to Ramirez's endorsement of in-class flipped learning is the individualization it provides to each student. Instead of delivering a live lecture, teachers record the material for students to access during class at their own pace. This method offers the support needed for the self-guided learning intrinsic to PBL, fostering an inclusive learning environment where students can grasp new concepts at their individual pace.

Ramirez emphasized that this foundational knowledge is particularly useful during PBL activities when students apply the concepts they've learned to handle complex projects. The immediate feedback provided by teachers in an in-class flip is invaluable to PBL, as it allows real-time support and on-the-spot adjustments to keep students on the right path.

In the wider context of PBL, Ramirez suggested that in-class flipped learning is an efficient method for introducing new content. For example, if the next project is about civilizations, teachers can flip this content ahead of time. This flexible approach also enables personal explanations of specific concepts if needed.

Ramirez stressed the benefits of in-class flipped learning in reducing teacher stress. Flipping instructions ensures all students have equal access to the instructional content, addressing a critical issue of equity. This equity extends to PBL, preparing all students, regardless of their resources at home, to effectively participate in project work. Moreover, it alleviates teacher exhaustion by reducing repetitiveness in explaining the same concepts or answering similar questions.

In conclusion, Ramirez emphasized that integrating in-class flipped learning into a PBL setting results in a more robust, flexible, and supportive learning environment. This combined approach not only enhances instructional effectiveness and supports differentiated learning but also decreases teacher burnout, placing students in control of their learning journey. This blend of methods not only makes learning more efficient but, according to Ramirez, also enhances students' understanding and enjoyment of their education (Ramirez, M., personal communication, July 12, 2023).

Success Stories: Flipped Learning Enhances PBL

Sean Moran, a social studies teacher at Bangor Area School District, shared the following story with me:

> In my journey as a social studies teacher, adopting flipped and project-based learning has been transformative, not just for me but also for my students. Among them, Emily's story stands out as a vivid testament to the potential of this teaching approach. Emily was initially a reluctant learner, a student with a learning disability who once described history as nothing but "names and dates" and "dead people I couldn't care less about."
>
> At the beginning of the semester, Emily was skeptical of the changes I'd implemented in my teaching style. She was used to a system of "learned helplessness," where she could say, "I can't do this," and be met with immediate answers, allowing her to pass with minimal effort. My flipped, blended, and project-based classroom was a jolt to her system.

The tipping point came during one of our routine class check-ins. Frustrated, Emily questioned why she wasn't getting credit just for completing a task. I explained, "You must demonstrate mastery of every task to prove you've comprehended the content." When she asked about the consequences of not mastering a task, I said, "You redo it until you demonstrate mastery." Her eyes widened as she began to grasp the implication. She exclaimed, "So I can't fail?" I affirmed, "Failure only comes when you stop trying, but you must also manage your time wisely."

This conversation was a breakthrough for Emily. From that point on, she invested real effort into the class, transforming from a reluctant learner to an enthusiastic participant. By the second semester, she was excelling, not just meeting but exceeding expectations. This transformation didn't go unnoticed; her parents, case manager, and even other teachers were amazed by her newfound enthusiasm and academic prowess.

Emily's journey is more than just a personal triumph; it's a compelling endorsement of the teaching model I've adopted. Her story confirms that flipped and project-based learning can be transformative, not just as a pedagogical method but as a catalyst for lifelong learning (Moran, S., personal communication, July 11, 2023).

Plan, Personalize, and Pursue

Begin your exploration by reflecting on the profound quote: "If we teach today as we taught yesterday, we rob our children of tomorrow" by John Dewey. As you ponder on its implications in the context of modern education, initiate the creation of a mind map. This visual tool will serve as the foundation for your exploration. You can use the one below, or you can create your own. Label the central idea of your mind map as "Flipped Learning."

Figure 8.10

Flipped Learning Mind Map

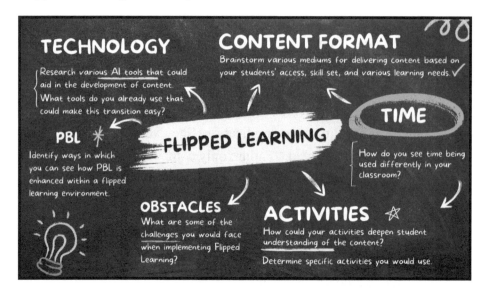

Plan

Start your exploration by considering the **content format**. Before diving into the tools and technologies, it's essential to understand the diverse ways content can be presented in a flipped classroom setting. This could range from instructional videos and curated readings to engaging podcasts and interactive modules. Each format offers a unique way to engage students, so consider the preferences and needs of your learners.

Once you've determined the format, delve into the **technology** that will support it. Research various technological tools apt for flipped learning. Platforms dedicated to video creation, interactive quiz tools, or content curation platforms might be particularly relevant. Evaluate each tool based on its potential benefits and limitations for your teaching context.

With a grasp of the content and technology, reflect on **time** management. How will you allocate time in this model? Consider the duration students might need for outside content versus the in-class time. Also, ponder the opportunities for self-paced learning, ensuring students have the flexibility they might require.

Integrating with **project-based learning** is the next step. Reflect on how the principles of flipped learning can seamlessly merge with PBL. Consider how flipped content can set the stage for meaningful projects, the strategies you might employ to assess PBL, and the ways in which real-world applications can be embedded into the learning experience.

With the foundation set, plan your in-class **activities**. These should complement and deepen the understanding of the flipped content. Activities could encompass group discussions, hands-on experiments, peer teaching sessions, or debates, ensuring active, collaborative learning during face-to-face sessions.

Lastly, anticipate potential **obstacles**. Every teaching model has its challenges, and it's crucial to be prepared. This could relate to technological accessibility for all students, ensuring consistent student motivation, or the time investment required for content creation.

Personalize

To effectively personalize flipped learning for a specific standard, begin by establishing the standard and context. Clearly identify the standard to be taught, ensuring that your lesson or unit aligns with educational objectives. This serves as the foundation of your flipped lesson. Next, assign a descriptive unit title that encapsulates the essence of the content. Determining the duration is equally crucial, as it sets the pace and depth of instruction, ensuring that students have ample time to engage both independently and collaboratively.

The heart of any lesson lies in its focus. Develop a topical essential question that acts as a guiding light for the unit. This open-ended question should provoke thought, guiding student inquiry and exploration throughout the unit, ensuring depth and relevance in their learning journey.

A paradigm shift in flipped learning is the emphasis on the independent space – the environment outside the traditional classroom where students engage with content autonomously. For many educators, planning for this space might be a novel experience. Traditionally, the focus has been on in-class activities, but in the flipped model, it's equally crucial to meticulously design how students will interact with content on their own.

Begin by outlining notes for instruction. These should capture the key concepts or ideas that form the backbone of your instructional material, ensuring clarity and coherence. With this foundation, proceed to instructional material creation. Whether you're crafting a video lecture, an interactive module, or a podcast, it's essential that this material is not just informative but also engaging, catering to diverse learning preferences and promoting active engagement.

Once your instructional material is ready, the next step is to decide on the method of resource sharing. Whether you opt for a class website, an LMS like Google Classroom, or email distribution, ensure that it's a platform accessible and familiar to all students. The goal is to make the transition to independent learning as seamless as possible.

In this independent space, students take charge of their learning, delving into content at their own pace, revisiting challenging sections, and preparing themselves for in-class activities. By planning effectively for this space, educators empower students, fostering autonomy, responsibility, and a deeper connection with the content.

The group space, the in-class environment, demands a different set of considerations. Begin with the peer review of instruction. Using Turn 'n' Talk cards facilitates peer discussions, allowing students to review and reflect on the flipped content collaboratively. These cards, equipped with prompts or questions, foster deeper understanding and critical thinking. Following this, design your classroom activities. These should be interactive, promoting hands-on learning, collaboration, and application of the content. Towards the end of the session, it's beneficial to regroup and debrief, providing a platform for students to share insights, ask questions, and consolidate their understanding. Lastly, establish a feedback mechanism. Whether through surveys, open discussions, or feedback boxes, this step is crucial. It offers insights into the effectiveness of the lesson, areas of improvement, and student perspectives, ensuring the continuous refinement of your flipped lessons.

Figure 8.11

Planning a Flipped Lesson Template

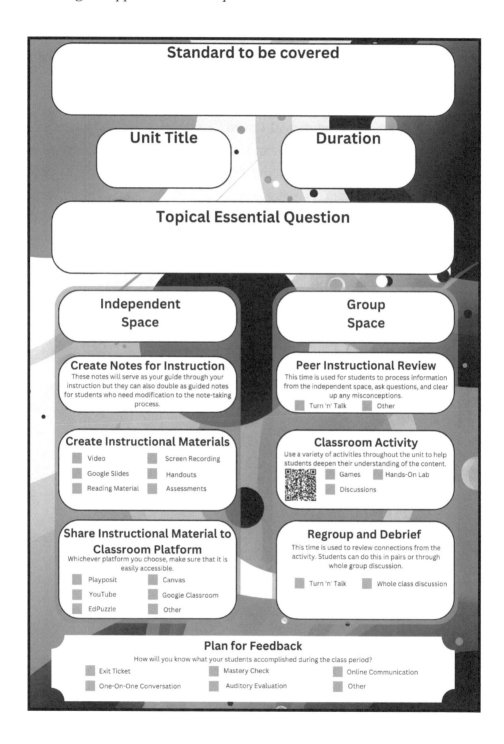

235

You can access the previous handout via Canva (left) or PDF for printing (right) by scanning the appropriate QR code.

Pursue

Ready to launch your flipped lesson? First, set your students up for success by clearly introducing them to the flipped learning concept. I've crafted an engaging video that demystifies flipped learning and sets clear expectations. Dive in and share it with your students or use it as an example for making your own. Let's empower them for this exciting journey ahead!

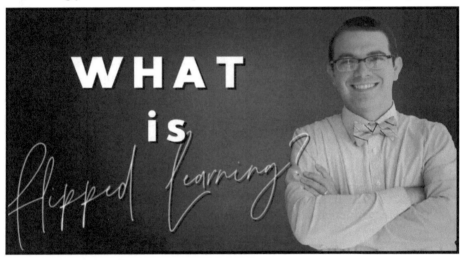

Scan the QR code to watch a video to learn more about flipped learning.

Now, action. After meticulous planning and personalization, it's time to implement your tailored flipped lesson. Dive in. Observe. How do students interact with the content in their independent space? Are they engaged? Do they grasp the concepts?

In the group space, the classroom, watch the dynamics. Peer

discussions using the Turn 'n' Talk cards should be lively. Are they? Classroom activities designed to deepen understanding should see students collaborating, questioning, and applying knowledge. Are they achieving the desired outcomes?

Then, the crucial step is feedback. It's a goldmine. Collect it. Surveys, open discussions, or simple exit tickets can be used. What worked? What didn't? Understand their perspectives. Refine. Adjust. Improve. Iterate.

Remember, the pursuit of excellence in flipped learning is ongoing. It's a journey. Embrace it. I have been flipping my classroom for over 10 years, and I am still going through these steps to refine what I am doing to better meet the needs of my students.

Chapter 9
Harnessing Artificial Intelligence
for Interactive Learning

 Interview with Phillip Alcock
AIxPBL Founder and Author

"We must not be afraid to push boundaries; instead, we should leverage our science and our technology, together with our creativity and our curiosity, to solve the world's problems."
—Jason Silva

At the heart of education lies a fundamental drive, which Jason Silva eloquently captures. This sentiment resonates profoundly with the ethos of project-based learning, especially in an era where artificial intelligence (AI) is becoming an integral part of our educational toolkit.and facilitate mastery?

What is AI?

Before we get too far, let's dig into what is meant by artificial intelligence. It is like a helpful friend in the world of technology, designed to make tasks easier and more efficient. It allows machines to act with a level of human-like understanding and problem-solving ability. You might not realize it, but you likely interact with AI regularly. When you ask Siri or Alexa for the weather or help to identify a random factoid, use "Hey Google" to play your favorite song, or get movie recommendations from Netflix, you're using AI! These systems learn from the vast amount of information they encounter to make better predictions and decisions, helping to personalize your experience. They can recognize patterns, understand commands, and even learn from your preferences over time. So, next time you see a route suggestion on your map app or receive a product recommendation while shopping online, remember that's AI at work! By understanding AI as a tool in your daily life, rather than a distant or complex or scary concept, it becomes less intimidating and more of a practical asset to embrace.

Moving from everyday life to the classroom, let's see how AI fits into PBL. Just as AI helps you with daily tasks, it can also support learning by making it more engaging and tailored to each student's needs. In a PBL classroom, where learning is active and centered around projects, AI can be a powerful tool. It can offer new ways for students to explore subjects and creative solutions to problems.

AI in a PBL Classroom

PBL, in essence, is a testament to this spirit of boundary-pushing. It's a pedagogical approach that defies traditional educational norms that often emphasize memorization and standardized testing. Instead, PBL places a premium on creation, application, and the transformative power of student-driven learning. In this context, AI is not merely a tool for obtaining answers; it is a catalyst for exploration and a beacon for innovation.

The incorporation of AI in PBL aligns perfectly with Silva's vision of harnessing technology and creativity to confront challenges. Students in a PBL environment are not passive recipients of predetermined knowledge. They are active participants, using AI to delve into complex problems, analyze and synthesize information, and evaluate their findings critically. This approach nurtures higher-order thinking, empowering students to use AI not just as a means to an end but as an extension of their creative and analytical capabilities. "Higher-order thinking refers to the top levels of cognitive thinking, as laid out in Bloom's Taxonomy model. When we use higher-order thinking, we push beyond basic memorization and recall to analyze and synthesize information. These are the skills that help us evaluate information and think critically. We also use these skills to develop new ideas and concepts, building on previous knowledge to create something entirely new" (Staake, 2023).

PBL is not a journey with a fixed destination. Rather, it is an open-ended exploration where the path is not linear but rich with opportunities for self-expression, discovery, and meaningful learning. Students are encouraged to demonstrate mastery of content in deeply personal ways and reflective of their passions. In this light, AI becomes a partner in their intellectual journey, expanding their capabilities and helping them bring their unique visions to life.

In the modern classroom, the integration of artificial intelligence is no longer a futuristic concept but a tangible reality that enhances the educational experience. However, to harness the full potential of AI in education, particularly in project-based learning, it's essential to establish a solid foundation. This foundation is built on the strategic frameworks of PREP and EDIT (Fitzpatrick, Fox, Weinstein, 2023, 91 and 116), which, when combined with AI in the PBL process, create a robust structure for AI integration.

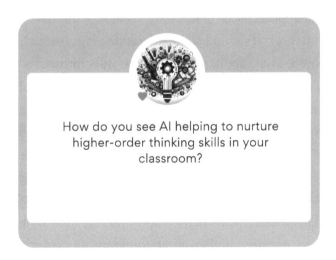

How do you see AI helping to nurture higher-order thinking skills in your classroom?

Journaling Your Journey

Use the space below to reflect on this question.

_____

_____

_____

_____

_____

_____

_____

_____

_____

_____

_____

Figure 9.1

Fitzpatrick et al. Prompt Engineering Framework

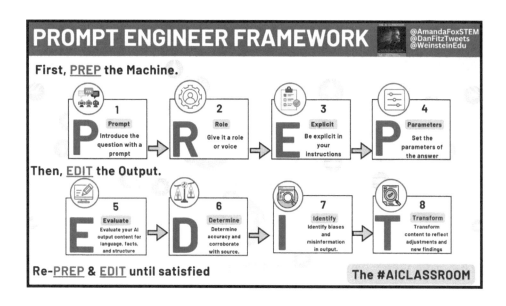

Originally featured in The AI Classroom, the above image represents how to effectively interact

with AI, ensuring that the output is educational, accurate, and useful for learning purposes.

The Necessity of PREP in AI-Infused PBL

The PREP framework acts as the bedrock for introducing AI into PBL. It ensures that students and educators start with a clear and purposeful direction, aligning AI's capabilities with the project's objectives. Each element of PREP - Prompt, Role, Explicit, Parameters - serves as a guiding principle, ensuring that AI tools are utilized with intent and relevance. By prompting AI with specific, goal-oriented questions and defining its role in the project, students set a clear path for AI's contributions. The effectiveness of AI in generating relevant scenarios largely depends on our ability to craft precise and contextually appropriate prompts. The limitations in AI's outputs often reflect our limitations in providing clear and comprehensive guidance. It's crucial that we, as educators, understand the community and context we are addressing to get the most out of AI's capabilities (Alcock, P., personal communication, December 19, 2023). Being explicit in instructions and setting defined parameters further refines AI's role, ensuring its outputs are meaningful and aligned with educational standards.

EDIT: Refining AI's Role in PBL

Once AI has provided its initial inputs, the EDIT framework comes into play. This reflective process involves:

- Evaluating AI's content
- Determining its validity
- Identifying any biases
- Transforming the findings to align with PBL objectives

EDIT encourages students to critically assess and responsibly use AI, fostering a deeper understanding of its capabilities and limitations. This critical engagement is crucial for the ethical and effective use of AI in education.

AI in PBL: A Tailored Approach for Dynamic Learning

Figure 9.2
AI in PBL

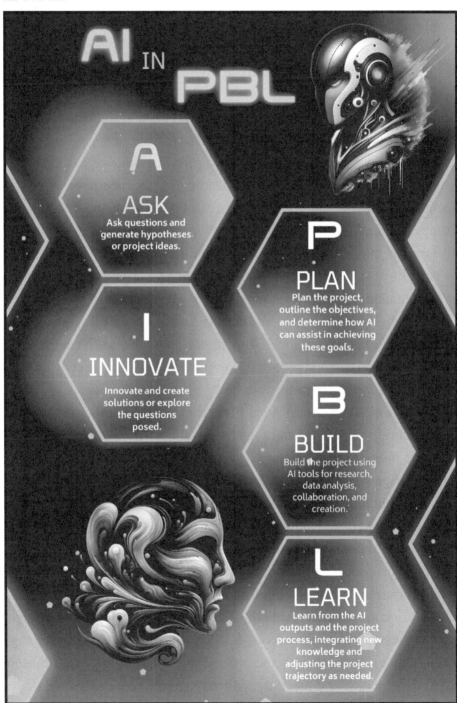

Building upon Fitzpatrick et al,'s (2023) framework, artificial intelligence in a project-based learning setting offers a tailored approach to integrate AI seamlessly into each phase of PBL - Ask, Innovate, Plan, Build, and Learn. This approach enhances each step of the PBL process, from formulating initial inquiries to planning, building, and reflecting on the project. It's not just about leveraging technology; it's about enriching the learning journey, promoting creativity, and facilitating a deeper understanding of the subject matter.

By implementing the frameworks as the foundation,students can view and use AI not merely as a technological tool but as a sophisticated ally in their learning journey. This approach prepares students to use AI creatively and ethically, ensuring their learning experience is enriched and their knowledge is applied to solve real-world problems. The visually compelling framework in Figure 9.1 provides a dynamic blueprint for this integration, capturing the vibrant and fluid nature of a PBL environment enriched by AI, a testament to its potential as a catalyst for creativity, critical thinking, and deep learning.

Building upon the structured interaction with AI provided by the PREP and EDIT frameworks, AI in PBL is employed as an assistive technology and an essential component of the learning process. This approach fosters active engagement and deepens understanding among students.

In the **ask (A)** phase of AI in PBL, students initiate their projects by formulating probing questions and generating hypotheses. This aligns with the prompt aspect of the PREP framework, marking the beginning of AI engagement. AI in this phase teaches students to view AI as a tool for exploration and expansion of curiosity, fostering a mindset geared towards discovery and inquiry rather than merely seeking quick solutions.

Moving to the **innovate (I)** stage, students use AI to explore potential solutions or to deepen their understanding of the posed questions. This phase corresponds to the role and parameters components of PREP, where the function and scope of AI within the project are established. The innovation phase encourages students to apply AI creatively, using technology for design, experimentation, and prototyping. This reinforces the concept of AI as a creation and practical application tool.

In the **plan (P)** stage, students outline their project's trajectory, objectives, and the role of AI in achieving these goals. Informed by the explicit element of PREP, this phase highlights the necessity of clear instructions for AI. Effective planning with AI equips students to strategically incorporate technology into their projects, enhancing organization and strategic thinking.

The **build (B)** phase involves the tangible creation and development of the project, utilizing AI for research, data analysis, collaboration, and creation. This phase reflects the 'evaluate' and 'determine' steps of EDIT, focusing on assessing the utility and accuracy of AI outputs. Building with AI in this context allows students to practically apply the technology, viewing it as an extension of their capabilities rather than a substitute for their efforts.

Finally, in the **learn (L)** stage, students reflect and adapt. They evaluate their project in the context of AI outputs and their learning process, integrating new knowledge and adjusting their project accordingly. This stage resonates with Fitzpatrick et al.'s (2023) EDIT's identify and transform aspects, emphasizing critical thinking and self-reflection, which are pivotal in PBL. Students learn to appreciate AI as a tool for learning and enhancement.

Each step in the AI in PBL framework builds upon the previous one, creating a comprehensive structure that guides students through their project from inception to reflection. By fully integrating AI into every phase of PBL and aligning it with the PREP and EDIT frameworks, students are equipped to use AI effectively and understand its role as a facilitator of deeper learning and creativity. This holistic approach ensures that AI is perceived as a tool to expand students' abilities, fostering an educational environment where technology serves to amplify human potential and creativity.

How can you see yourself integrating AI tools into your own classroom based on the frameworks and examples provided? What subjects or projects do you think would benefit most from AI augmentation?

Journaling Your Journey

Use the space below to reflect on this question.

_____

_____

_____

_____

_____

_____

_____

_____

Realizing the AI in PBL Vision Through Technology

The AI in PBL framework provides a strategic blueprint for integrating AI into student-directed learning. Thankfully, educators and students have access to innovative technologies that can empower this vision. AI writing assistants like Claude and Eduaide support the planning, building, and learning stages, providing feedback and analysis to enrich projects. Creative tools like Midjourney and DALLE-3 facilitate visual representations of concepts during the innovation phase. Conversational agents like ChatGPT and Gemini enable exploration and curiosity in the critical asking phase while also supporting reflection by answering student questions. We'll explore all of these tools more deeply further on.

These technologies align with the ethos of AI integration in PBL, not as a substitute for human effort and creativity but as an amplifier that expands possibilities. By combining emerging AI with the step-by-step integration outlined in the AI in PBL framework, educators are equipped to provide students with the best of both worlds: the boundless potential of artificial intelligence anchored by a human-centric pedagogical approach. This symbiotic integration promises to transform education into a journey of limitless growth and discovery for all.

AI in PBL in Action

Kindergarten to Grade 3 (K-3): Science Project

- **A**sk: Students explore the question, "What do different plants need to grow?" using an AI tool that suggests various plant types and their requirements.

- **I**nnovate: They use AI to design a simple garden layout on a computer, selecting plants based on their needs.

- **P**lan: Students plan their real garden, deciding where each plant will go, with AI helping to determine the best layout for sunlight and water access.

- **B**uild: They plant the garden, using AI to track plant growth and predict when to water or add nutrients.

- **L**earn: Students use AI to compare the growth of their plants against the predicted outcomes, learning about plant biology and ecology.

Grades 4-6: Social Studies Project

- **A**sk: Students use AI to help formulate a question about the local history of their town or city.

- **I**nnovate: AI assists in creating a digital timeline or map showcasing historical events or landmarks.

- **P**lan: Students plan a small exhibition, with AI helping to organize historical facts and images.

- **B**uild: They use AI tools to create and edit a digital presentation of their town's history.
- **L**earn: AI provides feedback on their presentation, helping students understand the impact of their local history on the present.

Grades 7-8: Mathematics Project

- **A**sk: Students explore "How can we use algebra to solve real-world problems?" using AI to find relevant problems like budgeting or distance calculations.
- **I**nnovate: They use AI to simulate real-life scenarios where algebra is applied, like planning a school event budget.
- **P**lan: Students plan their algebraic solutions, with AI suggesting different algebraic methods or equations.
- **B**uild: They solve problems using AI tools to check their work and suggest improvements.
- **L**earn: Students reflect on the accuracy and efficiency of their solutions, with AI providing an analysis of different problem-solving approaches.

Grades 9-12: English Language Arts Project

- **A**sk: High school students might explore "How does cultural context influence storytelling?" using AI to analyze different literature from various cultures.
- **I**nnovate: AI helps them create a blog or podcast discussing cultural influences in literature.
- **P**lan: They use AI to organize their content, plan their episodes or posts, and research literature.
- **B**uild: Students create their blog or podcast, with AI assisting in editing and improving their content.
- **L**earn: They use AI to gather feedback on their content and understand the diverse perspectives in storytelling.

In each example, AI is used to enhance the learning experience, tailored to the students' grade levels and subject matter. This approach demonstrates how AI can be integrated into PBL to support and enrich education across various ages and disciplines.

Assessing Tools and How Those Tools Are Used

Assessing Tools

As we begin to integrate AI into project-based learning environments, the responsibility falls on us to effectively evaluate AI tools before these tools are introduced to students. This preemptive assessment is crucial for ensuring AI's ethical and beneficial integration in the classroom. A teacher-focused rubric provides a structured methodology to appraise AI tools based on relevance, accuracy, complexity, fairness, and innovation. Such a rubric shifts the emphasis from passive adoption to critical analysis of AI's role in education.

By employing following rubric, teachers can objectively assess how AI tools align with and support PBL objectives. This is a key step in identifying and mitigating any potential biases or inaccuracies inherent in AI, ensuring that these tools are effective and ethically sound. The rubric empowers teachers to uphold high standards for AI functionality, minimizing risks and maximizing AI's capacity to enhance educational experiences through unique insights and creative contributions.

The implementation of a comprehensive AI evaluation rubric by teachers is essential. It fosters a discerning approach to utilizing AI, ensuring robust oversight and promoting the optimal pedagogical use of these tools. As AI becomes increasingly common in educational settings, teachers must cultivate a culture of critical assessment and accountability. This approach guarantees that AI tools are pre-vetted for classroom use, ensuring they serve as valuable aids in fostering student creativity and intellectual growth. By rigorously evaluating AI tools through a teacher-led rubric, we can ensure that AI's burgeoning presence in education enhances rather than hinders the rich tapestry of project-based learning.

Figure 9.3
AI Tool Rubric (Part 1)

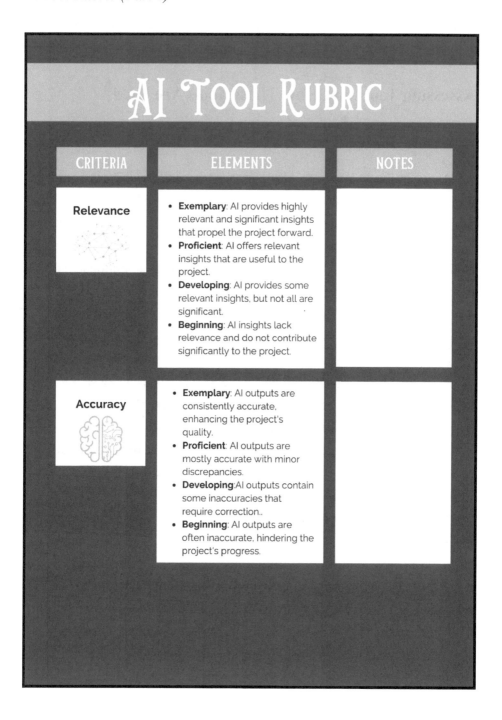

AI Tool Rubric

CRITERIA	ELEMENTS	NOTES
Relevance	• **Exemplary**: AI provides highly relevant and significant insights that propel the project forward. • **Proficient**: AI offers relevant insights that are useful to the project. • **Developing**: AI provides some relevant insights, but not all are significant. • **Beginning**: AI insights lack relevance and do not contribute significantly to the project.	
Accuracy	• **Exemplary**: AI outputs are consistently accurate, enhancing the project's quality. • **Proficient**: AI outputs are mostly accurate with minor discrepancies. • **Developing**:AI outputs contain some inaccuracies that require correction.. • **Beginning**: AI outputs are often inaccurate, hindering the project's progress.	

Figure 9.4
AI Tool Rubric (Part 2)

CRITERIA	ELEMENTS	NOTES
Complexity 	• **Exemplary**: AI handles complex tasks efficiently, providing nuanced contributions. • **Proficient**: AI manages tasks with a moderate level of complexity satisfactorily. • **Developing**: AI completes basic tasks but struggles with complexity. • **Beginning**: AI fails to handle complex tasks adequately.	
Bias and Fairness	• **Exemplary**: AI shows no signs of bias and treats all data with fairness. • **Proficient**: AI shows minimal bias and generally treats data fairly. • **Developing**: AI outputs show some bias or unfair treatment of data. • **Beginning**: AI outputs are biased and treat data unfairly.	
Innovation 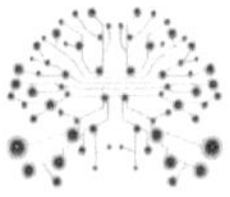	• **Exemplary**: AI contributes innovative ideas or processes that are novel to the project. • **Proficient**: AI provides some new ideas or processes that add value. • **Developing**: AI contributes few innovative aspects to the project. • **Beginning**: AI does not contribute innovative ideas or processes.	

Scan the QR code to download a copy of the AI Tool Ruibric.

Having established a framework for teachers to evaluate AI tools effectively, it's equally crucial to shift our focus to how students utilize these tools in their project-based learning endeavors. While teachers lay the groundwork by selecting appropriate AI tools, the ultimate success of AI integration in education largely depends on how students engage with and apply these tools in their projects.

Student Use of AI

Evaluating student use of AI is a critical component of fostering responsible and effective use of technology in the classroom. A student-centered rubric becomes an indispensable tool to ensure students are not only leveraging AI tools appropriately but also enhancing their learning experience. This rubric allows educators to assess various aspects of student interaction with AI, including:

- Integration and Application: How effectively are students integrating AI tools into their projects? This includes assessing whether AI is used as a genuine aid in learning or simply as a shortcut to completing tasks.

- Critical Thinking and Problem-Solving: Are students critically analyzing the information provided by AI? This involves evaluating how students interpret AI outputs, question potential biases, and apply AI-generated insights to solve complex problems in their projects.

- Creativity and Innovation: How are students using AI to foster creativity and innovation in their projects? This criterion looks at the extent to which AI is used to explore new ideas, create novel solutions, or add unique perspectives to their work.

- Ethical Considerations and Digital Literacy: Are students using AI tools ethically and responsibly? This includes understanding and respecting data privacy, recognizing the limitations of AI, and acknowledging the intellectual property rights associated with AI-generated content.

- Reflection and Adaptation: How do students reflect on the effectiveness of AI in their projects and adapt their work based on these reflections? This aspect assesses the student's ability to evaluate and iterate on their projects by incorporating feedback from AI tools.

Figure 9.5
Student Use of AI Rubric (Part 1)

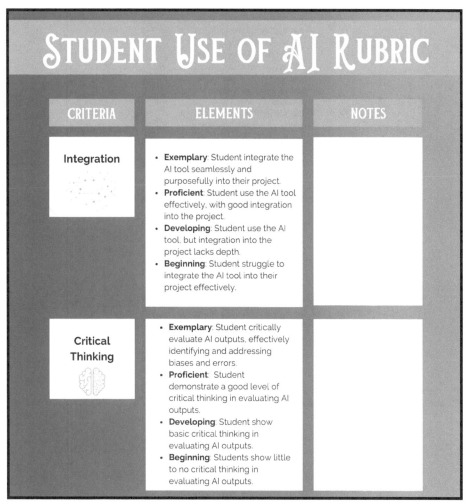

Figure 9.6
Student Use of AI Rubric (Part 2)

CRITERIA	ELEMENTS	NOTES
Problem Solving	• **Exemplary**: Student use the AI tool innovatively to solve complex project challenges. • **Proficient**: Student use the AI tool to address project challenges adequately. • **Developing**: Student use the AI tool for problem-solving but with limited success. • **Beginning**: Student fail to use the AI tool effectively for problem-solving.	
Collaboration	• **Exemplary**: Student collaboratively uses the AI tool, enhancing teamwork and project outcomes. • **Proficient**: Student generally uses the AI tool well in a team setting. • **Developing**: Student use of the AI tool is satisfactory but not fully collaborative. • **Beginning**: The AI tool is used individually, with little to no collaboration.	
Ethical Use	• **Exemplary**: Student consistently use the AI tool ethically, with a clear understanding of its impact. • **Proficient**: Student mostly use the AI tool ethically and consider its broader implications. • **Developing**: Student demonstrate a basic understanding of ethical use of the AI tool. • **Beginning**: Student demonstrate a lack of understanding of the ethical use of the AI tool.	

Scan the QR code to download a copy of the Student Use of AI Rubric.

This rubric encourages students to engage deeply with AI, going beyond superficial interaction to truly understand and harness the potential of these tools in a PBL context. It promotes a learning environment where AI is used thoughtfully and strategically, enhancing the educational experience while preparing students for a future where technology and human ingenuity coexist harmoniously. Through this careful evaluation of student use of AI, educators can guide students toward becoming proficient technology users, responsible digital citizens, and innovative problem-solvers.

The Research

The application of artificial intelligence in project-based learning is transforming the educational landscape. According to the eLearning Industry, AI in PBL primarily optimizes routine learning processes, enhancing their speed and efficiency. This integration of AI in PBL settings is not only changing the way learning occurs in many classrooms but also encourages the kind of thinking and collaboration necessary for working effectively with AI (Garbade, 2021).

Since its release, ChatGPT has significantly impacted education, prompting educators to reconsider their teaching methods and assessments. Viewing AI's capabilities as complementary rather than competitive allows for creative collaboration, benefitting both students and teachers. Despite initial concerns, the tool presents an opportunity for creative and effective use in educational settings, potentially becoming an ally rather than a challenge in the learning process (Larmer, 2023).

In a PBL context, the use of AI entails creating and studying machines and software to simulate human intelligence processes, with the main goal being to improve the efficiency of standard learning processes (Garbade, 2021). These findings indicate that AI's role in PBL is to streamline and enhance educational methodologies, facilitating a more engaging and efficient learning environment. I developed a chatbot for my students to interact with within their unit on The Decline of Feudalism in Medieval Europe. This chatbot allowed students to have their questions and personalized wonderings answered immediately, and it was not disruptive to the classroom environment.

By leveraging the power of AI, educators can enhance the PBL experience and improve student learning outcomes (Frąckiewicz, 2023). As a form of AI support in PBL, intelligent tutoring systems analyze students' progress and offer personalized feedback, guidance, and resources. This individualized support, particularly beneficial in large classrooms, helps bridge gaps in teacher-student interaction, ensuring focused attention for each student's success (Frąckiewicz, 2023). As discussed later in this chapter, SchoolAI is designed to not only help students with immediate understanding, but also provide teachers with insights into how their students are using the AI platform. Teachers will get updates that say, "Gwyneth is asking great questions and is showing a deep understanding of the content," or "Steven appears to be off task and is providing very short responses." This feedback provides you with the necessary insights to know exactly who needs additional support. While intelligent systems demonstrate the benefits AI can provide in a PBL context, educators must also consider how to thoughtfully integrate these tools in alignment with the fundamental principles of project-based learning.

With its focus on real-world problems and extended inquiry, project-based learning incorporates inherent features that reduce the likelihood of misusing tools like ChatGPT. Educators can guide students in using AI-generated content as a starting point, adding their ideas and sources. This approach aligns with the core principles of high-quality PBL, which involves complex inquiry processes and the creation of authentic products for specific audiences and purposes (Larmer, 2023). When a student struggled to conceptualize a project on European explorers, I asked if she wanted to use ChatGPT to spark ideas. ChatGPT suggested soccer jerseys representing explorers, which the student expanded by designing Native American jerseys, too, noting they were the "home team." This gave a launching point while maintaining student inquiry and interest.

The creations within PBL are an assemblage of diverse products beyond traditional essays or reports, such as infographics, multimedia pieces, or physical artifacts. This diversity in outputs necessitates a deeper understanding of the subject matter, which cannot be fully replaced by AI-generated content (Larmer, 2023). Often, I have 15 or more unique projects for any given unit. A game that has transformed some of my students' interest in social studies is Minecraft. It was a game I had heard my students rave about, but it wasn't until one student asked if he could bring in his copy of the game to use for his project on ancient Rome that I truly had an "aha!" moment. My student invested over 40 hours into his project. He rebuilt Rome and created a voice-over video of his project. He built roads according to Rome's designs as well as the Roman Colosseum. No student would have invested that kind of time into that project if I had designed it. When students design their projects, their buy-in and ownership of the learning goes through the roof!

Figure 9.7
Minecraft Project on Rome

Another significant AI application in PBL is in assessment. Traditional evaluation methods in PBL, which can be time-consuming and subjective, are transformed by AI-powered tools that provide objective, data-driven feedback on student performance. This innovation aids teachers in identifying areas for additional student support and tailoring their teaching strategies effectively (Frąckiewicz, 2023). For example, AI assessment platforms can track multiple metrics on student work, flagging potential problem areas for teachers to address. The data can be used to offer targeted recommendations for each learner. Curipod (2022), which we will look at later in this chapter, offers a variety of formative assessments that provide teachers with the immediate feedback needed to make in-the-moment adjustments:

- Entry and exit tickets
- Think-pair-share templates
- Feedback templates
- Draw and emoji activities

Key elements of PBL, like public product creation, frequent formative assessments, and the need for work to be shared and revised openly, further mitigate the risk of overreliance on AI. This transparency ensures that the student substantially revises and personalizes any AI-assisted work. Additionally, emphasizing explaining and defending one's work in PBL fosters critical thinking and deep learning, which cannot be achieved solely through AI-generated content (Larmer, 2023). My students typically work on their projects in class, and this gives them the opportunity to get feedback, both from their peers as well as from myself. While they work, I am able to inquire about their project and offer support if they hit roadblocks.

While AI tools like ChatGPT present new challenges and opportunities in education, their integration into PBL can enhance the learning experience by providing personalized support, streamlining assessment, and encouraging collaboration and creativity. It is essential, however, to approach this integration with a focus on enhancing human capabilities and maintaining the core principles of PBL.

This theoretical understanding of AI's role in education is vividly illustrated in real-world classroom settings. The following stories from the field offer tangible examples of how AI can be applied practically and creatively, enhancing both the teaching and learning experiences.

AI in the Classroom: Enhancing Learning Through Practical Applications and Creative Exploration

How Students are Using AI in the Classroom

Heather Sanson, a high school criminal justice teacher at Franklin County Schools in Tennessee, implemented an innovative approach to AI in her classroom. Her first-year students used OpenAI to create elements of a mock trial, including opening statements, direct examination questions, and closing arguments. This project exemplifies the practical application of AI in education.

The AI tools provided foundational examples for legal communication, crucial for students unfamiliar with the nuances of a trial. Students actively engaged with the material, tailoring AI-generated content to fit the context of their mock trial. This process deepened their understanding of legal procedures and the importance of strategic questioning and argumentation.

The exercise was a success, teaching students about the trial process and the revelation of facts through witness testimony. Heather plans to use this AI-integrated approach in future semesters, highlighting the value of AI in enhancing the learning experience and fostering critical thinking.

Transitioning from the practical application of AI in Heather's classroom to a more creative use, we have Lacey's project. Lacey, a student in my social studies class, aspired to create a *Where's Waldo?* style of book to illustrate the influence of the Roman Catholic Church on medieval Europe. Utilizing her notes, she crafted prompts for MidJourney, an AI image creator, to generate relevant images.

Lacey's project was an iterative learning journey. She evaluated and modified each AI-generated image for historical accuracy and relevance, demonstrating her deep engagement with the subject matter. This process was about creating a stunning image and personalizing her learning experience, allowing her to represent complex historical concepts meaningfully.

Lacey's final product was a personalized, informative book that showcased her understanding and interpretation of medieval European history.

This project underlines how AI can be a powerful ally in project-based learning, enabling students to explore, visualize, and express their academic insights creatively.

Another student of mine, Shawn, created an exceptional project with AI. Shawn's journey in creating his Revolutionary War-themed rap project is a stellar example of how AI can play a pivotal role in guiding students toward innovative and meaningful educational experiences. Initially, Shawn faced a common student challenge: deciding on a project idea. He came to me, his teacher, feeling frustrated and uncertain about his direction. Recognizing his interests and the potential of AI, I suggested we use ChatGPT to brainstorm ideas related to our current content on the Revolutionary War and his passion for music.

As we fed his interests into ChatGPT, the AI tool generated ideas that helped Shawn make deeper connections between his love for music and the historical content. This interaction with AI was a crucial moment in Shawn's creative process. It was during this brainstorming session that Shawn experienced a eureka moment. His eyes lit up as the vision for his project crystallized. Suddenly, he had a clear path forward: a rap album that would creatively intertwine the historical narratives of the Revolutionary War with the modern medium of rap music.

Once the concept was solidified, Shawn began to utilize various AI tools to bring his vision to life. ChatGPT provided him with a valuable starting point for his lyrics. While a great foundation, these AI-generated lyrics required careful evaluation and manipulation by Shawn to ensure they accurately reflected the historical content he had researched. This process was not just about using AI-generated content; it was an exercise in critical thinking and creative adaptation, allowing Shawn to deepen his understanding of the subject matter and express it through his unique musical lens.

Shawn's use of AI tools extended beyond ChatGPT. With MidJourney, Soundtrap, Lalal.ai, and Uberduck, he designed his CD cover, created music, and produced vocals aligned with his project's theme. This multi-faceted use of AI in various production stages demonstrates AI's versatility as an educational tool.

Shawn's project underscores the role of AI in fostering student engagement, creativity, and learning. By leveraging AI for brainstorming, content creation, and production, Shawn could develop a project that was not only personally meaningful but also academically enriching. His experience is a testament to the power of AI in transforming the learning experience, guiding students from initial frustration to a moment of clarity and purpose, and supporting them throughout the creative process. This case study highlights how AI can be an invaluable ally in the classroom, helping students discover their passions, make meaningful connections, and bring their innovative ideas to fruition.

These diverse educational projects exemplify the transformative potential of AI in enhancing learning experiences. From Heather Sanson's practical use of AI in a mock trial to Lacey's creative illustration of historical themes and Shawn's unique blend of music and history, each case study demonstrates how AI can be a powerful tool in education. These projects highlight AI's ability to facilitate critical thinking, deepen subject matter understanding, and foster creativity. By integrating AI into their learning processes, students could explore and express their academic insights in novel and meaningful ways, showcasing AI's role not just as a technological aid but as a catalyst for innovative and personalized learning. These experiences affirm that when effectively integrated into educational settings, AI can be an invaluable resource in helping students realize their creative potential and academic goals.

Navigating AI in the Classroom

Integrating AI into your PBL classroom does not come without challenges or concerns. Educators can effectively integrate AI into their teaching practices by understanding and addressing these challenges and concerns.

Plagiarism

As AI becomes more sophisticated, there's a growing concern about students submitting AI-generated work as their own (Elgersma, 2023). Plagiarism is not new in the classroom, but AI tools such as ChatPGPT, Claude, and Gemini make copying and pasting text based on a single question not only tempting but an even more difficult-to-detect issue. A student could put in the prompt, "Write a five-paragraph essay that compares and contrasts two main characters in the novel The Lord of the Flies. Use text evidence. Include a few grammatical mistakes and one spelling error. Write in the style of an 8th grader." Within a matter of seconds, the essay is composed. So, what does this mean for educators as we move forward?

Integrating standards-based grading and higher-order thinking questions into the curriculum becomes crucial to combat the ease of AI-generated plagiarism. These approaches shift the focus from mere regurgitation of information to a more profound understanding and mastery of content. They encourage students to demonstrate their learning in diverse and intricate ways, going beyond the traditional written assignments.

For teachers not employing standards-based grading, adopting a portfolio approach can be particularly effective. Portfolios allow students to collect and reflect on a diverse range of work, demonstrating their learning journey over time. This can include various types of evidence, from essays and projects to reflections and presentations. Portfolios emphasize continuous learning and improvement, making it challenging for AI-generated content to replace the nuanced and personal nature of student work. When students showcase their learning journey, we can see the growth that has occurred, which allows us to see the degree of mastery rather than solely relying on an end-of-unit snapshot.

Encourage originality and creativity in project work. Use AI as a tool for idea generation rather than content creation. In PBL, where projects are often unique and personalized, the risk of plagiarism is reduced as students are more engaged in creating original content based on their experiences and interests. We must rethink what we ask our students to generate and for what purpose. No longer can we base mastery of content solely on a piece of writing. We must establish a sense of showing me what we know rather than just writing about what we know. If the written expression is a piece of mastery in your class, you may want to require revisions as a part of the process. Look through the history of a document that has been submitted to add more credibility to the work. Add micro-conversations to your process so that you can have conversations with students and dialogue with them about their understanding of the content. It is vital to be proactive in the classroom and not reactive. Before your students begin writing, see what AI will produce based on the questions you are asking or the assignment that has been assigned (Elgersma, 2023). Know what is possible, and then modify assignments based on those results.

Ethics

Plagiarism is just the tip of the iceberg regarding challenges and concerns about AI's usage in the classroom. Incorporating AI, particularly generative AI, into a project-based learning classroom presents various ethical challenges and concerns. Ethical issues tend to come in the forms of plagiarism, bias, misinformation (sometimes referred to as hallucinations), and data privacy information. AI in education raises concerns about data privacy, especially when AI models are trained on datasets containing personal information.

> The best thing you can do when trying out new technologies is to loop your tech department in early and often. The education community will eventually have regulations and standards to address these concerns. Still, in the meantime, it will be up to district tech teams to make the right decisions for their students (Jennings, 2023).

Incorporating discussions about ethical use into teaching various educational technology tools is essential across all grade levels, each tailored to the students' developmental stage and comprehension.

For students in grades K-4, the focus is on foundational understanding, covering basic digital citizenship concepts like online safety, privacy, and respect. Teaching methods include simple, interactive activities such as storytelling and role-playing to convey concepts like keeping personal information private, understanding right and wrong online behaviors, and being respectful online.

In grades 5-8, the approach evolves to developing critical awareness. The teachers should introduce concepts of plagiarism, online etiquette, and data privacy basics. Methods involve interactive lessons and group discussions to encourage critical thinking about information shared and encountered online, discussing the ethics of using internet resources, understanding online sharing impacts, and identifying misinformation.

For grades 9-12, the focus shifts to advanced application and ethics. The exploration deepens into digital ethics, data privacy, intellectual property, and technology's societal impact. Teaching methods such as seminars, debates, and research projects encourage independent thinking and ethical application. Content covers the ethical implications of AI and machine learning, intellectual property protection, countering biases in digital content, and understanding the long-term consequences of digital footprints.

The teaching approach is age-appropriate at each educational level, gradually building students' understanding and ability to engage with technology critically. This strategy ensures that students are proficient in using technology tools responsibly and understand the importance of ethical practices, preparing them to navigate the digital world as informed and responsible digital citizens.

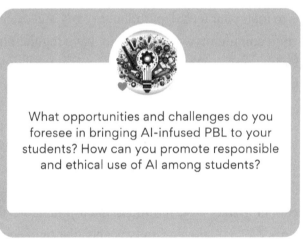

What opportunities and challenges do you foresee in bringing AI-infused PBL to your students? How can you promote responsible and ethical use of AI among students?

Journaling Your Journey

Use the space below to reflect on this question.

_____

_____

_____

_____

_____

Bias and Misinformation

Alcock shared with me regarding bias in AI that it's evident in scenarios where the output reflects specific cultural or gender biases. For example, historical training data might lead to AI associating certain professions like doctors with males. Although there's progress towards more inclusive and multicultural representations, it's essential to recognize and address these biases in AI-generated content (Alcock, P., personal communication, December 19, 2023). Caroline Fell Kurban, a professor at MEF University in Istanbul, Turkey, shared with me that her students could identify that image generators tended to have gender and racial biases. She shared that when her students asked the AI to generate an image of a nurse, the images were always of white women. This was very concerning (Fell Kurban, C., personal communication, November 11, 2023). Also, Tom Menella, a professor at Western New England University, shared that when using AI to grade research papers, AI tended to grade female-written work lower than male-written work (Menella, T., personal communication, November 11, 2023).

Addressing bias and misinformation in AI is a critical challenge in its application, especially in educational settings. A key solution to this issue is fostering open and ongoing conversations about these biases. As Phillip Alcock, Caroline Fell Kurban, and Tom Menella (2023) highlighted, AI can exhibit gender and racial biases, such as image generators predominantly depicting nurses as white women or AI grading systems showing bias against female-authored work. The first step in addressing these biases is awareness and acknowledgment. Educators should encourage students to identify and discuss instances of bias in AI-generated content actively. This can be facilitated through PBL activities where students critically analyze AI outputs, conduct experiments to uncover biases and engage in reflective discussions on their findings. Moreover, integrating these discussions into the curriculum can help develop critical thinking skills and an understanding of ethical AI use. Students can be guided to explore the origins of these biases and understand how AI training data can influence outcomes. Such conversations raise awareness and empower students to think about ways to mitigate these biases, fostering a culture of ethical AI usage. Through these approaches, the educational community can work towards more equitable and accurate AI applications, ensuring that technology serves as a tool for learning and advancement rather than perpetuating existing societal biases.

AI Tools for Teachers and Students

MagicSchool.ai

 Free as well as FERPA compliant
Users: Must be 18 years old or older to create an account.
Teachers, however, can share tools with their students to use.

MagicSchool is an AI-powered educational platform designed to deliver personalized learning experiences spanning kindergarten to college levels. Leveraging advanced machine learning capabilities, it tailors content, monitors progress, and enriches engagement and effectiveness across this diverse educational spectrum (Reimers, 2023). MagicSchool even has a section dedicated to the development of PBL units. This can provide a good starting point as you develop your unit.

The project-based learning generator used by MagicSchool.ai is

> a valuable asset for educators looking to create authentic, standards-aligned project-based learning experiences. By adhering to PBL principles, offering topic flexibility, and ensuring standards alignment, this tool simplifies the creation of immersive projects that promote meaningful learning and student engagement (Magic School, n.d.).

While this tool is effective in fostering meaningful learning, integrating it with the modern PBL approach, which incorporates passion as a central element, could further enhance its impact. This integration would not diminish the value of the Magic School's method but rather augment it, ensuring that learning experiences are not only standards-focused but also deeply resonant with students' interests and aspirations. This tool can provide educators with a great starting point when planning a PBL unit.

Figure 9.8
MagicSchool PBL

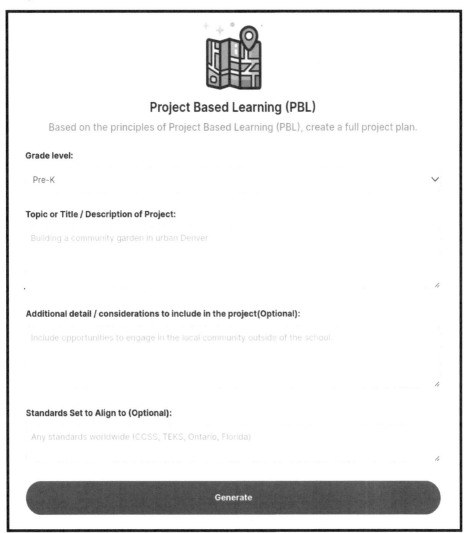

The Magic Student platform complements MagicSchool.ai's project-based learning generator by incorporating student passion as a central element in the modern PBL approach. While Magic School provides a valuable starting point for creating standards-aligned PBL units, Magic Student offers a dedicated student portal where teachers can provide access to curated tools and resources tailored to each project, ensuring learning experiences resonate deeply with students' interests and aspirations. Within this portal, teachers can select specific tools, create virtual collaboration spaces, and monitor student tool usage, empowering educators to facilitate passion-driven projects with oversight and support. This integration of Magic School's standards-focused generator and Magic Student's passion-centric portal elevates PBL, promoting both academic rigor and personal investment for immersive, multidimensional learning experiences.

Figure 9.9
Magic Student Preview

Schoolai.com

Free as well as FERPA and COPPA compliant
Users: Designed for teachers and education leaders,
but the AI is designed to engage students and educators.
Students of all ages may explore using this platform.

SchoolAI creates personalized learning for students. Students are able to interact with various chatbots. These chatbots come in the form of numerous historical figures as well as tutors. Teachers are able to customize the chatbot so that it responds to specific topics as well as addresses scenarios you are covering with your students. The site allows you to create exit tickets and bell ringers, and also has a unique feature to keep students engaged: Choose Your Own Adventure. Students can experience your content via a story that asks them to make choices that impact the outcome. Once you have designed your chatbot, you will see a list of your students that are signed in. You can click on the students and review their ongoing conversation with the bot. Interestingly enough, because the chatbot is designed for a specific topic if a student tries to ask random questions, the chatbot will redirect the student to focus on the topic. The site will also provide you with insights regarding how your students are interacting with the bot and it will also indicate how well the students are responding to the chatbot.

Figure 9.10
School AI View

Schoolai.com offers a feature where teachers can develop their own chatbots to assist students during a PBL unit. I have personally created several chatbots for my students. These bots are programmed with the unit's topical essential questions and various driving questions. After inputting these details, I informed the chatbot about the students' task: to develop a project that addresses all driving questions fueled by their own passions and interests. This setup allows students to discuss their project ideas with the chatbot, which then provides feedback and suggestions on integrating the academic content. The chatbot is designed to engage in conversations about the content, prompting students on how to incorporate it into their projects. If a student is uncertain, the chatbot can offer creative suggestions to help bridge the gap between their ideas and the academic objectives.

ChatGPT

ChatGPT is an advanced language model developed by OpenAI, designed to understand and generate human-like text based on the input it receives. It's a form of artificial intelligence that can assist in various tasks, particularly in areas requiring natural language processing. It can be used by educators for personalized learning, help with writing and research assistance, act as a language learning tool, provide feedback and assessment, act as a resource for generating ideas, question-answering tool, and administrative assistance (OpenAI, 2023). Due to the fact that ChaptGPT was not designed for schools, it is not FERPA or COPPA compliant.

Figure 9.11
ChatGPT View

ChatGPT is an all-encompassing tool that streamlines the project development process for students. Initially, it aids in formulating project concepts, aligning them with the topical essential question and the driving questions of the project. This includes assistance in crafting detailed timelines to manage project execution effectively. Furthermore,

ChatGPT offers a unique feature where students can upload images of their projects, receiving critical feedback on the representation of the core content and suggestions for improvement to better fulfill project goals. Additionally, it plays a pivotal role in the development of presentations, guiding students to organize information coherently and present it in a logical, impactful manner.

Midjourney

 Subscription
Users: Must be at least 13 years old or older.

Midjourney is an image generator. It is an AI bot that functions through discord.com. Midjourney images are generated through prompts.

> A prompt is a short text phrase that the Midjourney Bot interprets to produce an image. The Midjourney Bot breaks down the words and phrases in a prompt into smaller pieces, called tokens, that can be compared to its training data and then used to generate an image. A well-crafted prompt can help make unique and exciting images (Midjourney, n.d.).

Like ChatGPT, Midjourney was not designed for a school setting. Therefore it is not FERPA or COPPA compliant.

In a PBL environment, Midjourney can be an incredibly versatile tool for students. For projects involving research and presentations, Midjourney's ability to generate images based on descriptive prompts can bring historical events, scientific concepts, or thematic studies to life, adding a visually engaging element to student presentations. This tool is particularly beneficial in creative writing and storytelling projects, where students can visually conceptualize characters, settings, or scenes, enhancing their narrative and fostering a deeper connection with their work. In art or design-focused projects, Midjourney allows students to experiment with various artistic styles and visual compositions, encouraging exploration and innovation in their creative process. Midjourney also introduces an opportunity for critical thinking and analysis. Students can engage in discussions about the accuracy and interpretation of AI-generated images, exploring how these visual representations align with or differ from their initial prompts. This aspect allows students to reflect on their understanding of the content compared to how AI has interpreted their prompt.

Figure 9.12
Midjourney Image

Eduaide.ai

 Free and subscription, FERPA and COPPA compliant
Users: Must be 18 years old or older to create an account.

This tool offers AI-assisted lesson development. You can input the grade level, topic, and keywords, and the tool generates a lesson plan with objectives, teaching strategies, activities, assessment ideas, and closure questions (Fecich, 2023).

> It offers the ability to translate the generated content into more than 15 languages instantly. Educators can generate a syllabus, create discussion prompts, use the 'teaching assistant' for help with creating individualized education

program plans, write emails, or even compile a list of accommodations for students. Eduaide.AI has a content generator, teaching assistant, feedback bot, free-form chat, and assessment builder (Dené Poth, 2023).

Figure 9.13
Eduaide Image

Eduaide.ai, much like MagicSchool.ai, integrates a traditional project-based learning framework within its platform. Educators begin by choosing a content area and grade level and opting for cooperative learning strategies. Following this, they have the opportunity to select the project-based learning feature. At this juncture, educators input the topic for the unit. With a simple click on "Add to workspace," Eduaide. ai generates a comprehensive plan. However, to align Eduaide.ai's output with the principles of modern PBL, some adaptation is necessary. By modifying the generated plans to infuse elements that resonate more deeply with students' interests and passions, educators can bridge the gap between traditional PBL structures and the more dynamic, passion-driven approach of Modern PBL. This adaptation not only maintains the structural integrity of Eduaide.ai's traditional PBL framework but also enriches it, ensuring that the learning experiences are both academically sound and personally meaningful for students.

Curipod

Free and premium plans, FERPA and COPPA compliant
Users: Individuals 13 years or older, those under 13
with parental supervision, or students of any age when
authorized by their school, as it does not collect personal
student data.

Curipod is a platform that utilizes AI to assist educators in creating diverse and engaging lesson plans suitable for various settings including traditional, remote, or hybrid classrooms. According to Dené Poth (2023), this website empowers teachers to develop interactive lessons in minutes. Educators can input a topic and immediately generate a comprehensive lesson featuring text, images, and various activities like polls, open-ended responses, word clouds, and more, including SEL check-in activities. Core to Curipod's philosophy is principles of curiosity, inclusivity, personalized learning, and collaborative activities, reinforced by a commitment to responsible AI use and strict data privacy. This approach enhances teachers' instructional capabilities without replacing them, making Curipod a transformative tool in modern education for a dynamic, inclusive, and effective learning experience (Curipod, n.d.).

Figure 9.14
Curipod Image

Curipod is an invaluable platform for teachers implementing project-based learning PBL, offering tools to develop and present content, uncover students'

prior knowledge, facilitate information processing, and create engaging activities that foster collaboration. It simplifies the integration of new learning with students' existing understanding and encourages active participation in group settings. This enhances not only the educational experience but also cultivates essential skills like teamwork and problem-solving, making Curipod a great resource for educators implementing PBL.

***

The AI tools discussed here represent just a small sampling of the rapidly evolving landscape in educational technology. As new AI tools continually emerge, it's crucial for educators to approach them with caution, applying the evaluation rubric provided in this chapter. For a more comprehensive exploration of AI tools that can significantly enhance the Project-Based Learning classroom, *The AI Classroom* by Dan Fitzpatrick, Amanda Fox, and Brad Weinstein is an invaluable resource. It offers a variety of tools and insights tailored to meet diverse teaching needs, ensuring that educators are well-equipped to integrate AI into their teaching strategies effectively.

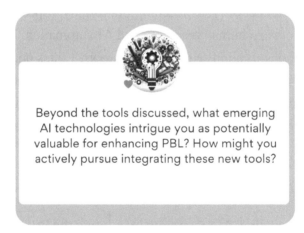

Beyond the tools discussed, what emerging AI technologies intrigue you as potentially valuable for enhancing PBL? How might you actively pursue integrating these new tools?

Journaling Your Journey

Use the space below to reflect on this question.

_____

_____

_____

_____

_____

Plan, Personalize, and Pursue

Plan

To effectively integrate AI into your project-based learning initiatives, begin by reviewing the AI in PBL framework and mapping out which tools can enhance specific phases of your upcoming projects. An audit of your curriculum is crucial to identify one or two opportunities for AI augmentation in an upcoming unit. Set tangible implementation goals for the semester, such as piloting two PBL projects with AI elements. Developing an inventory of available AI tools and ranking them based on their suitability for PBL needs is also essential. Additionally, create staff training sessions to establish comfort levels with leading AI solutions.

Personalize

Personalization is key to making progress in your unique educational environment. Reflect on your teaching philosophy, especially considering the balance between human creativity and AI automation. Tailor the PREP and EDIT rubrics to align with your classroom values and priorities. Co-develop PBL planning templates for students that incorporate AI reflection. Identify two or three subject areas or age groups where AI-infused PBL can impact the most. Customize assessment rubrics for responsible student use of AI technologies.

Pursue

Actively pursuing AI integration by piloting the PBL projects with AI augmentation that you identified in your plans. Gather student feedback on how AI is enhancing or hindering their learning process. Maintain an iterative journal documenting efforts to refine AI implementation and share successes and setbacks with peers to improve frameworks further. Continually learn about new advances in AI tools relevant to education.

By planning, personalizing, and actively pursuing AI integration in structured ways, you can lead a journey of sustained evolution that enriches PBL in your unique environment. The key lies in maintaining an open, discerning, and responsive approach that leverages AI to amplify human potential rather than simply automate established processes. This human-centric mindset, backed by organizational commitment to develop capacity in this emerging domain, will lead to next-generation learning experiences enhanced by AI's capabilities.

Continuous Learning and Adaptation

Engage with the latest advancements in artificial intelligence and project-based learning by leveraging a mix of specialized resources, communities, and strategies tailored to enhance your teaching practice.

Specialized Journals and Publications

Journal of Artificial Intelligence Research: Access peer-reviewed research on AI's cutting-edge developments.

TechTrends: Discover practical applications and technology reviews relevant to education.

Engaging Podcast

AI Café Podcast: Tune into dynamic discussions as Tom Mennella, Dr. Caroline Fell Kurban, Juli Ross-Kleinmann, Errol St. Clair Smith, and I explore the practicalities and vision of AI in education. Each episode dives into experiences, breakthroughs, and tools, offering a blend of academic insight and real-world application.

Targeted Webinars and Online Workshops

ISTE Webinars: Learn about AI's integration into education with webinars from leading technology educators.

EdSurge Digital Learning Network: Participate in workshops focusing on real-life PBL challenges and solutions.

Focused Professional Learning Communities

AI in Education Society: Connect with educators integrating AI into teaching.

Modern PBL: Project-based Learning in the Digital Age Facebook Group: Collaborate with a community dedicated to enhancing and sharing PBL strategies.

Practical Online Courses

Coursera's AI For Everyone: Understand AI's implications for education and beyond.

Project-Based Learning: Leading Meaningful Learning from edX: Gain insights into effective PBL implementation.

Conferences and Meetups with a Clear Focus

ISTE Conference & Expo: Engage with a global community of educators, exploring a comprehensive range of educational technology solutions and innovative teaching methods.

ASCD Conference on Educational Leadership: Gain insights into leadership, curriculum development, and educational innovation relevant to both AI and PBL.

Future of Education Technology Conference (FETC): Attend this renowned conference to explore the latest technologies, trends, and strategies in education, with a strong focus on the practical integration of AI and future-ready learning approaches.

Engaging with Specific AI Tools and Platforms

 Socrative: Utilize immediate feedback to adapt and enhance PBL activities.

- *Kahoot!:* Create interactive learning experiences with AI-driven content.

- *Curipod:* Utilize this innovative platform to create, share, and deliver engaging and personalized lessons. Its AI-driven features help automate lesson planning and adapt content to meet diverse student needs.

- *MagicSchool:* Dive into an immersive learning environment where AI personalizes the education experience, providing interactive and adaptive learning journeys for each student.

- *SchoolAI:* Leverage this platform to analyze educational data and improve learning outcomes. Develop chatbots that make the learning more personalized. Create Choose Your Own Adventure activities, and even have your students talk with historical figures such as Amelia Earhart, Abraham Lincoln, Frederick Douglass, and Nikola Tesla.

Seeking Feedback and Reflecting

- *Peer Observation:* Invite colleagues to observe and critique your PBL initiatives, focusing on integration and student engagement.

- *Implement and Reflect:* Introduce AI tools like Quizlet in your PBL projects and solicit detailed student feedback.

Use this QR code to view Quizlet mentioned previously.

As we reflect on the immense potential of AI to enrich project-based learning, our gaze must also shift to the horizon. How can we sustain this momentum of innovation? What new possibilities may emerge at the intersection of technology and student-driven learning? Chapter 10 explores the future directions for hands-on, passion-fueled education—one where students don't just master content but reshape it. We will look at strategies for bringing this vision to life and overcoming barriers through resourcefulness and community collaboration. For project-based learning to fulfill its dynamic promise, we must nurture a culture that values curiosity, creativity, and a willingness to challenge the status quo. Much like pioneers crossing into new frontiers, educators today have the opportunity to chart an educational landscape filled with possibilities—one where students acquire knowledge not just to repeat but to innovate.

Chapter 10
Looking To The Future:
Evolving Directions In Hands-On Learning

Daniel Jones
Author, Speaker, and Classroom Teacher

"The principal goal of education in the schools should be creating men and women who are capable of doing new things, not simply repeating what other generations have done."
- Jean Piaget

Piaget, a visionary in educational psychology, emphasized the importance of cultivating innovators and original thinkers, a philosophy that resonates deeply with the foundation of PBL. This approach to learning, infused with a student's passions, is not just about acquiring knowledge; it's about reshaping it, questioning it, and using it as a springboard for new ideas and solutions. PBL, with its focus on creative approaches, interdisciplinary connections, and collaborative efforts, aligns perfectly with Piaget's vision. It prepares learners not just to navigate the future but to actively shape it, fostering a generation of learners who are not content with the status quo but are empowered to create, innovate, and lead. This chapter delves into how PBL, enlivened by personal passions, becomes a powerful tool for transforming education, aligning with Piaget's aspiration for a future where education is the catalyst for genuine innovation and change.

Our world is undergoing rapid change, especially with the advent of artificial intelligence. As we contemplate the future and where it may lead us, my greatest hope is for a transformed education system that departs from the rigid, assembly-line model of the past. For too long, education has resembled a factory, with students organized in rows, expected to complete identical tasks in the same manner and at the same pace. While burnt out and ready to resign, I will never forget telling my principal and superintendent, "How else can you teach kids? You tell them what to memorize; they regurgitate it on a test, then you hit repeat." Their response: "I don't know, but you will find a different way." Project-based learning represents that shift.

As societal, industrial, and global needs evolve rapidly, so must our educational paradigm. We cannot cling to tradition merely because "we have always done it this way."

Change inspires both fear and promise. Yet, it remains necessary if we genuinely wish to become student-centered. The challenges and jobs of tomorrow may not exist today. To navigate these unknowns, students will require formidable creative problem-solving abilities. As evident throughout this book, innovation, collaboration, analysis, and real-world application form the core of project-based learning, equipping students with these skills. We have the opportunity and responsibility to empower students to innovate, discover, and invent solutions to global issues. Project-based learning repeatedly asks students to question and conceive unconventional solutions. To drive meaningful change, we must nurture resilience in confronting obstacles alongside a growth mindset that frames challenges as opportunities and curiosity as the engine of innovation.

If PBL is the Goal, How Do We Get There?

Advocate

Your journey as an educator embracing project-based learning is not just about adopting a new teaching method; it's about becoming an advocate for the transformative role of PBL in modern education. When I experienced a shift from professional burnout to a renewed sense of passion, I eagerly shared my enthusiasm for project-based. I flipped learning with anyone willing to listen. This excitement was so overwhelming that I couldn't keep it to myself.

Similarly, as you start to see the profound impact of PBL in kindling the enthusiasm and curiosity of students, you'll naturally find yourself wanting to spread the word. You'll feel compelled to share your experiences with colleagues, whether the teacher across the hall, friends on social media, or fellow educators through texts. The beauty of PBL is so compelling that once you witness its effects, you instinctively want others to see its value, too.

In my case, I often invite my administrators into my classroom. I am eager for them to witness firsthand my students' incredible work. Watching students deeply engaged in their projects is a testament to their learning and the effectiveness of PBL. By sharing these moments with my administrators, they become more than just observers; they become partners in understanding and supporting my teaching approach. They see the practical application and potential of resources in my classroom, making future discussions about needs and improvements more meaningful and informed.

The key message here is the importance of sharing your classroom experiences. If others don't see the dynamic and engaging learning environment you create through PBL, they won't fully understand or appreciate the reasons behind your teaching methods. Sharing your classroom's story is not just about showcasing student work; it's about advocating for a pedagogical approach that can redefine education.

Professional Development and Collaboration

The dialogues you engage in about project-based learning are crucial initial steps towards creating a vibrant PBL environment in your classroom. However, it's equally important to pursue professional development opportunities specifically tailored to PBL methodologies. This commitment to growth can take various forms, such as attending workshops, participating in seminars, or engaging in collaborative projects with colleagues with more PBL experience. These experiences enhance your understanding of PBL and equip you with practical skills and innovative strategies to implement effectively in your teaching.

Throughout this book, I've strongly encouraged collaboration with a colleague as you explore and work through the ideas presented. This collaborative approach is more than just a method of professional development; it's a powerful tool for reflection and adaptation. When you discuss and dissect the concepts of PBL with a fellow educator, it allows you to view these ideas through the specific context of your classroom. This perspective is invaluable, as it helps you tailor PBL strategies to suit your students' unique needs and dynamics.

Furthermore, engaging in these conversations provides an opportunity for mutual support and feedback, especially when you encounter ideas that challenge traditional teaching methods or your teaching style. When adopting a new educational approach, it's natural to face uncertainties or questions. Having a colleague to discuss these challenges can provide clarity, reassurance, and alternate viewpoints. This process of sharing and reflection is not just about finding solutions to immediate challenges; it's about growing as an educator and continuously evolving your teaching practices.

In essence, embracing PBL is a journey of continuous learning and adaptation. By seeking professional development opportunities and engaging in collaborative discussions, you are affirming your commitment to understanding PBL and mastering its implementation for the benefit of your students. This path of growth and exploration is a testament to your dedication as an educator, and it's a journey that promises to be as rewarding for you as it will be for your students.

Start With What is Already Working

Integrating project-based learning into your classroom is not about overhauling your entire teaching approach but rather creatively infusing your existing curricula with PBL elements. This process involves aligning your projects with educational standards while also adding aspects that ignite student curiosity and engagement. Embracing PBL doesn't mean discarding what you've already established or trying to reinvent your teaching methods completely. Instead, PBL encourages you to reflect on your current practices and consider ways to transform them into more student-centered and student-driven experiences.

You already possess a repertoire of effective units and lessons, and the shift toward PBL is an opportunity to enhance these existing elements. It's about reimagining how you can present these units and lessons in a way that encourages students to engage with them more actively and deeply. This could mean incorporating hands-on activities, encouraging inquiry-based learning, or integrating real-world problems that resonate with your students' interests and experiences.

The goal here is to grow and evolve the components of your teaching that are already working well. It's about providing students with opportunities to explore, investigate, and learn in meaningful ways. This approach enriches their learning experience and fosters skills like critical thinking, collaboration, and problem-solving.

Personalizing your classroom to include PBL isn't about starting from scratch; it's about building on the strong foundation you already have. It's a journey of enhancing and adapting your teaching methods to create a more dynamic, engaging, and student-focused learning environment. This process not only benefits the students but also brings a new dimension of fulfillment and growth to your role as an educator.

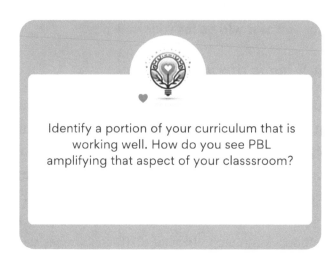

Identify a portion of your curriculum that is working well. How do you see PBL amplifying that aspect of your classsroom?

Journaling Your Journey

Use the space below to reflect on this question.

_____

_____

_____

_____

_____

_____

_____

_____

Getting the Community Involved

Resourcefulness plays a crucial role in enhancing the Project-Based Learning experience in your classroom. A key aspect of this is sourcing materials and forging connections with the community, which can significantly enrich your students' projects. This can involve contacting local businesses or utilizing online platforms to obtain resources that add depth and authenticity to student projects.

Actively seeking local grant opportunities can be particularly beneficial for acquiring essential materials like paint, canvases, brushes, hot glue guns, glue sticks, markers, colored pencils, scissors, and construction paper. These grants can provide the financial support needed to bring your PBL initiatives to life without straining your school's budget.

Engaging with businesses in your community is another valuable strategy. By sharing your classroom projects and goals with local businesses, you gain potential access to resources and build relationships that can have lasting impacts on your PBL implementation. These community connections can offer students real-world insights and opportunities, reinforcing the relevance and applicability of their learning.

Establishing these relationships within the community helps students see the value of their work beyond the classroom walls. It demonstrates that their projects and efforts are recognized and appreciated by the wider community. This external validation can motivate students, fostering a sense of pride and accomplishment in their work.

Being resourceful in gathering materials and leveraging community connections is not just about enriching the PBL experience; it's about showing students the real-world impact of their learning. The relationships you build and the resources you gather strengthen the PBL framework in your classroom, making the learning process more engaging and meaningful for your students.

Parents and the Public

Actively engaging families and the broader school community is a pivotal aspect of enhancing understanding and support for project-based learning. Involving parents and guardians in the PBL process is essential for ensuring a clear and cohesive understanding of expectations within and outside the classroom setting. This inclusive approach fosters a shared vision and collaboration between the school and families, thereby enriching the students' educational experience.

When families are informed and involved, they appreciate the myriad skills that PBL develops in their children. They recognize the value of an educational approach that sees and nurtures each student as an individual with unique passions and interests. This realization often leads to awe and pride as families witness the creativity and innovation their children display through PBL projects. Such family engagement supports students' learning and reinforces the significance of the skills being developed, like critical thinking, collaboration, and problem-solving.

Community involvement further enhances the validity and impact of PBL. Students interacting with professionals and community members gain invaluable real-world insights and connections. This exposure complements their classroom learning and prepares them for future professional and personal interactions. Engaging with the community sets the stage for PBL to become a more widely embraced and integral part of the educational landscape, shifting from being an exception to becoming a norm.

Engaging with families and the wider community transforms PBL from a classroom-centered approach to a community-supported educational experience. It creates a supportive network that not only backs the PBL initiatives but also actively contributes to the growth and success of the students. This collaborative approach lays a strong foundation for PBL to thrive, making it a more effective and impactful method of teaching and learning.

 Use the QR code to get the step-by-step guide for how to build community partnerships in a PBL classroom.

Voices from the Classroom

Parent Perspective

Many years of poster boards, papers, PowerPoints, and attempted art projects resulted in tears, anxiety, and self-doubt for my daughter, Alyvia. Although a straight-A student, these standard and typical projects requested by her teachers did not bring her more clarity on her textbook content which brought about major insecurities in herself. As a neurodivergent female, she was able to mask her needs by mimicking what others did while in school, yet coming home to tell me her school work and class experience was traumatizing.

At the age of 11, I decided to change schools and send her to a school that focused on teaching through the arts. Her first year was successful, yet a huge adjustment to a new culture and way of learning. The next year, she went to 7th grade where Mr. Jones became her social studies teacher. His class is project-based, yet gives the students the creative space to utilize their strengths in different art forms. These projects brought out a side of my daughter that, even as her parent, I had not witnessed.

My very introverted daughter absolutely loves writing and reading. In her first year at the art school, her teachers were very concerned that she sat alone at lunch and read books, removing herself from socializing with friends. Although no mother wanted to hear that, I knew this was where her happy place was. Where she reset and regrouped, lost in a story. She has been a writer and reader since she was 4 years old. Her imagination has always been one of my favorite things about her. For her projects in Mr. Jones's class, she has written scripts for sitcoms, commercials, and short films. What has transpired from her writings has been nothing short of incredible. Not only did she create the stories, but she filmed, edited, and I couldn't believe it myself, acted out every single character in her videos. I felt like I had the female Tyler Perry as my daughter! She completely engrosses herself in every character she writes about, no matter if it is the father in the story, the grandmother, or the newscaster. Seeing those dimensions of herself, the ability to transform and be the screaming father in her story while being the most quiet and introverted kid in real life, blew me away.

Alyvia herself reflects on a particular project, 'One of the best projects that I have done in this class came in the form of a Sitcom episode about a family living together. I am very proud of this project because it was very challenging yet fun and exciting, considering I have never done something like it before. I had a lot of fun including all of the information in the episode in fun and creative ways. This project helped me improve my cinematography and editing skills. I probably would have never done something like this had it not been for this class, and I will be forever grateful for Mr. Jones and his project-based learning!'

Mr. Jones' class has brought out a creative genius in my daughter. The biggest blessing is to see the growth of her personally. Her self-confidence has soared. She feels talented in a way she has not prior. She sits with her friends at lunch now and laughs and talks about teenage things. I feel these creative spaces Mr. Jones has provided has changed the trajectory for my daughter in more ways than I can count (Buckner, E., personal communication, January 4, 2024).

Reflecting on the Past

When I was in elementary school, 'Bare Minimum' was my middle name. My inability to comprehend content was not only the driving force in my lack of effort but also my mother's reasoning in switching schools. I had no idea that this one change in my life would make way for my career path.

During my middle school years, Dan Jones's project-based

learning classroom was by far my favorite. Through PBL, my intelligence was not limited to paper-pencil work. For the first time in my education, I had to take ownership of my work and was motivated to do so. Many hours were spent crafting board games, game shows, hand-sewn dresses, and even villages made of candy. Prior to this experience, my only goal was to meet the 'checklist' set by the standards of my former school, with the outcome being little retention. PBL pushed me to be fully immersed in the content gaining strength in comprehension and a love of learning. No longer was my motivation task-oriented but a creative joy. One of my favorite projects was a section titled 'Histories Mysteries.' The goal is to solve a historical mystery by investigating facts. I happened to receive Roanoke Island and its disappearance. My task went beyond simple research but included a delightful and insightful interview with an author who specialized in the island. Ten years later, despite the Island's disappearance, I have not forgotten its history nor the feeling of happiness during that interview.

Not only did I leave that classroom with the nickname of 'Overachiever,' but I went on to graduate at the top of my high school class and a determination to teach. I currently teach middle school and have never forgotten the impact of PBL (Baxter, B., personal communication, January 8, 2024).

Change Rests in Your Transformation

As educators, we stand at the forefront of a transformative educational journey. This journey is not solely about altering how our students learn; it extends far beyond that. It's about gradually reshaping the learning landscape into a more dynamic, relevant, and engaging environment. This transformation prepares our students to excel in a future brimming with possibilities.

Embracing change does not necessitate a complete overhaul of your current methods overnight. Instead, transformation can occur in small, manageable increments. It begins with you. Every small step towards integrating new ideas, techniques, or technologies into your teaching practices contributes to a larger shift in education. No matter how small, these steps are the building blocks of significant change.

Chinese philosopher Lao Tzu once said, "The journey of a thousand miles begins with a single step" (Lao Tzu, 2018, p. Chapter 64). Start with one aspect of your teaching that you wish to enhance. It could be as simple as incorporating a new discussion format, experimenting with a digital tool, or applying a different assessment strategy. Each incremental change you implement is a stride towards a more enriched educational experience for your students.

This transformation journey is a collective one, where each small change contributes to a larger educational evolution. By initiating change, even in the smallest ways, you become a catalyst for a broader movement toward an education system that truly meets the needs of the future.

As you embark on this path, know that every effort, every experiment, and every new approach you try adds a valuable thread to the tapestry of transformative education. The change rests in your transformation, and through your willingness to adapt and grow, you enhance your teaching and inspire your students to embrace a mindset of continuous learning and growth.

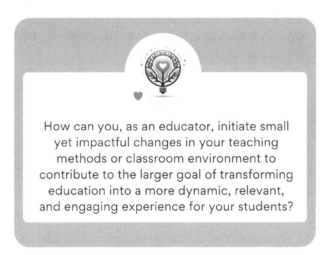

How can you, as an educator, initiate small yet impactful changes in your teaching methods or classroom environment to contribute to the larger goal of transforming education into a more dynamic, relevant, and engaging experience for your students?

Journaling Your Journey

Use the space below to reflect on this question.

_____

_____

_____

_____

_____

_____

_____

_____

My Endless Journey

Initially, my understanding of project-based learning was limited to guiding my students through meticulously designed projects, where they excelled in creating impressive tri-fold boards and PowerPoint presentations, occasionally experimenting with other innovative presentation software/applications. I prided myself on their ability to grasp the content and execute my vision, adding their flair through their choice of colors and topics. However, they were essentially bringing to life my concept of the project.

It was a pivotal moment when I realized I had fundamentally misunderstood PBL. I had equated mere project creation with PBL, missing its true essence, which lies in the project's purpose and who controls its design. This revelation marked the beginning of a transformative journey in my teaching practice.

My evolution in PBL has been a journey of reflection, feedback, and continuous adaptation. Listening to my students' experiences year after year, I reshaped our classroom, always considering how changes could enhance learning for all. This journey has been one of trial and error, and learning, embracing the true spirit of PBL by starting with significant questions, engaging in research, and exploring various approaches to meet standards.

I encountered numerous challenges when implementing PBL, often feeling like I was extinguishing one fire only for another to ignite. To address these issues, I developed a systematic approach: I began by listing all the challenges, from understanding students' knowledge levels to planning projects and determining the right balance of guidance. This led to a structured plan for each unit, spanning about two weeks, rooted in best practice methods and a student-centered approach.

The following are specific strategies that I employed to transform my PBL classroom:

1. Rubrics with Essential Questions: I introduced rubrics featuring an essential question to guide the entire unit, including topics and terminology. This encouraged students to come to class prepared, having researched the key concepts in advance.

2. Design Lab: This stage allowed students to share their findings about the essential question, learn from their peers, and plan their project representations.

3. Turn 'N' Talk Cards: Inspired by Grant Wiggins' Backwards Design, these cards facilitated discussions at the start of each class about the previous night's lesson. This focus eliminated off-topic questions and ensured the dialogue was targeted and relevant.

4. Micro-Conversations: By engaging in brief, focused interactions with each student, I could offer personalized support, helping those who needed more guidance and encouraging independent work, among others.

These strategies significantly enhanced my students' success, both individually and in group settings, laying a solid foundation for their projects.

My journey with PBL is a testament to evolution, adaptation, and the power of embracing a learning mindset. It's about constant innovation, learning from failures, and being committed to improving the educational experience for my students. This path, marked by ongoing growth and enthusiasm, inspires me as an educator.

How has your understanding of project-based learning grown or changed as you journeyed through this book?

Journaling Your Journey

Use the space below to reflect on this question.

_____
_____
_____
_____
_____
_____
_____
_____
_____

Common Obstacles and Strategies for Overcoming Them

Rapidly Evolving Technology

"Change is the only constant in life."
-Heraclitus

This notion that change is going to happen is ever present in the realm of technology. We can proactively do some things so that when it happens, we are ready for it. Caroline Ceniza-Levine's (2017) Forbes article "Avoiding Information Overload: Five Ways To Keep Up In Times Of Rapid Change" offers valuable insights. The article suggests strategies like scheduling learning time, prioritizing long-term development, getting support, and scheduling downtime. These approaches can help educators adapt to technological advancements in PBL, ensuring they remain current and avoid being left behind.

Schedule Learning Time

Scheduling time to learn about technology is crucial in a PBL classroom to keep up with rapid technological changes. This dedicated learning time ensures educators are up-to-date with the latest digital tools and educational technologies. Ceniza-Levine suggests setting aside 30 minutes a week to look at emerging trends and new technology tools. She also encourages people to look up to a year ahead for learning opportunities such as conferences or professional development (Ceniza-Levine, 2017). By staying informed, teachers can more effectively integrate these technologies into PBL environments, enhancing the learning experience for students. It also allows educators to adapt to new teaching methods and platforms, ensuring their PBL approaches remain relevant, engaging, and effective in a technology-driven educational landscape.

Prioritizing Long-term Development

In a project-based learning classroom, prioritizing long-term technological development is essential for preparing students for a rapidly evolving digital future. This involves regularly incorporating cutting-edge technologies into PBL projects, giving students practical experience with the latest tools. Simultaneously, it's important to focus on developing students' adaptability and self-learning skills to navigate new technologies independently. Continuous professional development is crucial for teachers, ensuring they stay updated on technological advancements and pedagogical approaches. "You need to look ahead at what the most substantive changes will be for your area of expertise, and plan your classes, conferences, and other long-term investments for these changes" (Ceniza-Levine, 2017). This holistic strategy equips students with the technical skills and the adaptive mindset necessary for success in a technology-driven world.

Getting Support

The importance of gaining support and sharing insights is crucial, especially regarding evolving technology trends. Teachers should proactively engage with their principals, department chairs, or mentors, sharing new information and ideas from conferences, classes, or current educational trends. By sharing "what you're seeing in the market,... s/he may have additional news and ideas, as well as counsel on where you should focus" (Ceniza-Levine, 2017). This collaboration ensures the entire educational team is informed about the latest technological advancements and pedagogical strategies. Creating a shared learning and support culture within the school community fosters a more dynamic and informed PBL environment, benefitting educators and students.

Schedule Downtime

In the fast-paced environment of a PBL classroom, especially when dealing with rapid technological changes, the value of downtime extends beyond preventing burnout. It offers educators a critical pause for reflection and perspective. "When upheaval is happening is exactly when you don't feel like you have the time to take a break. So you must build downtime into your schedule the same way you build learning time into your schedule" (Ceniza-Levine, 2017). This break allows time to fully assimilate new technological knowledge and integrate these learnings into teaching practices before moving on to the next innovation. Therefore, scheduling downtime refreshes the mind and enhances one's ability to work more effectively with new technology, contributing to a more thoughtful and efficient educational approach.

Cultivating Teacher Readiness

In *A Case Study Of Three Universities Preparing Teachers For Project Based Learning,* several key approaches emerge to enhance teacher readiness for project-based learning. First, assessing the readiness of schools and districts is crucial, focusing on factors such as a culture of innovation, leadership support, and effective partnerships between educational stakeholders (Denton et al., 2021). This assessment helps identify the necessary conditions for successful PBL implementation. Second, teachers require support through practical examples of PBL in their specific educational contexts and guidance on integrating these methodologies into their existing teaching practices and curricula (Denton et al., 2021).

Throughout this book, you have had the opportunity to work through PBL processes that will enable you to tailor PBL to your specific class. Addressing the challenges of PBL implementation is also vital, particularly in adapting it to fit existing curricular structures and developing strategies for engaging diverse student groups effectively. This is one of the reasons why PBL is not just a simple "follow this formula" pedagogy. Rather, due to its complexity, it requires you to look at your classroom, instruction, student engagement, and assessments holistically to create the best PBL experience for your students. Furthermore, teachers, especially those new to PBL, may benefit from additional training in classroom management and PBL techniques. This training can equip them to manage dynamic, student-centered learning environments more effectively (Denton et al., 2021). PBL can create a chaotic classroom environment, but a well-run PBL classroom manages controlled chaos. Students are up and moving and talking with purpose, and together as a class, you all have designed those interactions to have the most meaning. Last, promoting system-level changes in schools, such as modifying teaching practices, curricula, and assessment methods, is essential to align with PBL approaches.

Scalability and Sustainability

In regard to project-based learning, the concepts of scalability and sustainability are pivotal for ensuring long-term success and

298

effectiveness in educational settings. Insights from two significant sources, a report by Cynthia E. Coburn (2003) and a report by Poulos, Chalmers, Culbertson, Fried, and d'Entremont (2016), offer comprehensive strategies and considerations.

Coburn (2003) emphasizes the need for "consequential change [to] be sustained" (Page 6), highlighting the importance of maintaining the effectiveness of educational reforms like PBL over time. It stresses the depth of teacher engagement in these reforms, advocating for strategies that effectively develop and nurture this depth (Coburn, 2003). The document also underscores the importance of creating supportive school environments and utilizing systematic data collection methods, such as student work samples or teacher logs, to track the impact of PBL (Coburn, 2003).

Complementing these insights, Poulos et al. (2016) outline key action steps for enhancing educational practices. They advocate for establishing a shared vision and high expectations through collaborative processes involving teachers, leaders, families, and students. Building leadership capacity and fostering teacher collaboration are also crucial, as is using data to drive decisions. Engaging families in the vision, considering the context, balancing priorities, and continuously reflecting and improving upon practices are integral to the successful implementation and sustainability of PBL.

A Final Charge

As we conclude our exploration of project-based learning, let's take a moment to honor the hard work, dedication, and passion you've invested throughout this book. Embracing PBL is more than adopting a set of strategies; it's about committing to a journey of continuous growth, exploration, and transformation. This journey, fueled by your passion and perseverance, has the power to reshape education one student, one project at a time. Remember, the most profound changes often begin with the dedication you bring to your classroom each day, grounded in the innovative spirit of PBL.

You, as educators, are the catalysts for this transformative change. The journey you've embarked upon is challenging but immensely rewarding. Your commitment to this path is a testament to your belief in the potential of every student and the transformative power of education. As you continue to implement the principles of project-based learning, embrace the hard work you've put forth. It's this very effort that will light the way for your students, inspiring them to embark on their own journeys of discovery and growth.

But remember, no educator is an island. As you delve deeper into the world of PBL, do so with the understanding that being part of a community is not just beneficial; it's essential. Connect with fellow educators who share your passion and commitment. Journey together, support each other and grow as a collective. When challenges arise, as they inevitably will, lean on this community for support, inspiration, and shared wisdom. Together, you can navigate the complexities of innovative teaching, share successes, learn from setbacks, and continually evolve your practice.

Encourage one another to stay the course, to keep the flame of passion alive, and to remember the profound impact you are making. Celebrate your victories, no matter how small, and approach setbacks as opportunities to learn and grow. This journey of PBL is not just about reaching a destination; it's about the shared experiences, the collective growth, and the community you build along the way.

As we close this book and you continue to forge ahead, do so with a renewed commitment to your mission and an open invitation to collaborate and connect with others. Let this charge serve as a reminder of the hard work you've invested and the exciting path that lies ahead. Embrace the challenges, cherish the journey, and always, always lean on the strength of your community.

Carry forward the passion, dedication, and collaborative spirit that have brought you to this point. Continue to inspire, challenge, and nurture your students with the knowledge that they are part of a larger community of change-makers. Together, let's continue to shape a future that is bright with curiosity, engagement, and lifelong learning. Here's to you, the educators, the community builders, the passionate pioneers of project-based learning. The journey continues, and you are never alone.

Glossary

21st Century Skills: 12 abilities that today's students need to succeed in their careers during the Information Age. The twelve 21st-century skills are critical thinking, creativity, collaboration, communication, information literacy, media literacy, technology literacy, flexibility, leadership, initiative, productivity, and social skills (Stauffer, 2022).

Active Learning: a learning method in which students are actively or experientially involved in the learning process (Unangst, 2021).

Assistive Technology: any item, piece of equipment, software program, or product system used to increase, maintain, or improve the functional capabilities of persons with disabilities (Connecticut's Official State Website, n.d.).

Authentic Assessment: applying knowledge and skills in real-world situations, scenarios, or problems. Authentic assessments create a student-centered learning experience by providing students with opportunities to problem-solve, inquire, and create new knowledge and meaning (Messier, 2022).

Authentic Learning: actively engaging with problems and materials constitutes the best way to learn (Mayo, 2010).

Blended Learning: a learning model that combines in-person classroom instruction with online and virtual components to reap both benefits. The result is an enhancement of in-person teaching with the ease, flexibility, and accessibility of technology (Banger, 2022).

Cognitive Load Theory: a concept that explains how the amount of information and mental effort required in a learning task can affect a person's ability to process and understand new information. It suggests that if a task demands too much mental effort, it can overwhelm the learner's mind and make learning less effective (Sweller, 1988).

Collaborative Learning: group-structured, whereby the students organize and divide the work between themselves. Each student is responsible for his/her work separately but is also in charge of the team's work as a whole (Lew, 2020).

Cooperative Learning: students work in small groups for a few minutes to help them process what has been taught, think about a particular question, assist the teacher in identifying and addressing any misunderstandings about the content, and quickly recap on the key points in the lesson (Gillies, 2020).

Children's Online Privacy Protection Act (COPPA):
"applies to personal information collected online by operators of both websites and online services. The term 'online service' broadly covers any service available over the Internet or that connects to the Internet or a wide-area network. Examples of online services include services that allow users to play network-connected games, engage in social networking activities, purchase goods or services online, receive online advertisements, or interact with other online content or services. Mobile applications that connect to the Internet, Internet-enabled gaming platforms, connected toys, smart speakers, voice assistants, voice-over-Internet protocol services, and Internet-enabled location-based services also are online services covered by COPPA (Federal Trade Commission, 2020).

Differentiated Instruction: tailoring instruction to meet individual needs. Whether teachers differentiate content, process, products, or the learning environment, ongoing assessment and flexible grouping make this a successful approach to instruction (Tomlinson, 2023).

Digital Collaboration Tools: online collaboration tools are apps, software programs, or platforms that help businesses and their people streamline the creative process and work together more effectively and efficiently (Bynder, n.d.).

Digital Literacy: the skills you need to live, learn, and work in a society where communication and access to information are increasingly through digital technologies like internet platforms, social media, and mobile devices (Western Sydney University, 2020).

Essential Questions: open-ended questions that require students to engage in higher-order thinking and lead to a deeper understanding about a unit of study or specific subject area (Summit Learning, 2019).

Experiential Learning: an engaged learning process whereby students "learn by doing" and by reflecting on the experience (Boston University, 2023).

FERPA: The Family Educational Rights and Privacy Act (FERPA) is a federal law that affords   parents the right to have access to their children's education records, the right to seek to have the records amended, and the right to have some control over the disclosure of personally identifiable information from the education records (U.S. Department of Education, n.d.).

Flipped Learning: a framework that enables educators to reach every student. The Flipped approach inverts the traditional classroom model by introducing course concepts before class, allowing educators to use class time to guide each student through active, practical, innovative applications of the course principles (Flipped Learning Global Initiative, n.d.).

Formative Assessment: refers to the gathering of information or data about student learning during a course or program that is used to guide improvements in teaching and learning. Activities are usually low-stakes or no-stakes; they do not contribute substantially to the final evaluation or grade of the student or may not even be assessed at the individual student level (Carnegie Mellon University, 2019).

Inquiry-Based Learning: a learning process that engages students by making real-world connections through exploration and high-level questioning. It is an approach to learning that encourages students to engage in problem-solving and experiential learning (Santa Ana College, n.d.).

Interdisciplinary Learning: a process by which learners integrate information, data, techniques, tools, perspectives, concepts, and/or theories from two or more disciplines to craft products, explain phenomena, or solve problems in ways that would have been unlikely through single-disciplinary means (Mansilla, 2010, p. 288-306).

Iterative Learning: a process children use to master new skills like walking, feeding themselves, reading, and more. The cycle involves making an attempt, failing, evaluating what went wrong, refining the approach, and starting the cycle again. This process values failure and self-assessment (Johnson, 2023).

Metacognition: thinking about one's thinking. It refers to the processes used to plan, monitor, and assess one's understanding and performance. Metacognition includes a critical awareness of one's thinking and learning as well as oneself as a thinker and learner (Chick, 2013).

Mind Maps: a visual diagram that organizes information into a hierarchy. It's often created around a single concept, drawn as an image in the center of a blank page. The concept then branches out into subtopics and related ideas. Each branch can have multiple sub-branches (mindmaps.com, 2023).

Passion-Based Learning (PsBL): the process of facilitating learning by harnessing and focusing on the students' passions as well as creating a passion within the students (Network Support, 2023).

Passive Learning: a method of learning or instruction where students receive information from the instructor and internalize it (Unangst, G., 2021).

Personalized Learning: an educational approach that aims to customize learning for each student's strengths, needs, skills, and interests. Each student gets a learning plan based on what they know and how they learn best. It doesn't replace an IEP, a 504 plan, or intervention programs (Morin, 2019).

Problem-Based Learning (PmBL): a student-centered approach to learning that involves groups of students working to solve a real-world problem (Kurt, D.S., 2020).

Project-Based Learning (PBL): the act of using a project to develop hands-on engagement where students, fueled by their curiosity and passion, work collaboratively to explore, absorb, and internalize classroom content beyond rote memorization.

Real-World Application: something that happens in the world or someone's life rather than in a book or the imagination (Cambridge Dictionary, 2023).

Scaffolding: supports are provided to students to help them access and strengthen a new concept or skill (Field, 2021).

Social and Emotional Learning (SEL): the process through which all young people and adults acquire and apply the knowledge, skills, and attitudes to develop healthy identities, manage emotions and achieve personal and collective goals, feel and show empathy for others, establish and maintain supportive relationships, and make responsible and caring decisions (Collaborative for Academic, Social, and Emotional Learning [CASEL], 2022).

Student Agency: relates to the student having an active role in their learning through voice, and often a choice, in the process (Reese, 2023).

Student-Centered Learning: a wide variety of educational programs, learning experiences, instructional approaches, and academic-support strategies intended to address the distinct learning needs, interests, aspirations, or cultural backgrounds of individual students and groups of students (Great Schools Partnership, 2013).

Bibliography

Almulla, M. A. (2020). The Effectiveness of the Project-Based Learning (PBL) Approach as a Way to Engage Students in Learning. *SAGE Open*, 10(3). https://doi.org/10.1177/2158244020938702

Anderman, E. M., & Hicks Anderman, L. (2021). *Classroom motivation: linking research to teacher practice*. Routledge.

Badalamenti, J. (2016, May 2). *The 4 essential elements of passion-based learning. ESchool News; eSchoolMedia. https://www.eschoolnew*s.com/eclassroomnews/2016/05/02/the-4-essential-elements-of-passion-based-learning/

Banger, C. (2022, March 1). *The Importance of Blended Learning in K-12 Classrooms*. D2L. https://www.d2l.com/blog/importance-blended-learning-k12-classrooms/#:~:text=Blended%20learning%20is%20a%20learning

Boston University. (2023). *Experiential Learning*. www.bu.edu. https://www.bu.edu/ctl/guides/experiential-learning/

Bowen, R. S. (2017). *Understanding by Design*. Vanderbilt University. https://cft.vanderbilt.edu/guides-sub-pages/understanding-by-design/#:~:text=Understanding%20by%20Design%20is%20a

Buck Institute for Education. (n.d.). *What is PBL?* PBLWorks; Buck Institute for Education. Retrieved February 14, 2024, from https://www.pblworks.org/what-is-pbl

Buljan, M. (2022, March 7). *The Truth About Immersive Learning and Its Sharp Benefits*. ELearning Industry. https://elearningindustry.com/the-truth-about-immersive-learning-and-its-sharp-benefits

Bynder. (n.d.). *What are collaboration tools? Glossary*. Bynder. https://www.bynder.com/en/glossary/collaboration-tools/#:~:text=Online%20collaboration%20tools%20are%20apps

Cambridge Dictionary. (2023, April 5). *real-world application collocation | meaning and examples of use*. @CambridgeWords. https://dictionary.cambridge.org/example/english/real-world-application

Carnegie Mellon University. (2019). *Common Assessment Terms - Eberly Center - Carnegie Mellon University*. Cmu.edu. https://www.cmu.edu/teaching/assessment/basics/glossary.html

Ceniza-Levine, C. (2017, May 15). *Avoiding Information Overload: Five Ways To Keep Up In Times Of Rapid Change*. Forbes. https://www.forbes.com/sites/carolinecenizalevine/2017/05/15/avoiding-information-overload-five-ways-to-keep-up-in-times-of-rapid-change/?sh=714a8092212f

Chick, N. (2013, February 10). *Metacognition*. Vanderbilt University; Vanderbilt University. https://cft.vanderbilt.edu/guides-sub-pages/metacognition/#:~:text=Metacognition%2C%20put%20simply%2C%20thinking

Coburn, C. E. (2003). Rethinking Scale: Moving Beyond Numbers to Deep and Lasting Change. *Educational Researcher, 32*(6), 3–12. https://doi.org/10.3102/0013189x032006003

Collaborative for Academic, Social, and Emotional Learning (CASEL). (2022). *Fundamentals of SEL*. CASEL. https://casel.org/fundamentals-of-sel/

Connecticut's Official State Website. (n.d.). *What is Assistive Technology*. CT.gov - Connecticut's Official State Website. https://portal.ct.gov/DDS/General/AssistiveTechnology/What-is-Assistive-Technology#:~:text=Assistive%20technology%20(AT)%20is%20any

Cooper, L. A. (2022). Designing the Project-Based Learning Experience using Motivation Theory. *American Society for Engineering Education, 36661*.

Cornell University. (2022). *Problem-Based learning | center for teaching innovation*. Teaching.cornell.edu. https://teaching.cornell.edu/teaching-resources/

engaging-students/problem-based-learning#:~:text=Problem%2Dbased%20
learning%20(PBL)

Curipod. (n.d.). *Home.* Curipod. Retrieved December 21, 2023, from https://curipod.com/

Curipod. (2022). *10 Formative Assessment Examples.* Curipod. https://
curipod.com/blog/Ten%20Formative%20Assessment%20
Examples-e2c120693f184f9d8e98ba95e9fd72c3

d.school, S. (2019). *Stanford d.school.* Stanford D.school. https://dschool.stanford.edu/

Dabrowski, J., & Reed Marshall, T. (2018). *Motivation and Engagement in Student
Assignments: The Role of Student Choice and Relevancy.* The Education Trust.
https://files.eric.ed.gov/fulltext/ED593328.pdf

Dené Poth, R. (2023, October 20). *7 AI Tools That Help Teachers Work More
Efficiently.* Edutopia; George Lucas Educational Foundation. https://www.
edutopia.org/article/7-ai-tools-that-help-teachers-work-more-efficiently/

Denton, A., Hodara, M., Petrokubi, J., Merrill, B., & Velie, Z. (2021). *Preparing
Teachers for Project Based Learning.* Education Northwest. https://www.
pblworks.org/sites/default/files/2021-07/OutoftheGate_Case_Study_
Report_2021.pdf

Dorian, G. T. (1981). *There's a SMART Way to Write Management's Goals and
Objectives.* Journal of Management Review. https://community.mis.temple.
edu/mis0855002fall2015/files/2015/10/S.M.A.R.T-Way-Management-Review.
pdf

Elgersma, C. (2023, February 14). *ChatGPT and Beyond: How to Handle AI in
Schools | Common Sense Education.* Www.commonsense.org; Common
Sense Media. https://www.commonsense.org/education/articles/
chatgpt-and-beyond-how-to-handle-ai-in-schools

Epstein, J. L. (2010). School/Family/Community Partnerships: Caring for
the Children We Share. *Phi Delta Kappan,* 92(3), 81–96. https://doi.
org/10.1177/003172171009200326

Fecich, S. (2023, July 12). *The Future of Danielson Domain 1: How AI is
Revolutionizing the Way We Plan and Prep.* EduMagic. https://www.
sfecich.com/post/the-future-of-danielson-domain-1-how-ai-is-rev-
olutionizing-the-way-we-plan-and-prep#:~:text=AI%20lesson%20
plan-

Federal Trade Commission. (2020, July 20). *Complying with COPPA: Frequently Asked Questions.* Federal Trade Commission. https://www.ftc.gov/business-guidance/resources/complying-coppa-frequently-asked-questions#:~:text=Mobile%20applications%20that%20connect%20to

Field, S. (2021, March 10). *How to Scaffold in Project Based Learning.* PBLWorks. https://www.pblworks.org/blog/how-scaffold-project-ect-based-learning#:~:text=The%20term%20scaffolding%20is%20used

Fitzpatrick, D., Fox, A., & Weinstein, B. (2023). *The AI Classroom.* Teacher Goals.

Flipped Learning Global Initiative. (n.d.). *Flipped Learning International Definition.* Flipped Learning Global Initiative: The Exchange.

Frąckiewicz, M. (2023, May 4). *Exploring the Synergy of AI and Project-Based Learning.* TS2 SPACE. https://ts2.space/en/exploring-the-synergy-of-ai-and-project-based-learning/#gsc.tab=0

Garbade, M. J. (2021, August 15). *Artificial Intelligence and the Rise of Project-Based Learning.* ELearning Industry. https://elearningindustry.com/artificial-intelligence-and-the-rise-of-project-based-learning

Gillies, R. M. (2020, March 9). *An introduction to cooperative learning.* THE EDUCATION HUB. https://theeducationhub.org.nz/an-introduction-to-cooperative-learning/

Great Schools Partnership. (2013, May 15). Student-Centered Learning Definition. *The Glossary of Education Reform.* https://www.edglossary.org/student-centered-learning/#:~:text=The%20term%20student%2Dcentered%20learning

Hendry, G. D., & Jukic, K. (2014). Learning About the Quality of Work that Teachers Expect: Students' Perceptions of Exemplar Marking Versus Teacher Explanation. *Journal of University Teaching and Learning Practice*, 11(2), 58–68. https://doi.org/10.53761/1.11.2.5

Hernández-Ramos, P., & De La Paz, S. (2009). Learning History in Middle School by Designing Multimedia in a Project-Based Learning Experience. *Journal of Research on Technology in Education,* 42(2), 151–173. https://doi.org/10.1080/15391523.2009.10782545

Jennings, J. (2023, September 12). *AI in Education: Privacy and Security - EdTech Evolved.* ESpark; eSpark Learning. https://www.esparklearning.com/blog/ai-in-education-privacy-and-security/

Johnson, J. (2023, April 6). *The Iterative Learning Cycle | Playvolution HQ.* Playvolution HQ. https://playvolutionhq.com/handout-the-iterative-learning-cycle/#:~:text=The%20iterative%20learning%20cycle%20is

Kingston, S. (2018). Project Based Learning & Student Achievement: What Does the Research Tell Us? *PBL Evidence Matters,* 1(1), 1–11. https://files.eric.ed.gov/fulltext/ED590832.pdf

Kurt, D. S. (2020, January 8). *Problem-Based Learning (PBL).* Educational Technology. https://educationaltechnology.net/problem-based-learning-pbl/#:~:text=What%20is%20Problem%2DBased%20Learning

Lam, S., Cheng, R. W., & Ma, W. Y. K. (2008). Teacher and student intrinsic motivation in project-based learning. *Instructional Science,* 37(6), 565–578. https://doi.org/10.1007/s11251-008-9070-9

Lao Tzu. (2018). *Tao Te Ching.* (p. Chapter 64).

Larmer, J. (2023). *ChatGPT & PBL: How Project Based Learning Can Help Teachers Battle (or Befriend) the Bots.* Blog.definedlearning.com. https://blog.definedlearning.com/chatgpt-pbl-how-project-based-learning-can-help-teachers-battle-or-befriend-the-bots

Lew, G. K. (2020). Collaborative Learning Theory. *Pressbooks.pub.* https://pressbooks.pub/elearning2020/chapter/collaborative-learning-theory/#:~:text=Collaborative%20learning%20is%20group%2Dstructured

Lucas Education Research. (2021). *RIGOROUS PROJECT-BASED LEARNING IS A POWERFUL LEVER FOR IMPROVING EQUITY IN SCHOOLS.* George Lucas Educational Foundation. https://www.lucasedresearch.org/wp-content/uploads/2021/08/Equity-Research-Brief.pdf

Magic School. (n.d.). *Project Based Learning (PBL) Generator.* www.magicschool.ai. Retrieved January 8, 2024, from https://www.magicschool.ai/tools/project-based-learning-pbl-generator

Mansilla, V. B. (2010). Learning to synthesize: The development of interdisciplinary understanding. In R. Frodeman, J. T. Klein, & R. C. S. Pacheco (Eds.). The Oxford handbook of interdisciplinarity (pp. 288-306). Oxford University Press.

Marenus, M. (2023, September 7). *Gardner's Theory of Multiple Intelligences.* Simply Psychology. https://www.simplypsychology.org/multiple-intelligences.html

Marzilli, A. (2019, October 9). *Making Project Based Learning a Gift for the Gifted.* PBLWorks. https://www.pblworks.org/blog/making-project-based-learning-gift-gifted

Mas'ud, B., Fachruddin, A. T. C., & Syamsinar, S. (2019). Promoting Passion-Based Learning as a Solution of Improving Creativity in English Classroom. *Inspiring: English Education Journal*, 2(2), 165–179. https://doi.org/10.35905/inspiring.v2i2.1273

Mayo, J. A. (2010). Constructing Undergraduate Psychology Curricula: Promoting Authentic Learning and Assessment in the Teaching of Psychology. In JSTOR. American Psychological Association. https://www.jstor.org/stable/j.ctv1chrszd

McGraw-Hill Education. (2023, August 31). *How immersive technology can empower students (and teachers) to learn.* ESchool News. https://www.eschoolnews.com/featured/2023/08/31/immersive-technology-empower-students-teachers/

McNeil, E. (2015, October 29). Survey Explores Why People Go Into Teaching in the First Place. *Education Week.* https://www.edweek.org/teaching-learning/survey-explores-why-people-go-into-teaching-in-the-first-place/2015/10

Mctighe, J., & Wiggins, G. P. (1998). *Understanding by design handbook.* Association For Supervision And Curriculum Development.

Messier, N. (2022, April 15). *Authentic Assessments | Center for the Advancement of Teaching Excellence | University of Illinois Chicago.* Authentic Assessments. https://teaching.uic.edu/resources/teaching-guides/assessment-grading-practices/authentic-assessments/#:~:text=Authentic%20assessments%20involve%20the%20application%20of%20knowledge

Meta Platforms Technologies, LLC. (n.d.). SAFETY AND WARRANTY GUIDE. *In Meta Quest 3 Health & Safety* (p. 5). Meta Platforms Technologies, LLC. Retrieved April 17, 2024, from https://scontent.fosu2-1.fna.fbcdn.net/v/t39.8562-6/386330719_831186342036212_3090846158777998057_n.

pdf?_nc_cat=100&ccb=1-7&_nc_sid=b8d81d&_nc_ohc=iE-iZrkk4lroAb6SOKQh&_nc_ht=scontent.fosu2-1.fna&oh=00_AfD3XOCe_sBfOyfmi1jvfZNZfVl6A39HcmcRSy6t8Lt-V7A&oe=662576E1

Midjourney. (n.d.). *Midjourney Prompts.* Docs.midjourney.com. https://docs.midjourney.com/docs/prompts

Mindmaps.com. (2023). *What is Mind Mapping? What Are Its Uses?* Mindmaps.com. https://www.mindmaps.com/what-is-mind-mapping/#:~:text=Keyword%20 Focused

Morin, A. (2019, August 5). *What Is Personalized Learning.* Understood. https://www.understood.org/articles/personalized-learning-what-you-need-to-know

Network Support. (2023). *Passion-Based Learning for a Thriving Classroom.* K12teacherstaffdevelopment.com. https://k12teacherstaffdevelopment.com/tlb/passion-based-learning-for-a-thriving-classroom/#:~:text=Passion%2DBased%20Learning%20is%20 the

OpenAI. (2023). *ChatGPT.* Chat.openai.com. http://chat.openai.com

Pink, D. (2023, June 20). *Interview with Daniel Pink* [Email to Dan Jones].

Possi, M., & Reginard Milinga, J. (2017). Learner Diversity in Inclusive Classrooms: The Interplay of Language of Instruction, Gender and Disability. *In Malaysian Online Journal of Educational Sciences.* https://files.eric.ed.gov/fulltext/EJ1150435.pdf

Poulos, J., Chalmers, S., Culbertson, N., Fried, S., & d'Entremont, C. (2016). *STAYING THE COURSE.* https://www.edvestors.org/wp-content/uploads/2016/05/Staying-the-Course-Full-Report-Web-Version.pdf

Reese, D. (2023). *What is Student Agency?* Blog.definedlearning.com. https://blog.definedlearning.com/blog/what-is-student-agency

Reimers, P. (2023, September 11). *MagicSchool Offers 40+ Time-Saving AI Tools for Teachers.* TechNotes Blog. https://blog.tcea.org/magicschool/#:~:text=MagicSchool%20is%20an%20AI%2Dpowered

Rosenzweig, E. Q., Wigfield, A., & Eccles, J. S. (2019). *Expectancy-Value Theory and Its Relevance for Student Motivation and Learning* (K. A. Renninger & S. E. Hidi, Eds.). Cambridge University Press; Cambridge University Press. https://www.cambridge.org/core/books/abs/cambridge-handbook-of-motivation-and-learning/expectancyvalue-theory-and-its-relevance-for-student-motivation-and-learning/3BED2523308E8BBC6BC1C6F359628BC2

Santa Ana College. (n.d.). *Inquiry-Based Learning.* Sac.edu. Retrieved October 30, 2023, from https://sac.edu/AcademicAffairs/TracDat/Pages/Inquiry-Based-Learning-.aspx#:~:text=Inquiry%2Dbased%20learning%20is%20a

Sembiring, A. K., & Harahap, H. F. (2015, November 1). *Effectiveness of Mind-Map Based-Project Based Learning and Concept Map Based-Project Based Learning on Environmental Science Course at Universitas Lancang Kuning Pekanbaru.* www.neliti.com; Sebelas Maret University. https://www.neliti.com/publications/175258/effectiveness-of-mind-map-based-project-based-learning-and-concept-map-based-pro#cite

Staake, J. (2023, May 22). *What Is Higher-Order Thinking? An Overview for Educators.* We Are Teachers; We Are Teachers. https://www.weareteachers.com/higher-order-thinking/

Stauffer, B. (2022, January 10). *What Are 21st Century Skills?* www.icevonline.com. https://www.icevonline.com/blog/what-are-21st-century-skills

Summit Learning. (2019, August 23). *What Is an Essential Question?* Summit Learning Blog. https://blog.summitlearning.org/2019/08/essentialquestions/#:~:text=Essential%20questions%20are%20open%2Dended

Sweller, J. (1988). Cognitive Load during Problem Solving: Effects on Learning. Cognitive Science, 12, p.257-285.

TED. (2013, May 3). *Rita Pierson: Every kid needs a champion | TED.* Www.youtube.com. https://youtu.be/SFnMTHhKdkw?si=Fj5CFSG-1alI5vFr

Tomlinson, C. A. (2023). *What Is Differentiated Instruction? | Reading Rockets.* Www.readingrockets.org. https://www.readingrockets.org/topics/differentiated-instruction/articles/what-differentiated-instruction#:~:text=By%3A

U.S. Department of Education. (n.d.). *What is FERPA? | Protecting Student Privacy.* Studentprivacy.ed.gov. Retrieved December 21, 2023, from https://student-privacy.ed.gov/faq/what-ferpa#:~:text=The%20Family%20Educational%20Rights%20and

Unangst, G. (2021, April 15). *Passive Learning vs Active Learning.* ASU Prep Digital. https://www.asuprepdigital.org/student_blog/passive-learning-vs-active-learning/

University of Illinois. (2023). *Problem-Based Learning (PBL).* Citl.illinois.edu. https://citl.illinois.edu/citl-101/teaching-learning/resources/teaching-strategies/problem-based-learning-(pbl)#:~:text=Problem%2DBased%20Learning%20(PBL)%20is%20a%20teaching%20method%20in

Wang, Q., & Xue, M. (2022). The implications of expectancy-value theory of motivation in language education. *Frontiers in Psychology*, 13(992372), 1–8. https://doi.org/10.3389/fpsyg.2022.992372

Western Sydney University. (2020). *What is digital literacy?* www.westernsydney.edu.au. https://www.westernsydney.edu.au/studysmart/home/study_skills_guides/digital_literacy/what_is_digital_literacy#:~:text=Digital%20literacy%20means%20having%20the

Williams, A. (2020, February 26). I Wish All My Teachers Taught Like This. *Flipped Learning Review Magazine.* https://flr.flglobal.org/i-wish-all-of-my-teachers-taught-like-this/

Zhao, X., Ren, Y., & Cheah, K. (2023). Leading Virtual Reality (VR) and Augmented Reality (AR) in Education: Bibliometric and Content Analysis From the Web of Science (2018–2022). *SAGE Open,* 13(3). https://doi.org/10.1177/21582440231190821

About the Author

Dan Jones is a dynamic force in the realm of education, with nearly two decades of bringing the past to life for his 7th and 8th-grade students. Beyond the traditional classroom, Dan has become a beacon of innovation, creating spaces where every student feels valued and inspired. His journey has woven through the diverse landscapes of private, public, and urban charter schools, each step enriching his approach to teaching and learning.

What truly sets Dan apart is his pioneering spirit. He guided his students to break new ground in the U.S., connecting them with national treasures like The National Archives, The U.S. Capitol and The White House Historical Association through pioneering distance learning sessions. His role as the President of the k-12 advisory board for the Flipped Learning Global Initiative has transformed educational practices, influencing educators around the globe to rethink how teaching and learning happen.

Dan's commitment to the forefront of educational innovation is evident in his exploration of project-based learning and digital technology, leading the charge in integrating AI into the classroom. His work has not only been recognized in publications like The AI Classroom but has also established him as a thought leader, stirring conversations about the future of education on platforms like The AI Cafe podcast on the Bam Radio Network.

At the heart of Dan's work is a profound commitment to education—a dedication to not just teaching students, but to igniting a lifelong curiosity and passion for learning. He is not just an educator; he's a trailblazer, reshaping the educational landscape with his experience, innovative approaches, and an unwavering belief in the transformative power of education.

More From TeacherGoals

The Science of Reading in Action
By Malia Holowell

This is not just a book. It's a teaching movement! With 67 % of U.S. kids not proficient in reading, according to 2022 data, the status quo isn't working.

This book tackles the main obstacles: training, tools and support offering:
- Evidence-based insights on teaching, reading, dispelling social media myths
- Solutions for common challenges facing struggling readers
- Ready-to-use activities and strategies that simplify brain-friendly reading instruction
- A method to help students memorize words 10x faster than with flashcards
- Techniques to ensure no student falls behind

Written by Malia Hollowell, a certified educator and Stanford alum, this book is your all-in-one guide for making reading instruction effective and engaging.

The AI Classroom
By Dan Fitzpatrick, Amanda Fox, and Brad Weinstein

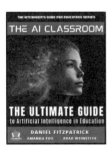

Are you an educator looking to stay ahead in the ever-changing world of education? Look no further than *The AI Classroom*, the ultimate guide for navigating the complexities of AI in education.

In *The AI Classroom* you will find:
- PREP and EDIT prompting frameworks
- 40+ prompts for educators
- 20+ AI tools to aide UDL guidelines
- 30+ AI tools educators can use NOW
- AI educational policy templates

Teaching In Sync
By Erica N. Terry and Dr. Lynea Laws

Teaching In Sync is a comprehensive guide to co-teaching success, covering everything from building a strong relationship with your co-teacher to utilizing AI for co-planning and incorporating technology for progress monitoring. With research-backed advice and a touch of NSYNC inspiration, this book will help you hit all the right notes in co-teaching.

Unlock the power of co-teaching with:
- 20+ downloadable resources
- Time-saving strategies to efficiently co-plan & progress monitor
- 50+ assistive and instructional technology resources
- 15+ AI prompts designed for co-teachers
- *In Sync* co-teaching framework

317

Upcoming Titles

Blueprint for Inclusion
By Rebekah Poe

Discover the essential guide to inclusive education in *Blueprint for Inclusion*. This concise, practical book offers educators research-backed strategies to support all students effectively, especially those with IEPs. Learn to navigate legal frameworks, foster collaborative teamwork, and create supportive classroom environments through actionable insights and real-world case studies.

Empower your teaching journey with strategies and wisdom that make inclusive education not just a goal but a reality.

Body and Brain Brilliance
By Dr. Lori Desautels

Discover the transformative power of *Body and Brain Brilliance*. Navigate through today's unprecedented stress with essential neuro-educational tools. Empower adults and children to cultivate emotional resilience and social connection, fostering classrooms where everyone feels seen, heard, and understood.

Dive in, and embark on a journey of healing and comprehensive well-being.

Unlocking SEL: The Blueprint to Social and Emotional Learning
By Lana Penley

Unlocking SEL by Lana Penley offers a transformative blueprint for education, seamlessly integrating Social and Emotional Learning (SEL) into classrooms. This guide explores essential strategies and real-life applications designed to cultivate mindfulness and foster a caring community. Dive into this invaluable resource for a journey that elevates the well-being of students and educators, ultimately creating a ripple effect of positive change in our educational landscape.

TeacherGoals Publishing, LLC offers bulk orders for any of our titles. A minimum of 25 copies must be ordered for bulk orders, and orders qualify for discounts. You can also request information about signed copies, book studies, and more. Scan the QR code for more information.

Made in United States
Troutdale, OR
06/15/2024